LOCKING UP CHILDREN

To the late Jim Dixon

Locking up children

Secure provision within the child-care system

SPENCER MILLHAM, ROGER BULLOCK
KENNETH HOSIE
Dartington Social Research Unit

SAXON HOUSE

Published by
Saxon House, Teakfield Limited,
Westmead, Farnborough, Hants, England
Reprinted 1980

British Library Cataloguing in Publication Data

Millham, Spencer
  Locking up children.
  1. Juvenile detention homes – Great Britain
  I. Title   II. Bullock, Roger   III. Hosie, Kenneth
  365'.42'0941   HV9146

ISBN 0 566 00170 5

Printed in Great Britain by Biddles Limited, Guildford, Surrey

Contents

Tables

Figures

Acknowledgements

In undertaking this research, the Dartington Social Research Unit has received invaluable assistance from a large number of people without whom the project could not have been completed.

We are most grateful to those who have allowed us to visit the numerous establishments mentioned in this report and we wish to thank the following: D. Benger, M. Born, D. Dennis, J. Dickie, the late J. Dixon, T. Edwards, C. Ford, W. Gregory, J. Henderson, Dr M. Hoghugi, J. Howells, Dr E. Irwin, K. Mallett, J. McCreadie, C. Mordue, R. Potter. M. Rose, M. Seddon, Dr D. Sime, Dr J. Tidmarsh and R. Webley. We are also indebted to: J. Burns, A. Childs, T. Collinson, L. Crew, J. Flackett, C. Holtom, S. Humphries, S. Imlach, C. Murray, N. Pyatt, T. Riddoch, G. Shaber, J. Smith, N. Whiskin, M. White and S. Woollock, all of whom ensured that our visits were fruitful.

We should also like to thank the many members of the Department of Health and Social Security who have guided this research and provided us with essential material. We are especially indebted to: P. Allen, Miss P. Cawson, L. Davies, Miss J. Gilbert, Mrs M. Jobbins, Mrs B. Kahan, E. Laws, J. Locke, Miss M. Martell, Dr M. Rodda, Dr N. Tutt and G. Whittaker. Invaluable information has also been provided by the Home, Scottish and Northern Ireland Offices and we are most grateful for this help to: Dr R. Clarke, Miss M. Deloney, Dr V. Holloway, A. McBrown, E. McClay, Miss M. Peck, R. Percival and Mrs S. Spiers.

Many other colleagues who are interested in secure provision have offered us advice as well as allowing us to see their own research material. We are particularly indebted for this cooperation to: H. Crowcombe, Miss L. Durwood, W. Forsythe, J. Freeman, Dr M. Gay, P. Griffiths, Miss H. Land, Dr W. Lumsden Walker, R. Marshall, Dr D. Martin, J. McCreadie, M. Power, R. Potter and J. Selosse.

We should also like to thank the Earl of Snowdon and Sir Denis Hamilton for the use of the cover photograph which originally appeared in *The Sunday Times*.

At Dartington, our deepest gratitude is due to Margot Blake, Ruth Frankenberg and Penny Hardwicke, to the Dartington Hall Trustees and to Professor R. A. Parker for their essential contributions to the work of the Unit.

Foreword

Locking up Children may strike some people as an unduly dramatic way of describing secure accommodation within the child-care system; but turning keys *is* the distinguishing feature of security. It is taken for granted as far as prison establishments are concerned, even for young offenders. By contrast the *caring* system is expected to adopt a treatment or nurturing perspective which is hardly compatible with locking up.

This form of provision, therefore, raises uncomfortable issues about the relationship between care and punishment and about whether they can ever be reconciled. Secure accommodation draws together in sharp relief each facet of the perennial dilemma of what should be done about difficult and troublesome children. For that reason it provides an extremely sensitive reflector of the more general issue and of the prevailing balance of solutions.

Who are the children considered to require secure accommodation? Does their behaviour differ in a pronounced fashion from that of other children living in community homes? This study begins to offer some answers. Few differences are found to exist between boys in these two groups. Might not the reasons for a boy arriving in security be found instead in social service interventions at earlier stages and, particularly, by looking at the kinds of circumstances which give rise to referral and acceptance? The study pursues these avenues of enquiry by looking in detail at two classes of behaviour which are liable to lead to custody: violence and repeated absconding.

Both designations tend to be regarded as simple and homogeneous. Yet just what is violent behaviour? How violent? How often does it happen? What are the injuries? Who is the aggressor and who the victim? And who forms the audience? The book does not deny violence, absconding or severely disturbed child behaviour. It *does* seek to describe, classify and compare and, on that basis, explore why behaviour which seems to call for security at one place or time can be contained and managed in open settings at another. Do all children allocated to security need to be there or to stay there as long as they do?

Such questions are of particular importance with respect to 'Section 53' cases. These are the children who have committed grave offences and are held in security for indefinite periods: in effect, at 'Her Majesty's pleasure'. Though small in number they test the real limits of our 'liberal' convictions about offending children. Just *how* are they to be cared for as growing children? Who do we ask to do it and what impossible responsibilities do they have to carry?

There is a growing number of children in secure accommodation in the caring system. Alongside this stands the prison department which handles thousands of 14-16 year olds, mostly in security. Clearly the present and future of secure accommodation cannot be adequately considered without including this group. What are the implications if, as the 1969 Children and Young Persons' Act might eventually permit, responsibility for these younger children, in the penal system is transferred to the Department of Health and Social Security and to local social services departments? How many of them will require security and why?

There is a long history of locking up children. The grounds for doing so have shifted and the numbers have fluctuated. Today, in the last quarter of the twentieth century, there are probably as many children being locked up at any one time as at the beginning of the century. We must be absolutely sure that the grounds for such action are utterly convincing for each child – convincing both practically and, more especially, morally. This study contributes to that scrutiny in two important ways. First, simply by drawing attention to the issue as it manifests itself in the 'caring' sector and, second, by providing much needed evidence blended with sensitivity and great concern.

R. A. PARKER
Department of Social Administration
University of Bristol

1 Introduction

Since the implementation of the Children and Young Persons' Act of 1969, public concern over what to do with the recalcitrant and offending young has increased. It is maintained that children are more difficult, the number of young persons charged with offences is rising and something needs to be done. Many remedies are suggested, among them that locking up the troublemakers would have a salutory effect and that a short and uncomfortable period in confinement would be beneficial. It is argued that this is likely to be more effective than reliance on the care order, the main provision of the legislation and at least security would ensure that children do not run away from the control of a local authority.

Yet, contrary to popular supposition, since the early 1960s a small but increasing number of children over the age of 10 have found themselves locked up. Depending on their conduct, they can remain in security for a short time or for several years. The security they experience ranges from facilities for temporary withdrawal of the disruptive or hysterical child to secure remand places for volatile offenders awaiting trial or even to long-stay secure units and youth treatment centres which have therapeutic intentions. A short sharp shock can also be provided by a stay in a detention centre or Borstal, much of which provision is secure. However, in advancing demands for increased security for young people, it is noticeable that few voices distinguish between the different and contrasting functions which the detention of young people is intended to perform. For the majority, it is control that is sought but this is a constraint that is imprecisely defined and frequently hides behind the language of treatment. But coercion is not sought in vain, as is frequently supposed, for we shall note that each year more children endure a period under lock and key than at any time since they were taken out of prison by the Children's Charter of 1908.

A wide variety of children can find themselves in security. They range from young children who repeatedly abscond from residential homes to those who commit very serious offences and are sentenced by the high courts to long periods of detention. Some of the children have been extremely disruptive or aggressive to staff while in the care of the local authorities; others offer a threat to the public because of taking and driving away cars, malicious damage or arson. A few demand protection from themselves, such as the promiscuous, the suicidal and the drug addict while some simply cannot be relied upon to present themselves at court. All these young people can become candidates for security and, depending on the circumstances, all could find themselves in a prison, a remand centre, a child-care institution, a Borstal or a detention centre, an adolescent unit or the secure ward of a psychiatric hospital.

It is also noteworthy that the moves to security are not confined to the UK. Everyone seems to have problems with adolescents and the response is largely the same. Western Germany and France, which have long been without major legislative changes in their approach to young offenders, are developing more secure places for children. Belgium has recently completed a secure unit at Liège, while even the Scandinavians, the last hope of the progressives, are having second thoughts about their open and liberal provision. Across the Atlantic, while all may be well in Massachusetts, a little further south there are more juveniles below 15 under lock and key than in the whole of Western Europe. Clearly the issue of increasing security for juveniles is not a local one.

It is the unenviable task of government departments to sift these conflicting demands for firmer control and to decide what is the most advisable and enduring course of action. In the autumn of 1974, we had just completed a study of the approved schools.[1] These were boarding schools which attempted to reform delinquents sent to them by the courts. It was not, therefore, extraordinary for the Department of Health and Social Security (the DHSS) to ask us to extend our studies into the needs for security. We were asked to investigate the development, nature and effects of secure care on children. There is, of course, already an extensive range of secure provision for juveniles available in Home Office prison department institutions and in special hospitals. The focus of the inquiry was, therefore, to be closed accommodation within the child-care community home system and the relationship between this and the other services for disruptive juveniles. This means that we are chiefly concerned with the provision for children and young persons between the ages of 10 and 16. If an expansion of security is necessary, what form should it take and how many additional places should be made available? At a time when demands on the social services departments of local authorities were rapidly increasing and where resources were strictly limited, it was clear that the additional burden of providing security would diminish the support offered to other vulnerable groups.

There is no doubt that secure unit places are very expensive. While the annual cost to the local authorities of a place in a community home with education (a CHE) was running in 1975 at about £4,000, a secure place rose in price that year to about £8,000, irrespective of capital expenditure. Youth treatment centre accommodation, which is intended for highly disturbed children, is even more expensive, reaching over £12,000 per child. In the same way, building costs have increased. Aycliffe's new treatment complex is estimated to cost £¾m and a second entirely secure youth treatment centre at Birmingham is about to open at the cost of £1½m. As these new establishments will increase the number of secure places in the child-care system by only 70, any programme of expansion seems to be an expensive undertaking. While the estimates of security in some regional development plans are very ambitious, other local authorities are becoming increasingly restive at the costs involved. Rural authorities, for example, particularly resent the costs they share with neighbouring urban areas for sheltering city delinquents. In addition, the tendency for the rapidly increasing costs of all forms of residential care to take proportionately more and more of social service budgets is causing great anxiety.

The moves to security for children have also come under political scrutiny. For example, the expenditure committee (social services and employment sub-committee) of 1974, which concerned itself with the workings of the 1969 Children and Young Persons' Act as a whole, spent a disproportionate amount of its time questioning witnesses on who should be locked up and why.[2] The committee was concerned that important decisions were being taken without sufficient information. Obviously, some research was needed, although political conditions might outweigh any findings that it put forward.

We decided to look first at the ways in which present ideas on the confinement of juveniles have developed. Our previous studies have repeatedly emphasised the importance of historical tradition in influencing contemporary approaches to children. In the nineteenth century, security was viewed as largely punitive and retributive but the philosophy seemed to have changed considerably by the 1960s when the first secure units in the child-care system were opened. Today, any long-term security for adolescents is justified in terms of a treatment programme rather than in punitive terms.

In addition, it is important to know what types of children find themselves in secure accommodation. Any analysis of an institution's population, although time-consuming, is usually very rewarding, and in this case a detailed study of the intakes to the three large secure special units in the child-care system at Redbank, Redhill and Kingswood enabled us to throw light on a number of traditional beliefs – for example, whether the boys in CHEs are becoming more difficult than those previously in the approved schools or whether those admitted to secure units actually are the most disruptive children in the system.

Unfortunately, this information will only concern boys in secure units. This is because most of the establishments for girls which we visited were both small and subject to wide fluctuations in number and use. Thus, any statistical analysis of girls' backgrounds would be of little value. At the largest establishment for girls which we visited, the youth treatment centre, we were not able to collect any material about the young people who live there. Consequently, while we shall offer a number of findings about closed units for girls, this material has been less systematically gathered than the information on boys.

We shall also see that the pressure for security has changed during the last 15 years from modest requests generated within the child-care system to immoderate demands voiced from outside. It is maintained that the children are becoming more difficult. This study will, therefore, explore the problems posed by the difficult and disruptive minority of children in the care of the local authorities. We shall ask, for example, whether aggressive behaviour and repeated absconding have their origins in a child's deep disturbance, as so much provision has assumed, and if so, whether security is the best answer to counter such disruptive conduct. We shall also study the structure, workings and effectiveness of the wide variety of secure accommodation that is developing within the child-care system.

For policy makers, it may not be sufficient for us to demonstrate that secure provision is expensive or that in terms of 'success' there are only limited benefits to be gained from this intervention. In extreme cases, locking up children may be the only practical solution. Originally the secure units were viewed as enabling other open institutions to function and were not intended to provide a dazzling treatment initiative. Our inquiry must, therefore, explore whether any or all the difficulties presented by secure unit candidates can be moderated in open situations. We shall illustrate other modes of intervention by looking at some experiments which tackle the problems posed by these disruptive adolescents. Finally, we suggest the ways in which local authorities can estimate their need of secure places and we shall discuss the national requirements. This study, however, is more than a needs and numbers exercise, for it raises wider, disquieting questions on the way our child-care system functions, particularly for the small minority of difficult children and young people.

Our research approach to secure provision is similar to that adopted in our previous studies of residential establishments. This design was originally developed for our work on boarding schools and modified during subsequent studies of other residential establishments. Both these methodologies have been published separately and have been used in several books on ordinary boarding schools and a range of studies of residential care.[3] It is better for a reader to explore the many complexities of studying institutional structures in these separate publications where much more space is available. All we can do here is to describe the sorts of questions which the research will be answering, how we set about our investigations and which institutions we visited.

The research approach

The research team visited and lived in each of the institutions mentioned. In the large secure units we stayed for about two weeks while in the smaller establishments the stay was shorter. During that time, we scrutinised documentary material and interviewed staff and children. In the large secure units, we began with an analysis of the boys' backgrounds and charted their progress through the system. For those boys who were released, we explored the ways in which the decisions to let them out had been reached and followed their subsequent careers. We were much concerned with the establishment, development and day-to-day running of all types of secure accommodation and we were allowed access to the reports of inspectors and regional advisers, the correspondence between the units and the higher authorities and the minutes of staff and managers' meetings.

We had found during a previous visit to the Kingswood secure unit that the children in these units find individual testing or interviewing threatening. It is closely associated in their minds with assessment and other procedures which had repeatedly led to an uncomfortable transfer from home or from a benign institution. Hence, we relied more in this research on informal group discussions and interviews with them. Questionnaires were not set directly to the children. However, all staff, not only professionals but all who had a function in the institution, were interviewed individually.

The chief focus of the study is the secure units on the campuses of three large CHEs. These establishments had been in existence for more than 10 years and a large number of boys had passed through them. At the time of our visit, Redhill had 29 boys, Redbank 25 and Kingswood 26. This made a group of 80 boys for intensive study. The follow-up investigation covered the entire population which had passed through Kingswood and Redhill and 138 boys from Redbank (55 per cent of the total intake). For those boys who had been released and on whom there was insufficient information at the units, we had to approach the local authority for additional information on their progress.

The research team also visited a number of other units for shorter periods. The purpose was to explore the experience of senior staff or those who had worked long in secure situations. Rossie Farm School, Kenmuir St Mary, Royston House at Aycliffe School were visited and, abroad, the secure unit at Fraipont, Liège and at Rossendale, Massachusetts, also provided helpful material. Intensive care units, both open and closed, also gave us great assistance, particularly those at Sedbury Park and Headlands CHEs. St Charles youth treatment centre was visited as were a number of hospital units. Discussions with staff in the adolescent unit at Broadmoor hospital and visits to the open units at Hollymoor, Exe Vale and Langdon hospitals enabled us to assess psychiatric opinions about the settings needed to care for disruptive adolescents and gave us some indications of the sorts of difficult behaviour that can be approached in open conditions. We were also able to interview some of the staff who had worked in the secure units in the early days and who were now employed elsewhere. Those who had been involved in the setting up of the first units were particularly helpful.

In the prison system, we visited Pucklechurch remand centre, Portland and Guys Marsh Borstals and had contacts with Ashford remand centre. We were interested in whether the admission of younger boys in increasing numbers to these institutions posed particular problems. In addition, we received the greatest possible help from other research units, particularly the Home Office Research Unit and Young Offenders Psychology Unit, the Research Division at the Department of Health and Social Security and the Centre de Formation et de Recherche de l'Education Surveillée at Vaucresson. All these provided us with material that has complemented our own research.

The objectivity of research

It is important at the outset of this report to clarify the concept of objectivity and to comment on the place of personal values in research. Much research into deprived and delinquent adolescents can hide the fact that the function of such knowledge is to increase the efficiency of social control. Unlike policemen or judges, whose controlling roles are inescapable, social researchers can delude themselves into identifying with Mannheim's 'free floating intellectuals' rather than with other agents of social control.[4]

We doubt the validity of this rarified, value-free perspective of research. We agree more with Merton who argued that objectivity stems more from the institutional structure of science than the neutrality of any particular inquiry.[5] Truth is established in the arena of investigation when it is governed by values of universalism, communism, disinterestedness and organised scepticism, that is, where work is judged independently of the author, where material is public, where personal interests are put aside and where sceptical evaluation is continuous.

Howard Becker once suggested that every piece of research is inevitably value-laden, not so much because of any conscious bias in the data collection but more as a result of the questions asked and the concepts employed.[6] Frequently, he claims, we accept too readily the 'official' definitions used by those in power. We accept labels such as 'criminal' or 'disruptive' without considering the respondent's definition of the problem. As our discussions on violence and absconding will argue, the participant's views may be quite logical given the situation in which they find themselves, irrespective of the moral acceptability of such behaviour to us. We assume, says Becker, that lower participants in our services have no right to be heard and accept a situation where the power holders in society define both the problem and its solution. Nowhere is this clearer than in our approach to security for disruptive children.

Most social researchers can adopt the stance of the disinterested intellectual even though we have seen that such a position is highly dubious. When, however, the research topic is highly emotive, as is the locking up of children, this attitude becomes quite unacceptable. We simply cannot escape from the key question which Becker poses, namely, 'Whose side are we on?'

We have assumed in this respect the 'liberal' position, not a fashionable one for sociologists. We feel both distaste at the prospect of locking up difficult children and concern over the damage they do and the risks they encounter while on the run. We find it difficult to accept that any adolescent under the age of 16 needs to be locked up unless the damage to himself and others resulting from his freedom is serious and manifest. We feel the case for security has continually to be made out and critically scrutinised. Locking up the child must always be the last resort, taken when alternatives have been exhausted. Unlike our studies of other residential care, when it was possible to balance the advantages and disadvantages of boarding school life from a distance, security does not allow such a neutral stance. We shall only be convinced of the need to lock up children if sufficient evidence accumulates in the following chapters.

Notes

[1] S. Millham, R. Bullock and P. Cherrett, *After Grace – Teeth*, London, Human Context Books, Chaucer Publishing Company, 1975.

6

[2] *Expenditure Committee Report on 1969 Children and Young Persons' Act*, London, HMSO, 1975.

[3] See R. Lambert, S. Millham and R. Bullock, *A Manual to the Sociology of the School*, London, Weidenfeld & Nicolson, 1970; S. Millham, R. Bullock and P. Cherrett, 'A conceptual scheme for the comparative analysis of residential institutions', in J. Tizard, I. Sinclair and R. V. G. Clarke (eds), *Varieties of Residential Experience*, London, Routledge and Kegan Paul, 1975, pp. 203-24 and S. Millham, R. Bullock and P. Cherrett, methodological appendix to *A Comparative Study of Eighteen Boys' Approved Schools which compares their Stylistic Variety and the Commitment of Boys and Staff*, Dartington Social Research Unit, 1972.

[4] K. Mannheim, *Ideology and Utopia*, New York, Harcourt, Brace, 1936.

[5] R. K. Merton, 'Science and democratic social structure' in *Social Theory and Social Structure*, Glencoe, Free Press, 1957, pp. 550-61.

[6] H. S. Becker, 'Whose side are we on?', *Social Problems*, vol. XIV, 1967, pp. 239-47.

Part I
The historical context

These moral entrepeneurs were as concerned with the severity of the law towards delinquent children as they were with the consequences of locking them up. Indeed, their campaign failed to distinguish between public perspectives on delinquency, the consequences of severe sentences and high court appearances for juveniles, the appropriate legal intervention and the final suitable placement of the child. In ways similar to the 1969 Act, this confusion over ends and means blunted the impact of reformation and allowed scope for the development of alarm and coercive reaction to modest reformative proposals.

Admittedly, there were great difficulties inherent in tackling common law where children were tried and punished in much the same way as adults. Reform of the law was slow and piece-meal and over time children gained protection from accumulating statute. There were recommendations for change in the nature of a child's criminal responsibility in 1818, in 1827 and in 1828, all without success. Even the Law Commissioners' report of 1837, which recommended that a distinction be drawn between adults and those under 16 convicted of larceny, and that justices should have some summary powers on the punishment of children, took 10 years for modest implementation.

Although the reformers' zeal led them to confuse appropriate sentencing with the consequences of imprisoning juveniles, their campaigns had effect and they were fuelled by the continuous and disturbing reports on the conditions of young children in prison. Naturally, much debate centred on the reformative as opposed to the retributive intentions of locking up young people. Frequently the timid efforts of the government to separate the young from hardened criminals provoked more reforming wrath than the practice of long prison sentences for juveniles. Parkhurst Prison for boys, created in 1838, where boys wore leg irons until 1840, was long blistered by the pen of Mary Carpenter as wholly unsuitable. At least these boys enjoyed a preferable fate from those consigned to another state experiment, the juvenile prison hulks. These 'floating Bastilles' were located on HMS *Bellerophon* in 1823 and, two years later, on the *Euryalus*, retired from Trafalgar fame, to house boys too tender for adult prisons. Both in formal regime and informally, they were frightful. Boys of 9 chose solitary confinement to protect themselves from the 'nobs', other boys who terrorised the ship. Many self-inflicted injuries occurred to ensure transfer ashore to the convict prisons. Indeed, the young children had less protection under this 'improvement' than they had previously enjoyed among adult prisoners awaiting transportation. These hulks provided a rich and constant source of scandal until, largely unreformed, they were swallowed up in the creation of the reformatory and industrial schools.[5]

The deprived as well as the delinquent were receiving considerable attention in the early nineteenth century. Dissatisfaction had increased during the late eighteenth century with Poor Law provision for children. The laxity of the parish apprenticeship system was highlighted, particularly by William Hanway's skilful championing of boy chimney sweeps. Cheapness was the only criterion on which the boarding out of children or workhouse care was evaluated and, consequently, the mortality rates of children were sufficiently alarming to precipitate government action in 1762.

By 1818, the poor children of Portsmouth were attending John Pond's Ragged School and his example caught on. In the north, a tradition of helping the children of the poor was well-established. Some factory owners, echoing Robert Owen, tried to soften the impact of industrialisation on families and the Sunday school movement was flourishing. Thomas Coram's eighteenth century experiment at Coram Fields had many imitators. Indeed, much of this voluntary effort sprang from the clear inadequacies of the small, community-based, largely rural, child-care system to meet the needs of a rapidly expanding industrial society. The growth of towns, the migration from the countryside and demands for female and child labour disrupted families and increased child casualties.

Now it is not this slow and grudging shift to a benign stance towards the young that is our main concern. More revealing are the many familiar institutional features that these origins exhibit.

Initially, in spite of advancing solemn claims to be saving the children of the perishing classes, it is remarkable how selective were all the early child-care establishments. Mary Carpenter's Red Lodge, a reformatory for girls established in Bristol in 1854, would only accept girls below the age of 14 and not a 'penitentiary case'. Her Ragged School, founded earlier, down the hill at Lewin's Mead, was similarly exclusive. Mary Carpenter made a clear distinction between the destitute child and the juvenile offender. Older children were viewed as tainted by their associations or experiences and had little hope of salvation. In a situation where supply greatly exceeded provision, philanthropy inevitably concentrated on those where hope was greatest. The Royal Philanthropic School also discriminated carefully. In 1796 a committee recommended that no boy over the age of 13 should be admitted, because older boys were incorrigible and girls of 'unchaste manners' were to be excluded. The fact that these institutions could shelter only one in 10 of those children offered to them by magistrates put them in a strong negotiating position. It seems as if contemporary problems and current institutional strategies have considerable antecedents.

In an attempt to improve the management of children, an internal classifying system was rapidly adopted at Redhill in the last decade of the eighteenth century. The more hopeful candidates, bearing a strong resemblance to John Gittins's 'A' boys, were cherished while the less promising boys fared ill.[6] Girls were separated from boys, older children from younger, the deprived from the depraved. Parkhurst and Red Lodge followed suit and the reformatory schools that blossomed in the 1840s, particularly after the Act of 1854, sifted their boys in a similar way. Thus assessment was, in origin, nakedly organisational and had to wait for more than a century for its cloak of diagnosis and treatment.

Control in these institutions was largely utilitarian and coercive. Redhill had a system of rewards and privileges which was well established by 1800 and the reformatories which worked boys for a profit, offered visits from home, letters and access to the outside world as recompense to the orthodox and industrious. Children's pocket money was much manipulated as a reward; so was food and clothing.

Rudimentary education and trade training were an integral part of this controlling approach. The boys are described as able but lacking in application and the girls as feckless. All were deficient in attainment and were to be saved by learning some skill. Indeed, the hierarchy of trades, so familiar to community home staff, appeared early with, inevitably, kitchen work at the bottom and carpentry at the top.

In spite of optimistic statements by the principals about the value of inspired staff and religious conviction, the successive removal of key adults from many schools in the early days would suggest that, both in control and moral exemplar, they were lacking. As today, the problems of finding and keeping residential care staff preoccupied the early years.

Absconding was a major problem from the outset in all institutions for children. For example, the management committee of the Philanthropic Society reported in 1796 that of the 176 boys admitted up to that time, 51 had absconded. Because the institution had no legal right to retain children, the principal found it very difficult to get the absconders back. In contrast, girls were less footloose and less delinquent on the run. Of the first 60 girls admitted, only 5 had run away.[7] But absconding was not new; running away had plagued the charity schools in the two preceding centuries and it was highly contagious.

However, if absconding was early established, so was the answer to these runaways. In 1591 'a lumpen boy' ran away from Christ's Hospital and, on his return, was taken by the beadle to be locked up in the Bridewell.[8] It was one of this dignitary's Sunday functions to tour the region around St Paul's rounding up begging and vagrant children for the school. In Norwich runaways received punishment and 'a collar of yron at the Bridewell'. It seems that no child-care institution or workhouse worth its salt was without a cell in the seventeenth and eighteenth centuries.

At Redhill, while all might have been well in the fields, Sydney Turner, who did so much to establish the school, tells us in 1830 that, 'If the reward system fails, cells are used with a diet of bread and water for a period ranging from a few hours to a few days. The cells are unheated and should give the inmate just as much cold and privation and discomfort as proper regard to health, cleanliness and the making of a kindly impression on the offender will allow of'.[9]

Indeed, even before the move from London, the Royal Philanthropic had made part of St George's, Southwark, a secure 'prison', as it was called, and a little later had established a secure reform block at Bermondsey. These units were to provide a salutory check to the recalcitrant and the industrial and reformatory schools, 40 of which were built in the decade after 1854, all had cells. Indeed, as structures the schools were very secure in their own right, with bars on the windows and locked doors, many of which survived until the early days of this century. Not that their children were unacquainted with maximum security – many had lingered in prison for long periods before entry and a policy was adopted by the managers of the reformatory schools to keep children in prison by delaying their admission to the institutions. It rendered boys 'more malleable' and 'suitably respectful'. This prior imprisonment survived until 1899 and, linked with the gaunt enormity of the

15

reformatories and their boys' long and exploitative stay, did much to forfeit public esteem for the institutions.

Another gift to the present residential child-care system was a pattern of transfer and expulsion of difficult children. Anyone who disturbed institutional peace was quickly removed. Large numbers of children were returned to the prison system. Indeed, to read much of nineteenth and early twentieth century writing on the residential care of young offenders and other vulnerable children is to realise how much schools relied on a number of closed or distant alternatives into which the unattractive child could be thrust. The armed forces, the mercantile marine and, in the early nineteenth century, transportation greatly helped to solve the delinquency problem. Of Redhill's early releases nearly half went to sea and Sydney Turner felt that the army or the colonies were his boys' salvation. In many ways it was difficult to distinguish between assisted emigration to Australia, New Zealand and South Africa from compulsory transportation, for, under both systems boys and girls were apprenticed on arrival, often with great success, to settler families. It was a well-tried practice for as early as 1619 100 children had left the London Bridewell for Virginia and in 1703 an Act empowered magistrates to put boys aged 10 for sea service or to apprentice them abroad.

By the end of the nineteenth century, shipping out had become well established. In times of distress assisted emigration, particularly of the young, was the biggest contribution made by the Charity Organisation Society.[10] In 1891 Admiral Field, criticising the Under Secretary for the Home Department on the state of the ship schools, brought no gasps from Parliamentary members when he revealed mutinies on the TS *Akbar* in 1878 or the damp, swampy conditions on the TS *Havana*. Indeed, the following statement brought general approval; 'I only want to secure a supply of boys for our ships. The schools are intended to train boys for the mercantile marine, to supply a waste of life of 4,000 or 5,000 persons drowned every year'.[11] It was a spirit of supply and demand with which all members present concurred. Today such an obliging Davy Jones locker would transform the child-care scene and, it should be remembered that at the end of the nineteenth century, disease and accident were claiming as many sailors as drowning.

However, one final nineteenth century legacy should not go unnoticed although it affected a wider range of children than the delinquent group. There was a rapid growth in institutional care to meet a wide variety of needs in the nineteenth century. Applying the factory system to social problems, economies of size encouraged the growth of large institutions, particularly for the criminal, the sick and the destitute. Many of these were secure and isolated. As each new category of need was identified, so a residential solution was advanced.

Beside the railways, as they advanced from London, the Palladian domes and alien campaniles of a hundred institutions blossomed. What was good for the perishing classes was also good for the less perishable. There was an enormous expansion in boarding education in the nineteenth century and lonely lads, tanned with the suns of Empire, sat on trunks going everywhere.[12]

If young offenders had their share of reform and legislation, so did other children.[13] In the reign of Queen Victoria more than 100 acts were passed specifically concerned with the welfare of children. Educational debate was continuous and even the children of legislators had their own inquiries. The Public School Commission sat almost continuously through the mid-decades of the nineteenth century. Indeed, the Children's Acts of 1894 and 1908 had to elbow their way through an avalanche of benevolent legislation for children in a way that makes the 1969 Act look positively lonely. But as administrators and politicians eagerly seized on a new range of problems, at least the solution was ever with them. It was the boarding institution which had fashioned them into a distinguished, distant and incorruptible élite.

Thus, nearly two hundred years ago, much present child-care practice was established. We can note the ideas of an effective system bedevilled by a recalcitrant minority. There was careful selection of clients and the leaving of the unpalatable child to fortune. The need to classify those admitted for organisational reasons was recognised early, as was the use of secure rooms or consignment to prison, the ultimate deterrent in a battery of utilitarian and coercive controls. Finally, there was the wholesale shipping out of those who disturbed institutional peace and an expulsion of them to anything that was distant and secure.

The difficulties of change

It is also clear in reading much of the early history that benign approaches to juveniles are not cumulative. They are subject to changes associated with wider economic and social forces. Tudor society, concerned with the commonweal and the stability of the extended rural family, attempted a more comprehensive child-care policy than did the two subsequent centuries. In the eighteenth and early nineteenth centuries the needs of early industrial society for a cheap, malleable and expendable labour supply meant that pauperism was viewed as being as great a threat to the well-being of society as was child neglect or delinquency. This concern greatly hindered the efforts of reformers. It may be that the shrinkage of the birth rate at the end of the nineteenth century and the need for a nourished, educated proletariat led to the more conservationist policies towards the children of the poor, an approach we still enjoy today.

Change was not easy and did not develop from a general consensus that some benevolent action towards the disadvantaged young was necessary. As social policy, particularly towards children, is caring in its intentions, it is easily assumed that once ignorance is banished and improvements devised, dispute and opposition will diminish. Retrospectively this can often seem to be the case. Certainly the nineteenth century reformers did succeed in removing large numbers of children from prison and spared them sentences of transportation. For example, in 1844 389 boys between the ages of 14 and 17 were sentenced to transportation in London alone.[14] In 1853 in England and Wales 12,000 young persons were sent to prison in a single year. However, the protesters brought an end to transportation in 1859

17

and by 1900 the number of young people in prison had fallen to about 1,700. Radical alternatives to imprisonment also flourished for, in 1857, the reformatory and industrial schools housed just over 2,000 boys and girls, yet, by 1900, the children sheltered had increased in number to just under 30,000.

However, the ship of reform did not have an easy passage. It tacked frequently and jettisoned many a cherished ideal overboard to the sharks of reaction. Any ameliorative legislation was bitterly fought and even after Acts of Parliament, it took considerable time for new policies finally to be implemented and for the judiciary and administration to participate unreservedly. Indeed, the parallels with the Children and Young Persons' Act of 1969 are remarkable.

Throughout the nineteenth century politicians frequently cited public opinion as being resistant to change. In 1840, on a visit to the young prisoners at Parkhurst, the Home Secretary refused an appeal for clemency from the governor on behalf of an eight-year-old. He justified his inflexibility 'because of the suspicion in the public mind of the first advances at Parkhurst towards the better treatment of offenders'. As late as 1906 Mr Wedgwood, a Member of Parliament, was conducting a skilful campaign of embarrassment against the Home Secretary forcing him to concede that 1,028 persons under the age of 16 had been committed to prison in the previous year, the majority of these committals being for the non-payment of fines of less than ten shillings.[15] But many members resented the criticisms of Mr Wedgwood and particularly his implied strictures on magistrates.

Even after the Children's Act of 1908, young people were still being sent to prison and *Hansard* abounds with members' illustrations of the ways in which the intentions of the Act were being subvened. It is a pity that Mr Winston Churchill, as Home Secretary in 1908, is not with us today. He comments:

> I would ask the House to consider specially the case of youths between sixteen and twenty-one. There is a disaster in sending a lad of that age to prison and an old prison visitor told me that they often cry the first time. It is an evil which falls only on the sons of the working class. The sons of other classes may commit many of the same kinds of offence and in boisterous moments, whether at Oxford or anywhere else, may do things for which the working class lad would be committed to prison. Let the House remember that there are at least five thousand lads committed to prison for minor offences and rowdyism each year.[16]

Although change was slow and grudging, by the end of the nineteenth century the reforms had at least managed to educate the legislators and judiciary. For example, the report of the departmental committee on the industrial and reformatory schools of 1896 shows a change of perspective.[17] It concerned itself less with either juggling forms of custody or with the benefits of institutional care and concentrated more on the welfare of the child. It questioned the need to remove the child from his home, the wisdom of gathering delinquent children together and argued that offenders were the victims of social forces rather than moral weakness and needed care not punishment. This committee, by blurring the functions of the industrial and reformatory schools, emphasised the similarities between a delinquent and a deprived child. All subsequent legislation for children at risk has followed this departure.

The 1908 Children's Act reinforced this stance by aiming at a more child-centred legal system. As an alternative to imprisonment, the Act made a wide variety of provision available to magistrates and it initiated the juvenile courts to balance welfare and justice. Many subsequent Home Office reports and the Children's Acts of 1932 and 1933 merely consolidated this position.

Unfortunately, the incompatibility of the welfare and judicial perspectives was rarely explored. Indeed, the conflict was perversely recognised in many official reports by proclamations that it did not exist. During the next 50 years the efforts to keep children from prison and to provide alternative secure places for remand, the expansion of probation and the development of the Borstal system meant that there was little time for philosophic discussion of the care or custody dispute. Neither did the conflict arise in practice, because the welfare of the child in the juvenile courts rarely had priority.[18] Magistrates offered the erring adolescent an explicitly punitive menu with the approved school order as the chef's special.

Unfortunately, these diverting issues had withered by 1969 and, by overtly challenging the power of the judiciary, the Children and Young Persons' Act brought conflict into the open. It was all the more vociferous because, unlike nineteenth century legislation and the more recent legislation of 1948, the ship of reform sailed alone against a tide of increasing hostility to the young which had been running through the 1960s.

The institutional response

Unfortunately for those seeking radical alternative approaches to delinquency, another pressure group had emerged. With increasing political sophistication, the residential institutions set up to contain difficult children made their claims explicit, the chief of which has always been to stay in business.

The institutions never doubted their custodial role and responded to vicissitudes in public and administrative esteem in a time-honoured way. For example, while crime rates rose rapidly in the Great War, the chances of the young offender receiving a residential placement diminished.[19] Indeed, 40 industrial and reformatory schools were closed in the period immediately following the Great War and the institutions were subject to both general and official criticism. Ironically, this was the period of their greatest success. The managers and headmasters fought vigorously for their institutions in a way reminiscent of the campaign which preceded the 1969 Act. As schools closed they offered themselves as bizarre alternatives, suggesting that they act as 'mild Borstals' or 'schools for the maladjusted or physically handicapped'.[20] They stressed the problems created by the varied nature of their boy population and, above all, the schools justified themselves because of the increasingly difficult boys the magistrates finally decided to consign to them.

19

It was a powerful lobby and these claims were officially recognised in interwar Home Office reports. A committee of 1927 urged that the fullest possible information be provided to schools to aid their 'treatment task'.[21] Similarly, it recognised the problems posed by a small group of very difficult boys within the system. The committee urged that something had to be done.

A system of classification and allocation was introduced at Aycliffe in 1942 and spread rapidly.[22] Unfortunately, classification's optimistic intention of matching child need with institutional provision and the highlighting of problem boys set the schools off on a path diametrically opposed to that followed by legislation. The school system looked inward, towards increasingly sophisticated programmes of treatment for clearly differentiated types of clients. The legislators looked outward, focusing on the similarities between offenders and all other children at risk. They were seeking an integrated pattern of residential child care. As with the conflict just illustrated between the welfare and justice perspectives on young offenders, the differing viewpoints between the practice of the schools and the intentions of policy makers waited until 1969 for an airing.

The 1939–45 war with its rising crime rates kept the approved schools, as they were called after 1933, in business. The Curtis Report of 1946,[23] preoccupied with the general problems of children in residential care, let the approved schools off lightly. The committee felt that the boys' schools were 'well conducted and humane'. But they were less happy with the schools for senior girls. Incidentally, they strictured the general use of corporal punishment in schools and the practice of locking up children for long periods of time, particularly girl absconders, 'whose hair was cut short and who wore loose sacks as a punishment'. Even the reports of the Home Office Inspectorate mellowed considerably after the war and they became a vehicle for reassuring public opinion that all was well in the schools rather than offering criticism.

Unfortunately, all was not well. The school structures had changed very little during the interwar years and were less suited to the more sophisticated, postwar delinquent. Their success rates were falling, their boys and girls were absconding more frequently. The institutions embarked on yet another period of uncertainty for, again, many were closed and criticism mounted. Naturally, the schools' first line of defence was much as before. Their boys on arrival were becoming increasingly difficult and a series of scandals helped this image. In 1947, at Standon Farm School, a staff member was shot and the assassins absconded.[24] While the subsequent committee of inquiry revealed considerable deficiencies in the school, the report supported the idea of an intractable minority that disrupted the approved school system and rendered the treatment of other children impossible. What should be done with the violent and with the disruptive absconder? Unfortunately, there was a ready answer at hand, it was provided by the secure rooms that in many schools stored boxes, at Standon the rifles for the cadet force and elsewhere, already held the difficult child or the absconder.

As early as 1951–52 it can be noted in the Franklin Report that strong representations had been received by the committee from the heads of both boys' and girls'

[handwritten margin notes: abnormally narrowed tightened]

20

approved schools that a closed school or a closed block, attached to an open school, be established for the difficult child or the persistent absconders.[25] According to the Franklin Report, the children's department of the Home Office were, at that time, 'considering the possibility of a school with a closed block', and the report strongly recommended that 'the experiment should be undertaken as soon as possible'. It took 15 years of soul-searching hesitation before these suggestions were implemented and in the next chapter we will see how these experiments, now an integral part of the child-care system, were mounted.

In conclusion, it is useful to summarise the heritage of secure units. First, the isolation and locking up of the recalcitrant has a long and largely unbroken tradition in the care of deprived children. In times of stress, change or liberal reform, demands for security will form part of a wider reactive chorus which emphasises the need for caution and strictness. The behaviour problems that face the authorities in looking after difficult children today have changed very little. Absconding has always been a challenge and hostile, aggressive adolescents are a constant feature of a century of official reports. From time to time, violence and uncooperative behaviour has affected residential institutions and become public knowledge. However, the alternatives open to those caring for the recalcitrant have become increasingly circumscribed in recent years and the growth of alternative care provision for disturbed and handicapped children has left exposed a residual minority of difficult young people. Solutions are not so immediately obvious. We no longer have a voracious mercantile marine. The disappearance of cheap lodgings, the decline in unskilled occupations and the general increase in unemployment have magnified the disposal difficulties faced by authorities, particularly for boys in their mid-teens. The increasing selectivity and decline in numbers of the armed forces should also be noted for, until very recently, they took many vulnerable boys and did well with them. We would suggest that while the problems of difficult children have not changed, they have become increasingly visible.

Another strong influence can be noted. Because residential institutions do not enjoy uninterrupted esteem and official approval tends to be fitful, the schools are highly sensitive, collectively organised and politically astute. Thus, they have developed effective strategies for coping with change or threats of closure. The most cogent apologia has always been the 'dustbin' role of the schools, the problems posed by a heterogeneous group of boys, the lack of special facilities and the insoluble problems presented by an aggressive, hostile minority of inmates about whom something should be done.

The 1969 Children and Young Persons' Act generated considerable anxiety in the approved schools, particularly as they became the responsibility of the social services departments of the local authorities who had rather different ideas on what constituted care. The schools responded by emphasising their onerous task and the difficulties posed by the children.

While the development of the secure units came from within the system and was under way long before the Children and Young Persons' Act of 1969, the concept of security is today often used as a synonym for a general tightening of control and is increasingly advanced as the solution to a variety of manifest difficulties. Because of the strength of the institutional tradition in this country, we inevitably try to solve the problems of one set of institutions by creating another group, albeit smaller and more specialised. We would accept that these observations do not provide clear guidelines for practice but suggest that because security fulfils a wide variety of expectations, some of which are symbolic and unquantifiable, it seems likely that matching provision with demand will be difficult.

Notes

[1] Athelstan, *Judicia Civitatis Lundoniae sub rege Aethalstano edita*, 10th century.
[2] I. Pinchbeck·and M. Hewitt, *Children in English Society*, London, Routledge and Kegan Paul, 1973.
[3] I. Pinchbeck et al., *Children in English Society*, op. cit., pp. 137, 138, 141.
[4] For a full discussion of these developments, see J. Carlebach, *Caring for Children in Trouble*, London, Routledge and Kegan Paul, 1970 and H. Gaillac, *Les Maisons de Correction*, Paris, Edition Curjas, 1971.
[5] See W. Branch-Johnson, *The English Prison Hulks*, London, Phillimore, 1970.
[6] J. Gittins, *Approved School Boys*, London, HMSO, 1952.
[7] See J. Carlebach, *Caring for Children in Trouble*, op. cit., chap. 1.
[8] Quoted in the *Christ's Hospital Book*, London, Hamish Hamilton, 1953.
[9] Quoted in J. Carlebach, *Caring for Children in Trouble*, op. cit., p. 63.
[10] M. Roof, *One Hundred Years of Family Welfare*, London, Michael Joseph, 1972.
[11] Reported in *Hansard*, 23 March 1891.
[12] T. W. Bamford, *The Rise of the Public Schools*, London, Nelson, 1967.
[13] P. Boss, *Social Policy and the Young Delinquent*, London, Routledge and Kegan Paul, 1967.
[14] Compiled from an analysis of replies to Parliamentary questions between 1890 and 1914.
[15] See *Hansard* for 31 October and 19 November 1906.
[16] *Hansard*, 20 July 1910.
[17] *Report of the Departmental Committee on Reformatory and Industrial Schools*, C. 8204, London, HMSO, 1896.
[18] See J. Carlebach, *Caring for Children in Trouble*, op. cit., W. Elkin, *English Juvenile Courts*, London, Routledge and Kegan Paul, 1938 and M. Fry, *The Arms of the Law*, London, Gollancz, 1951. See also the debate following the 1927 Working Party Report and the 1933 Children's Act.
[19] See *First Report Home Office Children's Branch*, London, HMSO, 1923 and *Third Report*, 1925.
[20] A series of articles in the *Certified Schools Gazette* for 1920 discusses these problems.

[21] *Report of the Departmental Committee on the Treatment of Young Offenders*, Cmd 2831, London, HMSO, 1927.
[22] See J.Gittins, *Approved School Boys*, op. cit.
[23] *Report of the Care of Children Committee*, Cmd 6922, London, HMSO, 1946.
[24] *Report of the Committee of Inquiry into the Conduct of Standon Farm Approved School*, Cmnd 937, London, HMSO, 1947.
[25] *Report of a Committee to review Punishments in Prisons, Borstals, Approved Schools and Remand Homes*, London, HMSO, 1951.

3 The establishment of the secure units

Hesitation might characterise the English; it rarely crosses the northern border. The Scots soon established their secure units for, in 1958, a 15-year-old boy led a riot at Springboig, a Christian Brothers' school near Glasgow. The boy was extremely violent, though not particularly delinquent, and was destined for subsequent fulfilment as a bouncer in a Mecca ballroom. List D schools, as the Scottish approved schools are now known, were apprehensive and, bowing to their pressure, an Under Secretary set out from the Scottish Office to Rossie Farm School, a remote institution well known for its no-nonsense regime.

Originally a bothy, sheltering young boys released from Dundee prison, Rossie Farm had passed by way of a granite reformatory block to possess a dazzling building in the international style which was opened in 1939. With a wide terrace and Metro-Goldwyn staircase more suited, it seems, to Hedy Lamarr than Glasgow 'bother-boys', the institution rises unexpectedly from a blasted heath four miles off the road that links Arbroath to Montrose, closeness to home not having much priority in its treatment approaches. As a senior staff member said, 'We pointed out that security was unnecessary, most of our absconders would die of exposure anyway, but you don't have a visit from a top civil servant for nothing and when he left, we found ourselves the proud possessor of the first secure unit in the British Isles.'

Bars were added to the original reform block, still pristine after a thousand North Sea gales and a total of 26 boys, reputedly the most difficult in Scotland, were moved in. Supervised by six staff in two shifts of three, the boys rarely left the unit. The main exercise facilities were provided by the frenzied polishing of floors. The tensions within the unit in the first 18 months led to a mutiny. The boys turned on the duty staff and escaped while a small group of boys remained to offer assistance. The implications of these events were clear. Something different from prison was needed if children were to be locked up.

In the summer of 1959, while the secure unit was bubbling, a caravan from Bedfordshire pulled into the grounds of Rossie Farm. The headmaster of Carlton School had arrived for a family holiday, benefiting from that camaraderie which links approved school headmasters. Unfortunately, his long vacation became a mini-break, for his departure from Carlton gave the signal for a disturbance there. Boys climbed on the roof and, mixing tiles with abuse, defied the staff to get them down. Skilfully exploited by a local journalist with little love for the institution, the disturbance became public. However, as the headmaster of Carlton's caravan left Rossie for the awesome trek down the unreformed A1, he drove past a possible solution to problem boys – the newly created secure unit.

The Durand Report, which explored this disturbance,[1] recommended that 'the establishment of one or more schools (as necessary) with closed facilities should be considered for boys'. It also recommended that some way should be found of removing from the approved school system 'senior boys who are unruly or subversive and who have shown themselves quite unsuitable for approved school training'. A little later that year, the report of the committee on the law relating to children and young persons, recommended that the closed blocks should be associated with the classifying schools, mainly because they were cheaper to run, sharing facilities with the parent school.

In May of that same year, 1960, between the publication of the above two reports and probably affecting the content of the latter, the Approved Schools Central Advisory Committee Working Party on closed and other special facilities published its report. It recommended the following boys as candidates for security:

(a)   persistent absconders;
(b)   exceptionally unruly and uncooperative boys;
(c)   exceptionally disturbed boys requiring psychiatric help;
(d)   medical misfits, e.g. epileptics and diabetics.

Clearly, reading the report, one is forced to the conclusion that the units were to be a rag-bag of those boys who were disrupting the system, a function that was to be extended as new categories of threatening adolescents were created. For example, children who committed very serious crimes (Section 53 of the Children and Young Persons' Act 1933) were added in 1968 and boys with threatening homosexual behaviour in 1969. Treatment, even if known, could hardly be applied to such a varied group of children. But the committee had, in fact, nothing to say about treatment except to offer the usual platitudes about making it positive and making every practical effort to improve it. The committee also endorsed the Durand Report conclusion that unruly boys should be transferred to Borstal and that the use of one or two detention rooms might smooth the daily tasks of those approved schools taking older boys.

Three reports [2] in a year could not be ignored and negotiations were begun to establish secure units at the classifying schools. They were to shelter about twenty boys each from the age of 13 and they were to be explicitly punitive, although the term 'brisk' is used in the reports. Indeed, the timetable which the Home Office recommended to the schools closely mirrors that of the detention centres, a point we shall explore shortly. Rising at 6.30 a.m. the daily programme was to keep the boys as physically and mentally occupied as possible. Dress was to be carefully regulated and a respectful demeanour to be sought among the boys; home leaves were to be allowed only in exceptional circumstances and even the occasional television programme was to be strictly educational. Indeed, in planning the unit's regime and in finding staff for the unit, the prison department provided the Home Office with the only shoulder to lean on. 'We knew nothing about it and they did; in planning Redhill the Prison Inspector got out a cigarette packet and said "It should be shaped like this with a courtyard in the middle, the cells should be round the outside. That will stop the smell from slopping out".'

Even before the units opened, however, the approved schools' staff, particularly those in the classifying schools, were having second thoughts about security. Schools had increasingly justified themselves on treatment criteria, seeking a sophisticated system which could match boys' need with provision. Naturally, they disliked the 'dustbin' role assigned to the units. Aycliffe, learning from past experience, refused to have a unit. Kingswood managers hesitated, at least until they received assurance from the Home Office that a more treatment-oriented approach could be tried. Reluctantly, the Home Office accepted these reservations and the Kingswood special unit opened in 1964. The second secure unit at Redhill followed shortly in July 1965 and the third, at Redbank School, Newton le Willows, opened in 1966.

It is also worth noting that the introduction of maximum security for juveniles was part of an increasingly punitive approach to the young offender which can be traced back to the late 1950s. Nowhere is it more clearly demonstrated than in the development of the detention centres. While in the 1950s the approved schools had difficulty in maintaining their position because juvenile crime rates were relatively static, with the older adolescent offender things were very different. The White Paper, *Penal Practice in a Changing Society*,[3] published in February 1959, shows governmental concern over the steady increase in the convictions of young people aged roughly from 16 to 21. Their answer was to increase the number of detention centres; these were places intended to give the young offender a short, sharp shock of minimum duration and to keep the older boy out of prison or Borstal and the younger boy out of remand homes.

The detention centres had a healthy pedigree.[4] Their origins go back to the efforts in 1908 to provide an alternative place of detention for boys in prison. This 'place of detention', as it was rather vaguely called in 1908, was increasingly orchestrated in 1927, 1933 and 1938. But in 1948 the detention centres, which were explicitly punitive, were finally given the go-ahead, partly to offset the soft implications of abolishing judicial corporal punishment and partly to take the pressure off Borstals and prisons. When implemented, the centres were certainly more rigorous than anything envisaged in previous reports. They were administered by the prison department and the Home Secretary explicitly rejected any reformative or educative components in their regime or even a minimum of after-care.

Although the first detention centre to be opened had been a junior one at Kidlington, near Oxford in April 1952, it was reported in 1958 to have several vacancies. But if development of the centres was fitful and tardy in the early 1950s, it grew in significance at the end of the decade when seven were opened for senior boys and two for girls within the space of two years. In 1952, 75 boys were admitted to detention centres and during the next five years the figures crept slowly to over 1,000. However, by 1965 they had jumped in numbers to well over 6,000 places. All this was in spite of evidence that they were taking some boys who were quite unfitted for the experience and that, in any case, they were ineffective. Borstal and prison receptions, which the detention centres had originally been intended to reduce, similarly rose in number, Borstal places increasing from just over 2,000 in 1952 to 4,000 by 1965, while prison reception more than doubled in the same period.

26

Although the growing crime rate among older adolescents partly explains the growing use of custody, it can be seen that discussions on security for younger boys within the approved school system took place in a generally favourable climate.

However, this punitive approach towards the young offender did not go unchallenged, at least from within. It did not take long for the treatment philosophy of the approved schools and the containment intentions of the Home Office to conflict over their new secure units. The schools deftly rejected the custodial and punitive perspectives of their masters. At the end of two years, the working party set up to consider the units' progress commented that the units' custodial and punitive regimes had been much modified. Boys were allowed much more freedom; home leave and visits outside the units were common and some boys were working on the campus or in the neighbourhood. Instead of the younger boys dominating the institutions, older boys, many of them eligible for Borstal, were in the majority. They were staying much longer than originally intended and the disruptive boys that figured in the formative discussions setting up the units were sparsely represented. Neither had all the boys been tried in other residential settings; some were being admitted on court rather than school recommendations and were being returned direct to the outside world. This certainly did not suit the Home Office for security had ceased to be the priority and the more the units rejected their 'dustbin' role, the more the aggressive and psychologically disturbed boys were excluded from them.

In 1969, the reconvened Home Office working party was asked to produce a review of the special units' functioning to provide guidelines for the local authorities that were about to assume responsibility for the units. In their reports a number of old strands reappear. We read that the failure of the units – almost all of their boys were reconvicted – sprang from inadequate selection criteria. The report complains of the 'dustbin' functions of the units and the magistrates' ignorance of the treatment potential of these special facilities. Yet another institutional answer was offered to an institutional problem. Redhill, uneasily followed by Redbank and Kingswood, decided that padded cells were necessary for very disturbed boys. The practice of shipping out the difficult children also reappeared. We read of the need for an institution to cope with the severely disturbed boys and girls where long-term psychiatric care would be available. Those children who had committed serious crimes and who were detained under Section 53 of the Children and Young Persons' Act of 1933 were also reluctantly brought into the orbit of the units, although the inability of staff to offer any long-term treatment for the psychologically disturbed and dangerous young person was increasingly stressed. Inevitably, another set of institutions was envisaged and the indefatigable working parties began again. Their labours were to reach fruition in the provision of youth treatment centres, part of whose provision was to be secure. All that was needed was a catalyst. It fell to two sad children who had committed grave offences to make the problem one of national concern, highlighting the issue and legitimising the solution.

We can see that the units developed, from pressure within the system the idea that the effective care of the majority of children was prevented by a disruptive minority. It was linked with beliefs about the increasing difficulty of all children admitted to residential care. The strength of the institutional tradition meant that answers to difficulties were always sought in institutional contexts. The custodial and punitive heritage of the schools meant that security had always been seen as the way of meeting institutional disruption. In some residential schools the cell had even survived in use. However, the Home Office's acceptance of the schools' time-honoured defence in times of crisis finally presented the system with a set of custodial units which were difficult to reconcile with the schools' increasing 'treatment' rationale. The more the secure units moved towards treatment, the more they shipped out in philosophy and practice those children that did not fit.

However, by 1969 the units had been in existence several years. While their places were full and a small waiting list existed, there had been no overwhelming demand for places. Indeed, when the units were being planned, estimates were sought from the system as to how many children needed security and only 60 places were thought to be necessary. Yet, by March 1975, in a written reply to the expenditure committee (the social services sub-committee), the Department of Health and Social Security provided an estimate of 673 secure places which were planned or already in existence in the assessment centres or community homes system.[5] Nearly two-thirds of these places were intended for boys. In the same way the youth treatment centres were envisaged as sheltering 200 children by 1978. There seems to be a marked increase each time estimates of need for special facilities are given but the ways in which these estimates have been made is rarely explained.

Admittedly, in August 1970 a Home Office circular suggested that up to 500 places in security might be necessary in England and Wales. It is likely, however, that this figure was based on the assumption that the 1969 legislation regarding boys under the age of 17 in Borstals would be implemented. By 1975 when the Department of Health and Social Security estimates were made, this legislation had been indefinitely postponed. While the estimates are confusing, there is little doubt that the provision of security, both actual and envisaged, is increasing. A glance at the 1969 Act will suggest why.

The 1969 Act brought into the open many unresolved conflicts. Most important of these was the clash between the welfare perspectives of social work and the judicial/control perspectives of magistrates and police. Alison Morris has cogently argued that the welfare and control perspectives cannot meet.[6] She suggests that the expectations and role performances of liberal legislators, social workers, the judiciary and the police are in conflict and are irreconcilable. Certainly after the 1969 Act magistrates did feel that they had been deceived into thinking the survival of the juvenile court meant that they could still influence the future of young offenders. Similarly, the police, who had welcomed the Act and created juvenile liaison schemes and juvenile bureaux, found that their alerts on children at risk were largely ignored by social services departments.[7] Frustration mounted as it was felt that children in care appeared to get neither supervision nor residential placements and, inevitably, this produced demands for firmer control. The old approved school system that was demonstrably failing by 1969 became, in retrospect, a golden system. The fact that security was not an important feature of the approved school system seems largely to have been forgotten.

The 1969 Act was also bereft of other enabling legislation in a way very different from previous major changes in society's approach to children. Unfortunately, many of the 1969 Act's alternative interventions for juveniles, such as intermediate treatment, were very slow to develop. Interestingly, the 1969 Act offered no sop to Cerberus by providing symbolic 'hard' alternatives for the recalcitrant, a lesson that should have been learned from previous legislation, particularly the alternative 'place of detention' concession of the 1908 Act and the detention centre concessions of the Criminal Justice Act of 1948.

It is also likely that the 1969 Act misjudged the climate of reform. We have already noted that a chill wind had been blowing towards the young offender since the late 1950s. The well publicised antics of students and football hooligans in the late 1960s did little to warm public and political attitudes which believed that things were out of hand and a firm line was necessary. Inevitably, the demands for security rose, a demand that did not distinguish between age, function or the consequences of locking up children.

The liberal reformers were strangely silent, giving the critics an open field. To their chagrin, the philosophy behind social work was being questioned. Its Freudian stance had greatly influenced training and unified the profession and it certainly gave strength to the reformulation of child-care ideas between the White Papers of 1965 and 1968. Bottoms comments:

> the Longford Report [this fathered the 1969 Act] is an expression of general social democratic ideology. Nevertheless, social workers were not slow to appreciate how the tenor of the report chimed with their own ideology, particularly delinquency as a presenting symptom and the consequent adoption of the medical treatment analogy. Social workers also shared the Labour Party's hostility to the courts and the legal profession.[8]

But while this alliance between social workers and reforming politicians may have helped the successful passage of the 1969 Children and Young Persons' Act, it stored problems for the future. Younger social workers were more radical, murmuring sociological ideas, raising moral questions about the nature of social work and doubting their policeman role. Even the psychologists were less keen on Freud. Research was hammering the hospital model on which much of the social work approach to juveniles in trouble was based. The radicals were also embarrassed by political changes. The Conservatives returned to office in 1970 and, during opposition, had made clear their unease over certain aspects of the Bill. They chose not to implement certain key proposals, particularly the raising of the age of criminal responsibility and the eligibility of younger boys for Borstal. Those leading social work figures that had joined the newly formed Department of Health and

Social Security found themselves mute civil servants, tarnished with too close an association with Labour's Children's Charter of 1969. Saddest of all, the sudden death of Derek Morell robbed the reformers of their strongest voice and political wit in answering the chorus of reaction.

Neither did the local authority social services departments, which rapidly became the target of every critic, thrust back at the strictures on their supervision and placement of difficult children. The departments were sagging under an increased demand for services.[9] In the year 1973-74, over 400,000 children were referred to the social services departments for attention. In addition, the replacement of the approved school orders by care orders transferred the burden of work directly from probation and from the old approved schools to the social services departments. In the year ending March 1975, the number of care orders made by the courts rose to over 11,000, supervision orders rose to nearly 20,000 and there was an avalanche of notifications from the police of children at risk. Associated with problems of reorganisation and staffing, the social services simply could not cope. Unfortunately, difficult boys in their mid-teens were largely outside the experience of social work departments and the role of policeman/probation officer was, in personality, training and philosophy, alien to young social workers.

The social services departments found themselves in an end-of-the-line position and, understandably, reacted with the paranoia that characterises 'dustbins' under stress. Far from opposing demands for more security, the social services added their voice. Applications for security, often for the most bizarre reasons, rose rapidly at all the secure units and, saddest of all, the most vulnerable group of children, offenders in their mid-teens were sent to Borstal or detention centre with increasing frequency. Indeed, the counter-revolutionaries seemed to have won their battle against the 1969 Act almost by default.

Conclusions

We have now examined the ways in which the secure units came into being. A number of crises highlighted the problems caused in the schools by aggressive boys and persistent absconders. Official inquiries and reports repeatedly emphasised the need to make provision for a small minority of children who were disrupting the system. Thus, during the mid-1960s, a modest amount of secure provision, about 80 places, was created to meet the anxiety of the approved schools. The size of the provision largely reflected the schools' estimates of the need.

We have noted the sorts of boy that it was intended the units should contain. They were mainly those who were disrupting the life of open institutions. At the outset, the regimes envisaged for the units were custodial and punitive, reflecting the age-old use to which security had been put and echoing the detention centre approaches. But the staff quickly threw off this retributive stance and moved towards educational and treatment goals. They dismantled much of the strict security. Unfortunately, the more the units became oriented towards treatment, the more they were tempted to be selective. Almost before they opened, it was clear that a short period in security would not offer much help to those children with severe personality problems and the admission of Section 53 cases to the secure units highlighted this issue. Thus impetus was given to the creation of the youth treatment centres.

The units met adequately the requirements for secure places in the late 1960s but recent demands for security have risen considerably. We would suggest, and the following two chapters strongly support this argument, that this increased demand represents part of the inevitable reaction that follows liberal legislation. The 1969 Act inescapably revealed deep conflicts in our philosophy and practice towards young offenders. Many of these tensions had been long nurtured and were quite unresolved. Because the Act misjudged the tide of reform, which had been ebbing with regard to young offenders for nearly a decade the legislation failed to make any token appeasement to the forces of opposition. Indeed, by challenging the judiciary and leading magistrates to think that the juvenile court had some considerable residual power, the 1969 Act has reaped a whirlwind. Those social workers that might have rallied to its defence were either mute, politically ineffective or beleaguered and the critics held the field. We would suggest that present concerns over increased security for children are less related to young people's needs than to wider issues of social control. The following chapters will illustrate this proposition.

Notes

[1] *Disturbances at the Carlton Approved School*, Cmd 937, London, HMSO, 1959. An important history of the development of secure provision has been prepared by P. Cawson and M. Martell, *The Development of Closed Units and its Research Implication*, DHSS, Research Division. Unpublished paper.
[2] The third report was *The Report of the Committee on Children and Young Persons*, Cmd 1191, London, HMSO, 1960.
[3] *Penal Practice in a Changing Society: Aspects of Future Development*, Cmd 645, London, HMSO, 1959.
[4] See 'Detention Centres: the experiment which could not fail', in P. Hall, H. Land, R. Parker and A. Webb, *Change, Choice and Conflict in Social Policy*, London, Heinemann, 1975, pp. 311-10.
[5] *Eleventh Report from the Expenditure Committee*, vol. II, *The Children and Young Persons' Act 1969*, Cmd HC, 534-ii, London, HMSO, 1975, p. 409.
[6] See A. Morris's essay in R. Hood (ed.), *Crime, Criminology and Social Policy: Essays in Honour of Sir Leon Radzinowitz*, London, Heinemann, 1976.
[7] See report of National Children's Bureau Working Party on alternative forms of care, 1978, chap. 1.
[8] See T. Bottoms' essay in R. Hood (ed.), *Crime, Criminology and Social Policy*, op. cit.

[9] Evidence presented to National Children's Bureau Working Party on alternative forms of care, 1975.

Part II
The intake to the units

4 Characteristics of boys in secure provision

We saw in the introductory chapters that secure units were originally set up to care for boys whose persistent absconding or disruptive behaviour proved intolerable to the open schools. The first three units for boys in England at Redhill, Kingswood and Redbank, were opened at a time when the task of the approved schools was to shelter those who were persistently delinquent. At that time, the legal order under which those young offenders were detained was quite different from the constraints imposed on other children in the care of the local authority.

However, since the implementation of the 1969 Children and Young Persons' Act and the establishment of a national system of community homes, the legal distinction between deprivation and delinquency has diminished. The original secure units, along with others for boys and girls opened since, have become a specialised facility which is theoretically available to all children in care. Clearly, the effects of this change on the types of adolescent admitted to secure units could be considerable, particularly as there is no longer any specific requirement for referrals to have experienced a sequence of failed approved school placements. The children for whom security may be recommended today may, therefore, differ on a number of admission criteria from those admitted in the past. We shall see, for example, that there are few 16- and 17-year-old boys in the units at present although we have noted that they were significant in the early years. Many in this age group now go on to Borstal institutions and the age of boys entering secure units has fallen sharply in most establishments.

Marie Johnston undertook a careful analysis of the first 80 boys admitted to the Kingswood unit and a similar group of 60 boys entering Redhill.[1] Her research delineates the characteristics of these early entrants. Research into more recent admissions has been conducted by Pat Cawson who examined the histories of all boys referred to the DHSS for secure placements at Redhill and Kingswood between June 1972 and July 1974.[2] Of these 217 referrals, 74 were subsequently admitted to the units. At Redbank, a former headmaster, R. Potter, has compared all 262 admissions with the last 110 admissions to both Kingswood and Redhill secure units.[3] Subsequently, he contrasted the characteristics of secure unit boys with a further three groups of 100 matched for sex, age and date of admission, drawn from the assessment centres. A study from Aycliffe analyses the problems presented by 124 boys and girls admitted to the secure house at the regional assessment centre and makes a further comparison between these groups and a sample of 62 boys assessed under open conditions.[4] This study is particularly important as it offers, for the first time, extensive information about girls admitted to secure provision and establishes important contrasts between their backgrounds and those of boys. The girls, for example, generally had more medical problems, were less intelligent and provoked more disruption than did boys. But, even though a proportion of these adolescents stay in security for a long period, most of the admissions to the unit are for purposes of assessment rather than treatment. Consequently, the boys described in that report are not necessarily the same as those who remain for long periods in treatment settings provided by larger units although there are obviously many similarities.

Our own researches have extended these previous studies. We not only examined the backgrounds of the populations in the three larger secure units at the time of our visits but also looked at the characteristics and subsequent careers of all boys released between 1 July 1971 and 31 December 1972.

We selected these groups because they had been out of the units sufficiently long for us to undertake a meaningful follow-up study. To supplement and give depth to this information, there were also likely to be staff in the secure units who could remember these boys and help to build up a profile of their training experience. We have to restrict our discussions to boys who have passed through the three large units at Redbank, Redhill and Kingswood. This is because, to date, these units are the only secure establishments which have sheltered a sufficient number of clients for us to draw valid generalisations.

The following discussions on the type of boy admitted over time to the secure units at Redhill, Redbank and Kingswood will also help us in an assessment of the need for secure places in the community home system. It should help to distinguish boys that arrive in security for administrative convenience from those whose disruptive behaviour is extremely persistent and has defied a wide variety of support. We need to know whether the boys in security are different in significant areas from other children in open residential institutions. Are they particularly dangerous, delinquent or disruptive?

We have seen that secure units developed from a belief that the care of the majority was hindered by a disruptive minority of boys so, presumably, the secure units should be sheltering these dissidents. It has long been argued that the approved schools and their descendants, the community homes, were increasingly taking more recalcitrant children as alternatives to residential care were developed. Can this widespread belief be substantiated? Theoretically, places in secure units are available to all institutions faced with problem children so those admitted should have the most pressing needs. Is this what, in fact, occurs? It is these sorts of question that we now intend to explore.

Background of boys in secure units

Initially, it is the youth and immaturity of secure unit boys that comes as a surprise. They are inadequate adolescents rather than thugs. The average age on admission for our 1975 sample was 14 years exactly in all three units. For Redhill and Redbank, this figure represents a drop in average age since 1964–68. The boys we are now considering, therefore, are in general well below Borstal age and clearly much younger than the boys for whom the magistrates, police and others have recently been urging additional secure provision.[5] Table 4.1 illustrates these changes in the age of admission to the Redhill and Kingswood units. It can be seen for example, that in 1975, only 38 per cent of the boys were over 14½ compared with 65 per cent in 1971.

Table 4.1
Boys' ages on entry to Kingswood and Redhill units (figures are percentages)

	Johnston 1964–68	Our survey 1971	1975
Under 12½	1	1	7
12½–14½	31	33	55
Over 14½	68	66	38
N =	140	67	55

The second significant characteristic of these boys in the units is their persistent failure in a range of other residential settings. The range of placements and frequency of transfer experienced before the special unit experience is quite exceptional. Three-quarters have been to a CHE, for example, and one-fifth have been detained in a remand centre. It would be easy to explain these histories if it could be established that the boys were either severely disturbed or deeply delinquent at the beginnings of their careers in residential care. Such simple explanations do not emerge from the evidence. We shall see that while boys in security are *among* the most deprived groups within the CHE system, there are others in open establishments with equally grave problems. Table 4.2 shows the previous residential experiences of our 1971 and 1975 samples at Redbank, Redhill and Kingswood and compares these figures with results obtained during our 1969–70 study of 11 open schools for boys of a similar age.[6]

One of the most significant predictors of a boy's future delinquent behaviour is his previous history of offending. Much research has confirmed that the more convictions a boy receives, the more unlikely he is to escape trouble or further periods in custody. Most of the boys in the secure units have extensive delinquent histories and this makes them high-risk children although they share this characteristic with many boys in open conditions. However, they will have also absconded from open establishments and, frequently, will have committed offences in order to survive while on the run. We shall demonstrate later that boys' absconding patterns differ considerably so it is not easy to assess how enduring is a boy's delinquent identity when so much of the absconding crime has been situational. Therefore, comparisons of figures for previous offences between secure unit boys and others can tell us little except to confirm that the special unit population is among the most vulnerable of juvenile delinquents.

Table 4.2

Previous residential experiences of boys admitted to the
Redbank, Redhill and Kingswood units (figures are percentages)

	1971	1975	Junior and intermediate approved schools 1969–70
Detention centre	8	21	1
Community home	43	49	23
Community home with education	89	71	6
Boarding school	25	34	11
Mental hospital	8	6	1
Remand centre	26	14	0
Youth training centre	1	1	0
Prison (remand)	4	2	0
N=	114	80	617

The boys in the units share with high-risk children a number of other characteristics. They begin to offend early, cause concern to teachers and social workers
when at primary school and are persistently delinquent in a series of residential
placements. Two-thirds of the boys in our 1975 sample were already in a CHE by
their thirteenth birthday. This pattern of early offending is a characteristic of
highly delinquent boys. Indeed, these kinds of children were clearly identified in
our previous researches into the approved school system, particularly as a sub-group
in the old junior approved schools, and we noted then that they subsequently
moved through a range of institutions quite untouched by the reforming efforts of
residential social workers. The majority of these boys were destined for prison.

There does not appear to be anything exceptional about the offences which
secure unit boys have committed and previous crimes have usually been violations
of property, minor theft or burglary. Although the proportions of boys whose
offences include arson, violence and taking and driving away motor vehicles is
greater than might be found in an ordinary community home, it must be emphasised that only a minority, about 15 per cent of the boys in secure units have
committed grave crimes.

The majority of boys in secure units, 76 per cent in 1975, show a pattern of
early delinquency leading eventually to a series of residential placements each of
which breaks down because of persistent absconding, usually accompanied by some
socially provocative behaviour. Often it is the drama and cost of these offences
rather than their inherent danger that seems to cause the most administrative concern, particularly since a judgment made the Isle of Wight authority responsible for
the damage caused by an absconder.[7] We shall see, in fact, that as these 1975
boys are younger, they tend to be less delinquent and less institutionalised than
earlier admissions to the secure units.

The remaining quarter of the special unit population includes those boys who are guilty of grave crimes and who are detained under Section 53 of the 1933 Children and Young Persons' Act or other legislation which gives priority to the protection of the public. In 1975, there were 13 such boys at Redhill, Redbank and Kingswood and these accounted for 16 per cent of the population of the three units, a figure that has increased from less than 5 per cent for the 1971–72 sample. But, even here one must be careful when generalising about grave offenders. Some of the boys are persistent delinquents whose offences have escalated to rape and violent robbery while others have had trouble free lives until they unexpectedly commit a serious assault. Another group of emotionally disturbed boys have committed arson, frequently of little import, except that fire-raising understandably terrifies all residential institutions.

In addition to these serious offenders, there is a small but increasing group of children, about 8 per cent in 1975, who present severe and often bizarre behaviour problems. These children offer spasmodic violence to staff or have attempted suicide, but otherwise, are not particularly delinquent. Their previous placements have usually been in children's homes, special schools or adolescent units rather than the CHEs. Clearly the growth of this pattern of referral for secure care results from the 1969 legislation. These children are usually deeply disturbed and seem to need the intensive care offered by the units more than the security. They are more typical of the admissions to the youth treatment centres which have some secure accommodation or small secure units in assessment centres. The majority of these children will not have committed any offences and, presumably, could even be voluntarily in care.

Clearly, this situation raises serious questions about the applicability of single treatment settings for such diverse groups and we shall return to this in later chapters. Indeed, when we come to discuss other establishments which provide security, such as the coeducational youth treatment centre, which has one secure house among three, we shall see that there is an even greater range of presenting problems among the children. There are considerable differences between the deprivation and disturbances of boys and girls, for example, and this makes it difficult to see how security in itself can provide a solution to the treatment problem. In short, it depends on the uses to which security is put.

Family background of boys in secure units

Our earlier studies of approved school boys established that the unfavourable home conditions experienced by persistent offenders are clearly linked with continuous antisocial behaviour.[8] We found, for example, that boys returning home from their approved schools to families where parent–child relationships were tense broke down more frequently than those fortunate enough to go back to stable, accepting environments. The families of boys in the secure units are typical of those where delinquency is a common adaptation among the children. The boys in secure accommodation are likely to have: run away from home at an early age (26 per cent), been brought up by relatives (15 per cent), had step-parents (34 per cent), experienced cruelty and neglect (38 per cent), been separated from mother (31 per cent), been rejected by father (29 per cent) and mother (21 per cent) and have parents who are mentally unstable (38 per cent), violent (28 per cent), heavy drinkers (28 per cent), frequently absent from home (43 per cent) and who have had extra-marital affairs (50 per cent). It is important to stress, however, that the family backgrounds of young delinquents are generally more satisfactory than those of many other non-delinquent children coming into the care of the local authority.[9] The majority of secure unit boys (94 per cent) do, at least, return to a family of some kind and few pose problems of homelessness.

In *After Grace – Teeth*, we estimated that about one-third of the old approved school population consisted of very vulnerable children whose prognosis for rehabilitation was poor and who seemed to get little from the old system.[10] There is no doubt from the figures given above that the boys in security form part of this intractable group, yet it is difficult to identify any distinguishing characteristics for the few who end up in secure conditions. Their deprivations do not seem to be greater than other high-risk children in open CHEs. Among the old approved schools, we found wide differences in the levels of family disturbance experienced by boys with the result that some establishments had a more deprived and delinquent intake than did others. In three intermediate schools, described in *After Grace – Teeth*, the dislocations experienced by boys were every bit as great as those of the secure unit group, yet these schools were able to shelter their clients in an open setting.

There are many other indices that could illustrate this argument. For example, a glance at the levels of measured intelligence and educational attainment show a similar pattern. Boys in the unit display scores which are identical with the intelligence of other deprived children and their educational attainments, while well below their chronological ages, are no more deficient than those of the boys in the old approved schools. All studies, including Potter's extensive comparisons, our own intensive survey of particular groups of boys in security and the Aycliffe comparative study seem to reach similar conclusions. While the boys in the secure units are problematic and high-risk, they are very similar to a significant proportion of boys in open conditions.

It is not, therefore, the background of boys in secure units which explains the eventual need for security as much as the failure of social intervention and the cumulative nature of the control problem at each attempt to provide a solution. Indeed, the fact that several assessments have usually been undertaken on the boys in secure units may explain the frequency of recorded unfavourable characteristics. Features such as previous separation of parents or sibling delinquency only come to light during continuous casework. This raises interesting implications about the functions of repeated assessments on these children as this process may unintentionally strengthen the case for extreme measures such as admission to a secure unit.

Previous residential placements

If, as we have argued, the boys in secure units are part of a vulnerable core of 1,500 deprived delinquents, it is important to consider why only 100 or so of them end up in locked establishments. What else, we need to ask, contributes to the use of security for boys if delinquent history and family background fail to differentiate this minority? The answer seems to be in the *history of social intervention* experienced by these boys and their reaction to it. Here, we cannot find parallels among offenders in open establishments. The career patterns of the secure unit population are virtually unique. By the age of 14 these children have experienced considerable deprivation and accumulated many convictions. Where they do differ from other boys is that they seem unprepared to put up with care that they perceive as inadequate. We have commented in previous research that most intervention with this one-third of the boys in the system seemed to achieve very little. Secure unit candidates seem to be those who overtly demonstrate the failures of care.

Indeed, the reading of several hundred voluminous files on secure unit children is a sobering experience. They are an indictment of the child-care system. Children are shuffled from one short-term placement to another in the vague hope that they will stick somewhere. Some boys have had eight placements in a year, interspersed with periods on the run during which they experience every violation that our big cities can provide. They return occasionally to assessment centres for additional uncomplimentary labels and then they are on their way again. They find the experience disintegrating. 'You have got to have an identity when you go away', said one boy, 'and by the time you've got one you're put somewhere else.' 'You feel sick', said another boy, 'except you feel sick all the time.'

Not only is placement haphazard; it seems to be based on a series of panic responses. There is certainly no unifying treatment concept. Pat Cawson, too, notes that among referrals to secure places [11] 'many children never had a long term *treatment* placement under open conditions. A large proportion of the children's residential experience consisted of successive admissions to short term establishments which were supposed to have a single purpose: the assessment of long term placement needs.' She continues, 'A considerable number of children have been referred on the basis of behavioural problems in short term placements and little attempt has been made to find alternative long term situations.' Indeed, it seems that the troublesome child could equally well end up exploring relationships in a therapeutic community, jumping the box in a detention centre or sitting in a secure unit - approaches that would all be graced with the word 'treatment' and all result from chance.

Most boys in the units have considerable experience of all forms of residential care: 36 per cent of the 1975 sample have been to two or more CHEs and 45 per cent to other boarding schools. Their experience of closed provision in the penal system, too, is quite extensive: 21 per cent have been to detention centres and 14 per cent have been detained in remand centres: figures which have no parallel amongst boys in open community homes. Considering that most of these boys are only 13 years old, the onus on the local authority and social services department is quite inescapable.

The problems posed by boys in the units, therefore, are those of children whose prognosis is poor yet who have been further damaged by persistent caring error. Recent and disastrous institutional histories clearly distinguish this group of boys. In Cawson's sample of referrals, for example, 35 per cent of secure unit boys had five or more residential placements in the previous year. Each placement seems to intensify boys' problems and, as we shall see below, as children's experience of defeat grows, their stays become shorter.

Now, the time-honoured response is to blame the boy, suggesting that his problems make it impossible to contain him. But, we shall in later chapters explore the role of the institution in shaping all sorts of deviant conduct. We shall suggest that community homes help to send off the absconder and court the violence that they ostensibly find so violating. It is not, therefore, surprising that difficult children display no unique features that might account for their disruption.

The length of time that boys actually stay in each of their residential placements also confirms the importance of the residential experience. Although boys' stays get shorter by half for each subsequent placement, their stays are by no means short enough to enable us to discount the institutional impact. The boys in secure units stayed in their first CHE placement for nearly a year on average and this is quite sufficient for the absconding syndrome to be either aggravated or reduced in a way that we shall explain in a later chapter. Pat Cawson, too, comments:

> We were interested in learning how typical was the case of a boy who absconded 'before the ink which formed his name in the admissions register was dry'. In fact, it seemed to be comparatively rare for children to leave a placement by immediately absconding. Only 15% of boys lost placements due to absconding within two weeks of arrival and only 5% had lost more than one placement in such a manner. Most children, it seemed, did remain to see what an establishment was like before running away from it and few residential establishments refused to re-admit immediate absconders for a second chance.[12]

Placing these findings in the context of our early discussions, we can now see that the problematic 14-year-olds presented for treatment in secure conditions are very much casualties of the system, rather than uniquely disruptive individuals. This fact, of course, reflects a much wider theoretical debate about whether behaviour is understood in terms of individual psychological traits or by symbolic interaction between individuals. While such arguments need not concern us here, it does seem that perspectives derived from interactionist sociology are useful in helping us see the long process which leads children to secure settings.

Explanations in terms of the motivations of behaviour only take us so far and may only apply to the highly disturbed individuals, so, to complete the picture, we need to know more about the interactions between the adolescent and the control processes operating in the wider society. Secure units may be justified in terms of the treatment they offer but, equally, their functions are concerned with control. This was clear from our introductory chapters. While Cawson has established that formal requests for secure units by magistrates was a main factor in bringing about actual admission to the unit, the care aspects of such pronouncements have a hollow ring when we digest her finding that out of 202 requests made to the DHSS for secure places, only 77 asked for a place at a specific establishment.[13] Potter's equally alarming figures from Redbank also confirm this pattern.[14] Of 262 admissions, only 27 requested *treatment* in a secure unit in the application. It is security rather than treatment that dominates the perceived solution.

Conclusion

These findings on the sorts of boys admitted to secure units raise important issues. Generally, the boys' backgrounds do not differ markedly from those of other boys in the system and we can see that the problems of all of them have been greatly increased by haphazard transfer. However, to conclude that because many boys are casualties of the system, secure units are irrelevant to their needs, is probably unwise.

It would be a mistake to draw such implications because it is unduly optimistic to imagine that research findings, which identify the institutional process as creating problem children, are likely to have much impact on the process of referral. It also seems likely that however much we perfect the child-care system, casualties will always occur. Hoghugi, for example, echoes this point in his report on the secure house at Aycliffe by saying:

> The secure house would not be needed were it not for the 'inadequacies' of our present care system. However, it would betray a particularly unsophisticated view of the workings of a complex society such as ours to suggest that we would ever reach a point of adequacy to give . . . the kind of specialised help such problematic children need. Almost all of the factors we have isolated as being associated with these children's disturbances are on the increase at a rate and in a manner disproportionate to the increase in our society's resources.[15]

The successive accidents that boys in care receive will, therefore, eventually turn some of them into desperate cases for whom some crisis decision has to be taken. Watching and reading about the children in secure units is not a happy experience and when they arrive, most of them are 'in extremis'. At that moment, security or some drastic intervention is essential to keep vulnerable children off the streets. Where research can help is to distinguish those children who are casualties of the system, for whom intervention should have been earlier and more effective, from those disturbed and difficult adolescents for whom the secure institution is the only possibility.

It is extremely easy for anyone looking back over the decision-making process on difficult children to identify the errors and indifference of the social work services. It is certainly not quite so easy to balance the niceties of care or to work out a prognosis for boys when a screaming adolescent is in the next room.

There is certainly little excuse for the whimsical nature of boys' placements and for the failure of the caring authorities to recognise that they have a problem with some children and to work out some programme of care. There is no excuse for offering boys a dreary replica of their previous residential experience in the vague hope that they will at last respond. But, in the same way, there is no excuse for research to highlight the deficiencies of the system without suggesting some feasible alternative. We hope to do this in a later chapter.

Notes

[1] M. Johnston, *Summary of Information Collected on the First 80 Boys Admitted to the Kingswood Special Unit* and *Summary of Information Collected on the First 60 Boys Admitted to Redhill Special Unit*, unpublished mimeographs, Kingswood Schools, 1970.

[2] P. Cawson, *Referrals to the Units* and *Behaviour Prior to Referral*, unpublished mimeographs, DHSS, Research Division, 1975.

[3] R. S. Potter, *Factors Relating to Special (Secure) Unit Admissions, Redbank School which directly influence the Curriculum*, unpublished BEd thesis, Chorley College, 1974.

[4] M. Hoghugi and S. Nethercott, *Troubled and Troublesome: a comparative study of boys and girls under security*, Aycliffe Studies of Problem Children, 1977.

[5] See, for example, the articles reviewing the 1969 Act in *The Magistrate*, November 1974 and March 1975.

[6] See S. Millham, R. Bullock and P. Cherrett, *After Grace – Teeth*, London, Human Context Books, Chaucer Publishing Company, 1975.

[7] The judgement was made in 1974 and the boy was subsequently admitted to a special unit.

[8] S. Millham et al., *After Grace – Teeth*, op. cit.

[9] *First Year at Fairfield Lodge*, Social Services Research and Intelligence Unit, Portsmouth Polytechnic, 1976.

[10] See S. Millham et al., *After Grace – Teeth*, op. cit.

[11] P. Cawson, *Referrals to the Units*, op. cit., pp. 32 and 38.

[12] P. Cawson, *Behaviour Prior to Referral*, op. cit., p. 98.

[13] P. Cawson, *Referrals to the Units*, op. cit., p. 5.

[14] Personal communication with R. S. Potter who had collected the data as part of a survey undertaken for an MEd degree at Manchester University.

[15] M. Hoghugi et al., *Troubled and Troublesome*, op. cit., p. 61.

5 Secure units – a safety valve for the system?

Secure units are, as we have seen, closely related to the rest of community home provision and, inevitably, any change in the pattern of residential care will affect the functions of security. Theoretically, there could be an increasing need for secure accommodation if, generally among children in care, the numbers of difficult adolescents were increasing.

We have seen that ideas about the deterioration of the quality of children admitted to residential care are not new. It was the time-honoured institutional defence during periods of falling numbers and low public esteem. Cawson, too, reminds us that, long ago, staff at Parkhurst Boys' Prison expressed alarm that the newly established reformatory schools were creaming off the better children.[1] Nevertheless, such ideas are still firmly fixed among residential workers and at the time of our approved school studies in 1969–70, many staff talked about the deteriorating quality of trainees. We were unable to support this conclusion from any evidence because we found at that time that the characteristics of our population were remarkably similar in terms of delinquent history, levels of institutionalisation, family dislocation and emotional disturbance to those described in a Home Office study of 1962.[2] Earlier comparisons such as those by Rose and Gittins have also failed to distinguish any obvious deterioration in the quality of boys admitted.[3]

Since the implementation of the 1969 Children and Young Persons' Act, there have been too few comparative studies for us to be categoric about changes in the community home population. A study at Aycliffe suggests that boys passing through the regional assessment centre in 1973 were more disturbed and deprived than their predecessors but this, of course, says nothing about children in care generally.[4] Indeed, the functions of the old classifying schools have changed so radically since the 1969 Act that the findings of this Aycliffe research may simply reflect these differences.

The evidence from CHEs also offers little support for the notion of an increasingly difficult intake. Bevington's study of admissions to Quinta School in 1970 and 1973 suggests that boys' problems may be growing more complex but that there is no upsurge in the difficult behaviour they present or in their prognosis for ultimate rehabilitation.[5] Similarly, in our own studies of four former boys' approved schools, we were unable to establish any increase in the problems posed by boys between 1969 and 1974–75.[6] If anything, on a number of criteria, the boys had become less difficult. They were certainly less delinquent and their future prognosis tended to be favourably influenced by a reduction in the time spent in previous residential establishments. Two other recent developments also had the effect of improving the potential of the intake. Difficult boys now go on more frequently to Borstal at 15 than they did before 1969 and the increasing selectivity of community homes has led to the retention of some problematic youngsters in other residential establishments, particularly in assessment centres. In short, none of the evidence on the characteristics of the contemporary population in CHEs suggests any increase in the difficulties posed by the boys.

This view is confirmed when we look at the present population in the secure units for, in every respect, they are less problematic than earlier admissions. Pat Cawson found a similar pattern when she compared the characteristics of her sample with the early admissions to Redhill and Kingswood described by Marie Johnston. Pat Cawson writes:

> Compared to the 1964-68 admissions, the 1972-4 were younger and less intelligent. They were less likely to have been living with both natural parents but otherwise appeared to come from rather 'better' homes: levels of criminality and mental illness in their families were lower. As in the earlier studies very few had histories of prolonged institutional care and it appears probable that the 1972-74 boys were no more institutionalised than their predecessors. The recent admissions also appear to be less delinquent than their predecessors, with fewer court appearances, fewer findings of guilt and a possible later onset of delinquency.[7]

When we compare our own 1971-72 and 1975 groups of boys with Cawson's sample, we can agree with her that, compared with earlier admissions, the present boys at two of the three units are younger and, therefore, have committed fewer serious offences and been in fewer CHEs. However, our analysis failed to establish any fall in levels of intelligence, criminality and mental illness in the family or its members' experience of prison. But, while researchers may differ over details, Cawson's study, Martin's work at Redbank [8] and our own studies all demonstrate that the boys in the units at present are less problematic than they have ever been.

We cannot see, therefore, any aspects of boys' backgrounds that would lead us to suggest that there has been any marked change in the quality of boys coming into CHEs or to justify any demand for an extension of secure provision. In fact, we now have a new sort of client: the younger boy who is less problematic but who stays in custody longer than did his predecessors. All research seems to demonstrate this disturbing fact. It is, therefore, most useful in our view to forget boys' backgrounds and look more carefully at their institutional career and see how effective strategies might be developed to prevent the ultimate need for secure care.

The process of referral

While the effectiveness of residential care in achieving lasting behaviour modification has long been questioned, research writing such as *After Grace – Teeth*, *Hostels for Probationers* and *The Approved School Experience* confirm that, whatever the eventual outcome, the impact of the institution on behaviour inside the establishment is quite considerable.[9] There are wide variations among residential settings in the levels of staff and pupil commitment as there are in expressions of problematic behaviour. As so much of the difficult behaviour displayed by boys admitted to secure units has been in residential settings, it seems likely from the evidence we have considered that the regimes experienced by boys cannot be ignored. It does seem that certain schools are more ready than others to demand security and more likely to get their demands accepted.

The 1960 Home Office working party, for example, asked the old approved schools to estimate the number of boys who were absconders, disruptive or medical misfits. The total was 374 boys, or 5 per cent of the approved school population, but, Cawson says, 'There were immense regional variations between the number of boys considered by different schools to fit into the categories. Many schools said that they had none or only one or two boys while others recommended 25% of their population for placement in closed conditions.'[10] It may be, of course, that schools which presented the largest number of cases had admitted the most difficult boys in the first place, a point to which we shall return later. However, it does appear from our own studies and from Cawson's evidence that a stay in certain community homes guarantees that disruptive conduct will lead to a recommendation for security and it is just as clear that similar conduct elsewhere will not.

When we look at the approved schools or their successors, CHEs, attended by boys in the Kingswood and Redbank units, for example, there is considerable consistency in the pattern of previous placements experienced by boys. (The task is more complex at Redhill because of the wide catchment area which the unit serves.) But at Kingswood, five schools account for 39 per cent of boys' previous placements of over three months' duration in CHEs, a figure that is nearly as high, 31 per cent, for another five schools in the Redbank area. Yet, the proportion of junior and intermediate places provided by these schools in each of the regions is low, about 28 per cent of Kingswood's catchment area and 20 per cent of Redbank's, so the over-representation of these CHEs among the population admitted to the secure units is quite clear.

We would expect this pattern in the light of our earlier studies of 18 boys' approved schools where we found the rates for premature transfer of children also varied considerably. The rates ranged from 0 per cent to 32 per cent of the boys in the schools, a variation that has also been found in the London area in 1974 by Tutt where the rates varied from 15 per cent to 66 per cent.[11] But, even so, it is not easy to establish how far the pattern corresponds to what we would expect, as many schools have changed their size in recent years and the catchment areas of the secure units have been modified. Also the fall in the age of entry to the units has meant that nowadays new arrivals do not have experience of establishments for senior boys. But, in spite of these difficulties, it is still clear that certain feeding CHEs figured large on the list of boys' previous placements while others are conspicuously absent.

Support for this pattern comes, too, from Cawson's study of referrals. She finds clear patterns in the schools attended by the boys.[12] One establishment, for example, had recently sheltered 17 of her sample, while several schools were noticeably absent from her list. She finds also that those schools which recommended large numbers of boys for security in 1960 tend to be those most frequently attended by the present referrals. She concludes that while it may be possible to explain these differences in terms of the difficulty presented by boys' backgrounds, the varied ability of schools to hold such boys is equally significant.

However, before we ask the crucial question: 'Is there a link between the sorts of boys admitted to schools and the referral pattern?' it is important to note the distressing pattern revealed by our earlier analysis. It is clear that schools which receive boys on their first CHE placement and where breakdown is common have also received boys on their third and even fourth placements when the chances of their success must be very small. It suggests that boys who have broken down once are often reallocated to establishments where large numbers of other boys are already faring badly. Disruptive boys are transferred to other institutions whose failure with difficult children is already manifest. Most transfers, it seems, takes the boy from one mediocre place to another. Ironically, it is only on admission to a secure unit where control is an overt function that there seems to be any increase in the intensity of care provided.

The schools that feed the closed units, however, are by no means homogeneous and, clearly, certain establishments take more difficult boys than others. For example, two of the schools in our earlier study clearly offered themselves as a last open refuge for difficult boys. Naturally, we do not know at a national level the differences in school populations and there is little prospect of such information ever being available. However, we can look at the schools attended by all boys in the classifying region admitted to the Kingswood unit during the period of our previous research. This will answer the objection that it is the types of boys in the schools which determine how many go on to security.

Between 1969 and 1972, we compared the regimes of 18 schools in the Kingswood region and gathered much statistical material about the sorts of boys admitted, the schools they attended and their after-release careers. When we examine the entrants to Kingswood secure unit during 1970 and 1971, we find that they previously attended the following schools – identified by letters which are identical with those used in many of the tables in *After Grace – Teeth*.[13] Results for 1969–70 are given in Table 5.1.

When we correlate, as in the table, the background characteristics of the boys in each of these schools with the pattern of placements before admission to the secure unit, we find that there is no evidence to suggest that the schools which pass boys on to the secure unit are those with the most difficult boys on admission: that is, a high-risk group when measured by the frequency of boys' previous convictions and their previous experience of approved school training. School I, for example, had a highly delinquent intake at this time, yet they passed no one on to the secure unit. Similarly, size of school bears no significant relationship to the number of their pupils entering the Kingswood unit. We cannot, therefore, explain the greater likelihood of boys from certain schools ending up in security either in terms of the poor quality of intake to these establishments or to the sizes of the various schools involved. Schools seem to have a differential tendency to create problem children, irrespective of the quality of their admissions or their willingness and capacity to contain them.

Table 5.1
Schools feeding Kingswood secure unit, 1969–70

		First place-ment	Second place-ment	Total	Rate for premature transfer (per cent)	Percentage of boys with 4 or more con-victions on entry	Percentage of boys with previous approved school experi-ence	Size of school in 1969
Junior	A	3	0	3	17	3	3	36
schools	B	7	1	8	6	30	3	105
	C	2	1	3	18	16	7	43
	D	2	0	2	12	26	0	73
	E	3	1	4	9	23	3	66
Inter-	F	5	1	6	7	32	6	98
mediate	G	3	1	4	32	56	13	73
schools	H	5	4	9	13	35	10	71
	I	0	0	0	0	42	13	66
	J	4	5	9	8	40	7	84
	K	1	2	3	10	27	6	110

Note: Rank order coefficient (rho) for correlation with admissions to to unit

	Rate for premature transfer	4 or more convictions	previous approved school	Size of school
	–0.07	+0.26	+0.14	+0.38

It is equally significant that there seems to be little relationship between rates of premature transfer, that is, the removal of a boy to another school before completion of his training and admissions to the unit. This is a surprising finding, for it implies that schools which transfer a large number of problematic boys are not necessarily those which feed the secure units. Schools J and B, for example, show this pattern and although they transfer few boys, many of these go into security, whereas the losses from schools C, A, D and G are less likely to go to the secure unit. It is perhaps significant that schools G, A and D are only on the fringe of the Kingswood catchment area and there may be features in the referral process other than the numbers of difficult boys.

The geographical region of the school also seems to be a significant factor in determining the levels of referrals for secure places. Some areas of the country take a far larger share of the secure places than others. The immediate regions gain a disproportionate number of places in each of the units. The North West, for example, is over-represented at Redbank, whereas few boys who have been in the three units have come from East Anglia, the East Midlands or Yorkshire. This geographical bias is found even when we compare the home areas of these boys with the general distribution of both the adolescent population at large and the numbers in care. In each case the bias in the distribution among regions of the country is highly significant, confirming that the provision of secure places, to some extent, creates the local need.

These anomalies become even greater when we consider specific local authorities. Pat Cawson writes that referrals to the DHSS for placements at Redhill and Kingswood did not reflect the numbers of children in cities who were theoretically vulnerable. She writes:

> Inner London, which provided the largest number of referrals in the present sample, had by no means the largest number of children in care. Similarly, Outer London, while providing a large number of referrals to closed provision, had one of the lowest figures of children in care throughout the period. The range among London Boroughs, for example, was between three Boroughs which referred no children at all, to one Borough which referred ten children in the relevant period. Outside London, a number of authorities (including some highly industrialised areas) referred no one at all while one large Midland city referred fourteen cases and a South Eastern county authority referred sixteen cases.[14]

It is, of course, possible that those authorities which do not make many applications for placement in secure units hold on to their boys until they are old enough for Borstal. But, here again, there is no evidence to support such a suggestion. The distribution of the home areas of 15- and 16-year-old boys who are received into Borstal is not related to the patterns for placement in secure units.[15] Indeed, in the North West, the admissions to both secure units and Borstals is greater than would be expected from the overall juvenile population, indicating that the use of Borstals probably parallels, rather than substitutes for, the placement of boys in other secure institutions.

It seems, therefore, that not only the location of a boy's home but also the geographic position of CHEs can both contribute to the chances of a child's delinquent career leading him to a secure unit. Referral for secure care seems to be very much a *process* growing out of a situation where vulnerable children abscond from residential placements, commit offences and, eventually, pose such severe problems of control that locking them up seems the only solution.

A study of applications for secure unit places gives little support to notions about the existence of a reservoir of unmet need for security. While existing provision will occasionally be under pressure from a surge of applications, a close examination of referrals reveals that the number of adolescents who need security but who are not placed in such accommodation is small. Much publicity is frequently given to waiting lists of candidates for secure places but our own research shows that such concerns are misleading. For example, in March 1975, there were 30 files in the waiting tray at one of the units and during our visit a vacancy unexpectedly arose. As the headmaster is responsible for admissions to the unit, he invited us to review these applications with him. We found to our surprise that 20 of the referrals had not followed up their initial inquiry within the last three months and, as a stay at the unit is about six months, presumably a secure place was no longer a priority. Of the remaining 10 applications, half were eliminated because of age or presenting behaviour, leaving only five possible candidates. But, even then, the boy we selected did not arrive. After 'phoning the local authority, the headmaster was informed that the boy had settled elsewhere. So, from an apparent list of 30 applicants, there were only four cases of urgent need.

In 1974, 55 applications were made to the Redbank unit of which 25 were admitted and seven placed on the waiting list. Of the 23 who were refused admission, 10 clearly did not need secure placement, one went missing, three stayed at home, one went to hospital, two to detention centre, one to Borstal and five to open CHEs, indicating again that the real need for security forms only a small part of the total applications. Cawson has noted that panic referrals are often defused by the actual delay in finding secure places as the absence of provision forces the authorities to find an effective placement.

The referrals to Kingswood and Redhill special units coming to the DHSS also confirm this pattern.[17] In the first 10 months of 1975, the social work service officer responsible for referrals handled 77 applications of which 17 were placed and 13 added to a waiting list. However, the most urgent cases, called priority 'A' referrals, accounted for only one-third (26) of the total applications. Half of these were admitted. In 1976, the number of applications had fallen by one-third to 59. This decline in demand is significant as it represents the gap between existing provision and local authority referrals since Kingswood and Redhill can between them take in about 50 boys a year. If rigorous selection has reduced the numbers of annual referrals in this way, the needs for secure accommodation are almost met by existing provision.

It appears, therefore, that the extent of unmet need for secure accommodation is considerably less than might appear from a glance at the numbers of referrals. While there may be a need for a few regional planning areas to extend their facilities, the proposed increases to provide 262 secure places in observation and assessment centres and 411 in CHEs seems to be rather excessive.[18] We shall consider later the special needs of 15- and 16-year-olds in penal establishments but these, at the moment, do not feature in current referrals to the units.

Conclusion

Everything in this chapter would suggest that, if a difficult child enters some institutions and is in the care of some local authorities, he stands a much greater chance of ending up in security. Linked with the findings of our previous chapter it shows how important is the process by which decisions are made. To those working in residential care these revelations should be disturbing for they demonstrate how making out a cogent case for a nearby secure place succeeds in getting a child in. In administrative terms, the case is indistinguishable from the need. This point is illustrated by Cawson's finding that the factor correlating most strongly with entry was not anything to do with the child's need but was the number of letters written to request a place.[16]

Even if assessment procedures had a sound theoretical basis and professional authority, we still find it difficult to suggest how admissions to secure units or other specialised care can be effectively vetted. For almost all candidates for security there are no hard and fast criteria for admission other than their reported behaviour in other institutions. Unfortunately, we know from our studies of violence and absconding that what is outrageous, disturbed or unacceptable in one home can pass with little comment in another. If the units take those children who disrupt the system, they cannot escape their primary controlling function, treatments cannot be specific and will be largely secondary. If the units are primarily treatment institutions, in which security might be a necessary part, the evidence demonstrates that they are not getting the sort of child that needs it.

There may be some hope here for it is always possible to intervene in a process and to change its nature. We shall note in subsequent chapters when we look at children's aggressive behaviour or at their absconding that they are rarely propelled by inner drives and that much of their conduct is largely engendered by, and understandable in the context of the institutions in which they shelter. It is also clear that the majority of children in the secure units are not intractable cases that differ markedly from other children in open conditions, although the frequency of transfer from one place to another tends to create a disruptive candidate worthy of security. We have said elsewhere that transfer is highly disintegrating and that treatment consists of hanging on to children. Better residential care would greatly diminish the need for security because it would diminish the behaviour that makes for candidates in need of it.

We would be slightly less categoric in our comments had not the extensive studies of Cawson forced her to the same conclusions as ourselves. Potter's work at Redbank has yielded similar material. There is no evidence that boys in today's CHEs are more difficult or, in terms of likely recidivism, at greater risk than in previous years. If such reasons are advanced to justify an increase in secure places, they are misplaced. While candidates for security are largely casualties of the child-care system, this chapter raises the disquieting evidence that, regardless of the boys they admit, some institutions create more casualties than others. Many areas and many institutions seem to get along without provision for security, while others seek and take up a disproportionate number of places. Improvements in the quality of residential care should, therefore, considerably reduce the levels of need for secure accommodation.

Even without these improvements there is little evidence that there exists considerable unmet need for secure places. Most applications tend to be crisis referrals and any delay in making a decision, which is highly irritating to the applicant, often leads to a satisfactory open placement. This suggests that social workers should treat institutional demands for security or some other crisis intervention with caution. Transfer of children in care is a serious matter; it is damaging and should be less frequent than it is. Those residential homes which have high transfer rates, high failure rates with the boys they release and make frequent applications for secure places merit rapid and drastic intervention. Closure is preferable to damaging the child, particularly as Michael Zander's research and that of West would suggest that delinquent boys left in the community do as well as those put in residential care.[19]

We would recommend that the regional authorities creating secure facilities should not be allowed to lock up children without careful external scrutiny and final approval, preferably by the DHSS. This would enable applications to be carefully examined, reveal inadequacies in social services practice and fearlessly identify those institutions that are creating candidates. It would also ensure more equitable access to this expensive facility. Without some clear safeguards such as these, the confusion and inequalities that these opening chapters have revealed will increase and the problems of matching need and provision will become insuperable. One views with unease a situation whereby the regional authorities that create additional secure places would be the sole arbiters of who should be admitted to them. It is not a value judgement to remind readers that secure provision is finally about liberty, the cost of which has been considerable and purchased as much for difficult children as anyone else.

Notes

[1] P. Cawson, *The Development of Closed Units and its Research Implications*, unpublished mimeograph, DHSS, Research Division, 1975.

[2] E. Field, W. Hammond and J. Tizard, *Thirteen-Year-Old Approved School Boys in 1962*, London, HMSO, 1971.

[3] G. Rose, *Schools for Young Offenders*, London, Tavistock, 1967 and J. Gittins, *Approved School Boys*, London, HMSO, 1952.

[4] M. S. Hoghugi, *What's in a Name?*, Aycliffe Studies of Problem Children, 1972.

[5] P. Bevington, *Follow-up and Evaluation Project*, unpublished report for Dr Barnado's and Quinta School, 1976.

[6] See the Dartington Social Research Unit's reports: *Research at Risley Hall*, 1974; *Research at North Downs*, 1975 and *Research at Turners Court*, 1974.

[7] P. Cawson, *Changes in the Intakes of the Special Units at Kingswood and Redhill Schools since the Implementation of the 1969 Children and Young Persons' Act*, unpublished mimeograph, DHSS, Research Division, 1975, quote from p. 16.

[8] *Statistics to 31.7.69*, Redbank Special Unit, 1969.

[9] S. Millham, R. Bullock and P. Cherrett, *After Grace – Teeth*, London, Human Context Books, Chaucer Publishing Company, 1975; I. Sinclair, *Hostels for Probationers*, London, HMSO, 1971 and A. Dunlop, *The Approved School Experience*, London, HMSO, 1974.

[10] P. Cawson, *The Referral Process*, unpublished mimeograph, DHSS, Research Division, 1975, p. 2.

[11] See S. Millham et al., *After Grace – Teeth*, op. cit., chap. 9 and N. Tutt, 'Recommittals of juvenile offenders', *British Journal of Criminology*, vol. XVI, 1976, pp. 385–8.

[12] P. Cawson, *Referrals to the Units*, op. cit., pp. 36–7.

[13] S. Millham et al., *After Grace – Teeth*, op. cit.

[14] P. Cawson, *Referrals to the Units*, op. cit., pp. 7–8.

[15] Details provided by Home Office Young Offenders' Psychology Unit.

[16] P. Cawson, *Referrals to the Units*, op. cit.

[17] Details provided in DHSS internal reports prepared by social work service officers Mr G. Whittaker and Mrs M. Jobbins.

[18] Figures supplied in *Eleventh Report from the Expenditure Committee*, vol. 2, London, HMSO, HC 534 – ii, 1975, p. 409.

[19] M. Zander, 'What happens to young offenders in care', *New Society*, 24 July 1975, pp. 185–7 and D. West and D. Farrington, *The Delinquent Way of Life*, London, Heinemann, 1977.

Part III
The presenting behaviour
of difficult children

6 Violence

We have already cast doubts on some cherished beliefs in the residential care of difficult children. There is no evidence that boys are becoming increasingly difficult in the system; indeed, on well-established prediction criteria, the boys are now easier than when we looked at them in 1969. The boys in the units differ from other very deprived children in care so far as we can see only by the repeated and rapid transfers they have experienced from various placements. If a hard core of difficult children exists in the child-care system, there seems to be no guarantee that they will arrive in the special units. We have also suggested that security fails to take the pressure off the residential system as a whole, which was their original *raison d'être*.

Nevertheless, such findings do not demonstrate that security is unnecessary. We would accept that some boys in the present CHEs are very difficult: persistent absconding and aggressive behaviour aggravates the work load of staff, affects their job satisfaction and sours the institutional climate. We have noted that these were the pressures that led to the formation of the units and the problems presented by children have not changed. In addition, a number of children commit very grave offences and are given long periods of detention; while the majority of these stay in Home Office establishments, some of the youngest children are sheltered in secure units. Although it might be disputed that such children need maximum security, in a number of cases it is probably necessary and, in any case, outraged public feeling and administrative caution usually means that these grave offenders spend a period in confinement. It is the behaviour of these various categories of difficult children we now intend to examine and in so doing may seem to move away from a study of security as such.

However, we have noted that two factors greatly influenced the setting up of the secure units. First, was the widely held view that violence and aggressive behaviour amongst boys in the schools was increasing. Second, there was a well-documented relentless increase in absconding. Because both of these issues, violence and absconding, are extremely complex and have a wealth of research literature of their own, our first inclination was to take the behaviour as given. But any closer look at the disruptive behaviour of children in residential homes supports the general thesis of this study of secure provision: that frequently the care provided for vulnerable children helps create their problem behaviour. Although many workers in the field have maintained this for years, it is not an easy standpoint to demonstrate. In addition, a great deal of research, planning and institutional provision has rested on the belief that disruptive behaviour is inherent in the child; otherwise he would not require special care. It is important to question this idea. As both the subsequent sections on absconding and aggressive behaviour have wider implications than for the narrow field of child care, a detour to glance at them has value outside this study. For example, mental hospitals, open Borstals and armed service establishments suffer serious problems of absconding and, of course, the aggressive behaviour of adolescents is not only confined to residential institutions. But, the detour is not extensive and for a full discussion of the material and scrutiny of the research data, the reader should look at the papers already published which cover these areas.[1]

Violence in residential institutions

Our first task was to find out how much violence there actually was in CHEs and whether the trend was on the increase. By taking a large enough group of boys, by looking at a wide variety of residential styles and scrutinising over time the patterns of aggressive behaviour, we might be able to draw some conclusions. Our interest in the subject was not new, for in 1968 our research perspectives on the old approved schools system were initially influenced by a well-publicised letter sent by the Staffs' Association of these institutions to the Home Secretary. In this, they urged decisive action on the rising tide of violence amongst children which threatened the tranquillity of the schools. They also urged an increase in secure provision. Unfortunately, it is much easier to write letters about the problems of violence among adolescent children than it is to find out actually what is going on. The following material illustrates clearly why.

Reliability of evidence

An initial problem in our study of violence stems from the difficulties in using documentary evidence from schools but this is not because material is suppressed or unavailable.[2] On the contrary, violent incidents, when they occur, are reported at length to case conferences or in boys' records. However, such accounts are not written with research in mind; thus the actual details of any violent incident become difficult to unravel. This is important because when we set out to measure violence, we largely find what we look for.[3] It is interesting that staff anxiety over violent adolescents, which we shall shortly illustrate, bears little relation to the actual levels of violence in schools. There were several schools in our research where staff frequently hit children and where the formal punishment records underestimated the number of violent incidents that occurred, but which, nevertheless, were quite happy with their levels of violence. No one seemed particularly anxious in this rumbustious environment, except possibly a visitor, and in such schools violence was not defined as a problem.

In contrast, in several cosy family group homes for younger children, where staff were particularly sensitive to boys' needs, violent behaviour was often viewed as a major concern. Staff complained that children swore, that they hit each other, that they damaged property or were noisy and defiant. In contrast, staff perspectives in more permissive regimes are quite different. In such contexts, violence is frequently defined as acting-out behaviour and aggressive attacks on staff, even physical attacks, are viewed as valuable crisis moments for exploration and resolution. In such contexts, violence is written about and perceived in a way that is very different from that found in more rigid regimes such as those for boys of senior age. Thus, with all these real problems in the way of any investigation into violence among adolescents in residential schools, it is not surprising that so little empirical research has been undertaken.

Violence defined

Despite these research problems, we had gathered considerable material during our previous researches into boys' approved schools. We had complete case histories of the 1,120 boys in them and recently we have been studying closely four CHEs, two intermediate and two senior schools, as they made major changes in their regimes. So, notwithstanding all these deficiencies in approaching the number and nature of violent incidents in residential schools for young offenders, we made the following explorations.

We chose to define violence as 'the use of force in a social situation in a way that those in power define as illegitimate'.[4] In a school, usually the headmaster and staff are the power holders who define the sorts of force that are forbidden. In most schools physical attack of boy on boy, of boy on staff or of staff on boy are all areas that are defined as unacceptable. But, as we come to examine these situations, there are many problems.

It is very difficult to get a reliable set of figures for attacks of *boy on boy* in schools. Serious attacks which precipitate other crises, such as absconding, or which demand medical attention, are entered up with more reliability than others where there were no such effects. The actual dynamics of the boy-boy incident are difficult to follow, however, and all that is clear is that some violence occurred. Much more reliable are the figures and descriptions of boys' attacks on staff in residential institutions. Any striking of *staff by a boy*, even if a relatively minor incident, is carefully recorded. In therapeutic communities too, this pattern is adhered to, even though the interpretation that is given to the aggression is rather different. Careful reporting probably springs from the fact that such behaviour is viewed as having serious and unfortunate prognosis implications for the offender.

However, in one area, where violence is offered by *staff to children*, we suspect that the reporting is deficient. This is not only because it rests with staff themselves to make uncomplimentary reports on their own actions, but also because much of the violence that we as adults offer to children - the vigorous shove, the shaking of a little boy, the grabbing by the scruff of the neck and frequently the clout - are not perceived by us as violence. This is supported by the fact that every report that we found in the schools of assaults of staff on boys all seemed to have come to light as the result of some subsequent action on the part of the child. For example, he has absconded, he has refused to go into the class or workshop, or, of course, he has retaliated. In the school's subsequent investigation of these incidents, the initial involvement of the member of staff comes to light.

Levels of reported violence

We have commented in earlier chapters that the aggressive behaviour of adolescents was causing concern in the early 1960s and influenced the discussions on the setting up of secure units. This concern has not decreased and it is still important to know how much violence there actually is in CHEs.

The first thing that becomes apparent when we look at 17 boys' approved schools which we studied is that levels of violence differ considerably between each of the age groups and between individual schools. Also, the number of recorded incidents does not correspond in any direct way to concern expressed by staff over boys' violence or to boys' aggressive histories. It is clear that the schools themselves greatly influence the amount of violence they experience, a pattern which we shall find mirrored in boys' absconding behaviour. Using material gathered during our general survey, we can compare three contrasting aspects of violent behaviour in these residential communities: the concern about troublesome behaviour expressed by 187 staff during interviews, the proportion of boys defined as violent or aggressive during assessment and, thirdly, the number of violent incidents of all kinds reported in school records.

The greatest discrepancies between the three aspects we have described are found among the schools for junior boys. Although we find that juniors are twice as likely as others to be labelled violent or aggressive, both staff concern about young boys' behaviour and the recorded levels of violence in junior schools are low. But, as the boys grow older, the correlations between staff concern, the number of incidents and the proportion of boys with aggressive histories increases. Staff attached little significance to violent behaviour among younger children and many outbursts probably pass unrecorded but, as the boys grow older, adult concern increases. An initial assessment or reputation for aggression leads staff to be more cautious and, consequently, more conscientious in recording violent outbursts. Hence, schools for older boys appear to be more violent, particularly in incidents involving staff.

This evidence provides an example of the ways in which ideas on violence reflect people's underlying fears and insecurities rather than reality, for adult anxiety seems quite unrelated either to the actual number of incidents or to children's potential for aggression.

Importance of school regimes

Regimes, too, seem to influence violence. It seems that the more relaxed the regime, the greater the incidence of aggressive behaviour of all sorts. But the number of *serious* incidents is so small as to make such comparisons unreliable and it certainly does not follow that violent environments are necessarily anarchic or threatening to staff.

These changing patterns of violence can be more clearly seen if we look more closely at four schools which we have studied during the past three years. These establishments have all moved towards more open flexible structures, offering care in small groups and have all abandoned the training structure of the orthodox approved school which they had operated previously. All these schools display increased levels of violence during the changes but the rates for recorded incidents per boy still vary very widely, even among this small group, so that one school has a rate four times greater than the others.

If we look more closely at a typical CHE sheltering boys in their mid-teens, we note that, despite the increase mentioned, serious incidents of violence are few and far between and that almost three-quarters of the incidents recorded are boy–boy assaults. In a three-year period, 1972-4, boys hit staff on only 11 occasions. In those three years, nearly 220 boys will have been in the school, so the frequency of assaults on staff works out at one incident in every three months. This pattern is repeated in the other schools and hardly corroborates popular ideas of a surging tide of violence in residential establishments. Even in the closed unit where regular outbursts of violence might be expected, for example, there were in the first three years at Redbank only 79 violent incidents in a period equivalent to 714 boy-months.[5] What is more, only 21 of these assaults involved staff and all this during an unsettled period when routines were being established. These findings are important because assaults on staff are the most likely of all violent acts to be systematically recorded and attacks of this sort question the way in which the aggressor should be approached in the future. Such infrequent incidents are hardly what the staff of the old approved schools had in mind when they wrote to the Home Office in 1969 expressing concern about violence. More perturbing than all this and most certainly what staff did not suspect is the greater number of incidents of staff hitting boys which appears from our evidence, especially as the notification of such incidents is very likely to be an underestimate of the truth.

Trends in violence

Violent behaviour in residential establishments also appears to be cyclical. Because there are so very few serious incidents it is difficult to talk of cycles, but offences do seem to cluster, usually between home leaves. It is also noteworthy that the boy–boy incidents seem to cluster in senior establishments with changes in the leading group. There is also some evidence from our study of our four schools over time that violence is increasing. The number of incidents seems to have doubled over a couple of years and, although earlier figures are less reliable, 1974 rates seem to be about three times those of 1969, even when we take into account fluctuations in school populations. It is probably this rate of increase in violence that has alarmed the headmasters and staff of residential establishments rather than the actual levels but, again, it must be emphasised that very few of these incidents are serious and almost all the increase has been in violence between boys. In any case, we should be mindful of the fact that increasingly difficult behaviour does not correspond with a greater high-risk clientele.

Characteristics of violent boys

One of the tasks we faced with the 1,120 boys in our earlier studies of the approved schools was to decide which types of boy were being admitted to each of the schools. Those schools that took second-time-round offenders or the more disturbed children could hardly be expected to be as successful as those that were taking tranquil boys who were new to the residential experience. For each boy in our study 41 characteristics were relentlessly plotted, ranging from early separation from parents to aspects of personality, intelligence and educational attainments. This is a common technique when approaching such a research problem and by a process of multi-correlation we are able to see which types of boy have a history of being actively involved in at least one violent act during their stay.[6]

From these correlations, we learn that boys who are violent in their CHEs are more likely to be less intelligent than others, to have spent long periods in residential care, and to come from families which have other violent members, particularly the father. Paternal absence seems to affect boys more than girls, making the boys less aggressive when young, but more violent during adolescence.[7] It has also been demonstrated that those parents who condone violence, who are violent themselves or who reward aggression, are more likely to have aggressive children.[8] Parental discipline will have been fitful. The boy's father in particular will have been ambivalent in his attitude towards his sons, a point corroborated by the fact that aggressive examples are very likely to be copied by boys if violence is seen to be rewarded or goes unpunished.[9] There is also a suggestion that institutionalised boys and those with low self-esteem are particularly prone to this sort of modelling.[10] Correlations are also clear between violence in adolescence and boys displaying difficult behaviour from an early age, many of whom have been noted as being highly aggressive during their primary education.[11] In all these areas there are strong relationships between present aggression and previous displays of violence.

But, while we know much about the characteristics of aggressive children, equally interesting is the finding that certain features do not correlate with violence. Contrary to previous findings by Morris, nuances of working-class status do not seem to be significant.[12] We found that a proportion of violent boys in our population come from quite prosperous working-class families, a feature noted by Farrington and West in their comparative study of aggressive with delinquent boys.[13] Violent behaviour is much less related to other sorts of crime than some researches into older offenders have implied.[14] Boys who are violent are also rarely isolates and aggressive children seem to form a sub-group, certainly not one of low status, in our schools.

However, it is particularly important to note that in this exercise there was a strong correlation between past and present behaviour. While such lads are clearly subject to the influence of 'labelling', it does seem that boys who have been violent before are expected by staff to be violent again, and so frequently are. Almost half the boys concerned in violent incidents in one of the schools we studied had been previously involved more than once, suggesting that expectations can render conflict more likely and more fierce. Unfortunately, it is not possible to trace the parallel violent histories of adults in the schools, although there is considerable evidence that certain staff are more likely to be involved in violent acts than others.[15]

Group violence

Occasionally in residential institutions, violent outbursts involve large numbers of people. We can add little to what has already been written on group violence because, thankfully, no riots marred our many visits to these institutions. However, it is worth considering Clarke and Sinclair's valuable review of the available literature on violence as so much that they suggest is supported by our own work on school regimes. They comment:

> the likelihood of a riot is increased by such factors as the admission of new disruptive residents or the discharging of old stabilising ones, the formation of cliques of difficult residents and the existence of grievances among them. Such patterns are accompanied by a lack of communication between residents and staff which makes it difficult for grievances to be dealt with and which grow worse as the trouble begins. The two groups, staff and inmates, grow apart in mutual hostility. The riots frequently take place during a change from a strict to a more permissive regime and may be triggered off by the staff disunity which often accompanies these changes.

They comment that the reports on disturbances at Carlton and Standon Farm Schools revealed similar tensions, 'the existence of boredom, a wide-spread sense of grievance, the presence of a number of difficult boys, poor communications between boys and staff and among the staff themselves, the undermining of staff authority and the absence of key staff at crisis moments'.[16] Here again, we see from another source that the role of the institution is stressed and that the context has to be right for confrontation. This is especially important as we have seen just how influential the disturbances were at Carlton School in initiating the secure units.

Wider perspectives on adolescent violence

A good deal more can be learned about adolescent violence than that simply afforded by the statistics we have accumulated. These can be studied in greater detail elsewhere. First of all, it is clear from a careful examination of staff–boy conflicts that almost all are entirely avoidable. Unfortunately, it seems that few staff have had even the simplest instructions on how to take preventive action. Frequently they hasten into confrontations in which neither staff nor boy feels he can back down without significant loss of face. Such confrontation often takes place in group situations where the esteem of others will be lost by backing down and, inevitably, the chances of an aggressive response are heightened.[17]

Stress on the need for such an awareness on the part of staff is reinforced by the fact that in those incidents where staff hit boys, over half the boys involved had previous violent histories. The staff had quite clearly provoked violence in two-thirds of the incidents and were the ones who hit first.[18] Yet, people can be trained to avoid violence, either by side-stepping the confrontation or by meeting it in much the same way as violent patients are contained in mental hospitals. It is unfortunate that few of these strategies ever form part of the courses offered to students destined for posts in schools or residential homes.

Particularly interesting also is the whole area of the relationship between the hitter and the hit. It is not necessarily one of constant and mutual hostility. Often the fight is part of an ongoing friendship, sometimes an intense relationship, and only in rare cases the result of carefully nurtured hostility or indifference. We undertook a number of sociometric studies during our studies of CHEs to contrast the friendship patterns between block institutions and those which emphasised small group settings in house units, instruction and recreation.[19] Not only did highly aggressive boys have a wider friendship network but they were more likely to be involved in conflicts with their reciprocating friends. It seems that signals between boys in a paired or triangular relationship are often misinterpreted and a fight ensues.

It can be hypothesised that, in the light of these relationships, there may be links between sexual and violent behaviour among adolescent boys. We have noted that violent boys have not only suffered from the absence of father but also spend a long time in institutional care. This poses them with considerable problems, particularly those of sexual identity. We also know that single-sex communities tend to engender anxiety over masculinity.[20] This problem is aggravated for the young offenders by the fact that they are bound by strong and pervasive norms on what constitutes masculine behaviour.[21] This should not imply that these boys hasten into earrings and keep their high-heeled shoes under the bed – indeed, the situation might be less fraught if they did – but it does mean that, in residential settings, boys' masculine self-image is constantly being threatened by what they feel about other people and by what other people feel about them. They and their schools have developed none of the mechanisms which abound in more esteemed residential settings, and which release or displace such anxieties. Consequently, young offenders will be more difficult and will allay their tensions by overtly masculine display, of which aggressive, violent behaviour is the most immediate, as well as being an unmistakable badge of courage.

In a modified way some of these identity problems must affect male staff and would explain why women, on those rare occasions when they are allowed to intervene, seem so much more successful in handling boys' aggressive outbursts than are men. In coeducational settings it is noticeable that whatever problems may abound, the aggressive behaviour of boys and the belligerent stance of male staff is much reduced.[22]

Cultural perspectives on violence

We shall explore more precisely in the next chapter on absconding the ways in which our social position affects our views on problematic behaviour. But it should be apparent that the interpretation which we put on aggressive behaviour differs not only with age but also with social class. Generally, juvenile aggression is concerned with establishing position and forming relationships. Fights between juveniles are highly ritualised and do very little damage. They are an exciting, enjoyable experience which gains attention, informal status and, frequently, the bonus of adult disapproval. This is particularly true of working-class adolescents whose vehicles for aggression are more limited than those of their contemporaries in a higher social class.[23] In the outside world, the football excursion and the motor bike offer some chances for aggressive working-class youths to explode but, for children in residential care, opportunities are much more restricted. It is interesting to contrast the CHEs with independent boarding schools. Not only are the latter highly aggressive places but their release mechanisms are also intrinsic to their functions. The relentless competition, the myriad of status positions, fierce and particular loyalties and monastic isolation all create antagonism and conflict. Of course, such aggression is highly creative. Sporting, cultural, social, academic and even spiritual arenas abound where the drive, iconoclasm, hostility and brimming resentment of adolescents can find expression.[24]

However, the problem of adolescent aggression is not simply one of cultural relativism and some comment is necessary on the rate of increase of reported violent incidents in residential settings. Actual violence levels are not yet large but, if present trends continue, they could become a major issue in some schools and increase demands for secure accommodation.

Future trends in violence

Our own studies and much other research suggests that violence increases in the institution when the stability of the inmate's informal world is threatened. When radical changes in roles, perceptions and relationships are demanded, considerable disruptions result. This is why moves towards a more benevolent regime, such as the introduction of pastoral staff, changes in control or the release of informal leaders, all of which may be ameliorative, can initiate unrest.

It is also clear that in times of change the many components of an institution do not necessarily change at the same rate and this can lead to a state of confusion among staff and children. For example, the norms of one sub-unit, such as the residential house, may conflict with the expectations of education facilities. The frustrations arising from this state of anomie, when the normative demands of particular sub-systems are dissonant from those of the wider institution, can provoke aggressive outbursts.[25] This means that all changes in institutions, however immediately benevolent they may be, need very careful engineering, especially as disruptive behaviour by adolescents following liberal innovations not only strengthens the hand of those who dismiss change as permissive, but also saps the confidence of radical staff. Critics perhaps fail to realise that it is just as likely that change in a more custodial direction would have produced similar tremors of boy dissatisfaction. Whatever the views of the staff, it is clear that recent changes in the aims, administration, staffing patterns, accommodation and clientele that have faced CHEs must be partly responsible for the increasing conflict that is reported.[26]

While disturbances are usually short-lived, there is evidence which would suggest that moves towards more benign regimes in a wide variety of residential schools, not only the CHEs, have been accompanied by an increase in violence and disruptive behaviour. A number of explanations for this offer themselves. In settings where close relationships are encouraged between children and staff and where affective displays and involvement are mutually cherished, those sharing a relationship will have a strong interest in knowing all the activities of each other. With such boys as those sheltered by the CHEs, whose vulnerability, emotional deprivation and difficulties in relationships have been relentlessly chronicled elsewhere, the competition and jealousy over the attention of caring adults must add yet another dimension to unrest.[27]

Residential institutions differ from schools in the outside world, in that such boy–boy and boy–staff relationships are public and their development is scrutinised by all. Boys become jealous of their friends' involvements with others and also of the affections of staff. The widespread and successful efforts to bring about closer relationships between boys, and between staff and children in CHEs through small group living and working situations, must be related to the increase in conflict. It accounts for the frequency of violence which we have already noted as existing between reciprocating friends. It would seem reasonable to suggest that where adolescents are kept longer under scrutiny than ever before, such as in day schools, youth clubs and residential schools, where adolescents are maturing earlier and where children are encouraged to be open and communicative about their feelings, aggressive behaviour must increase.

All this implies that while violence to us may appear wanton, motiveless and spasmodic, it is none of these things. For the participants conflict is logical, frequently moral and fulfilling.[28] It is the essential logic of much adolescent violence that should give us the greatest encouragement. If it is a response to demanding social situations rather than an uncontrolled drive, then youthful aggression can be checked and confrontation can be manipulated by adults.

Conclusions

In our discussions of violence in institutions, we have suggested that serious incidents are not common, that attacks on staff are rare and that staff are as likely to initiate aggressive confrontations as boys. We have noted that although violent boys are identifiable by certain aspects of their background, institutional settings can greatly influence the levels of aggressive behaviour that occur. We have suggested that a complex interaction develops between aggressor and victim, where both have expectations of each other. Where staff are inexperienced and untrained, which is the case in many children's homes, conflicts are quite likely. The changes towards a more benign, psychotherapeutic regime in many CHEs is likely to raise the levels of aggression among boys but this does not mean that the institution is either threatened or ineffective. We would suggest that only repeated and extreme violence, which actually does physical damage to people, needs raise serious questions about a boy's continuance in the institution. In all case conferences, the boys' perspectives need very careful exploration because, in our experience, gratuitous attacks are extremely unusual. Even then, secure provision may not be the wisest answer because the demands on the tolerance and self-control of immature adolescents are likely to be greater in security than outside. We shall see later that Derek Miller maintains that security is quite unsuitable for violent adolescents as it dehumanises the aggressor and legitimises his subsequent dehumanisation of others.[29]

Possibly the most interesting point in the empirical findings is that the actual incidence of aggressive behaviour, levels of staff anxiety and the numbers of violence-prone boys in the institutions are unrelated. As we illustrated in our opening chapters, the drift towards security was pushed by various currents of which staff anxiety over aggression was one. While violence figured prominently in the discussions of the working parties, the evidence we have presented suggests that this anxiety was unrelated to school situations. Thus, it was not surprising that in the review of the working of the secure units in 1968, the Home Office found that few violent boys had been admitted.[30] The units faced the same problems as Professor Wolfgang whose study of violent adolescents in England never took off, as there were not enough violent boys to go round.

Notes

[1] The full report on this research can be seen in N. Tutt (ed.), *Violence*, London, HMSO, 1976, pp. 126-65.

[2] The problems of extracting research material from documents not prepared for the researcher are fully discussed in S. Millham, R. Bullock and P. Cherrett, *After Grace - Teeth*, London, Human Context Books, Chaucer Publishing Company, 1975, chap. 12.

[3] Numerous studies have demonstrated the tendency for a self-fulfilling prophecy to operate in institutions. See for example, D. Hargreaves, *Social Relations in a Secondary School*, London, Routledge and Kegan Paul, 1967; C. Lacey, *Hightown Grammar*, Manchester, University Press, 1970 and C. Werthman, 'Delinquency in schools: a test case for the legitimacy of authority', *Berkeley Journal of Sociology*, vol. VIII, 1963, pp. 39-60.

[4] This definition is very similar to that of Skolnik in *The Politics of Protest*, New York, Simon and Shuster, 1969, p. 4 and discussed by Cohen in

'Directions for research on adolescent group violence and vandalism', *British Journal of Criminology*, vol. XI, 1971, pp. 319-40.

[5] Redbank Special Unit, *Statistics to 31.7.69*, mimeograph, 1969.

[6] See for example, D. West and D. Farrington, *Who Becomes Delinquent?*, London, Heinemann, 1973; D. Street, R. Vinter and C. Perrow, *Organisations for Treatment*, Glencoe, Free Press, 1966; R. V. G. Clarke and D. N. Martin, *Absconding from Approved Schools*, op. cit. and A. Dunlop, *The Approved School Experience*, London, HMSO, 1975.

[7] E. Zigler and I. L. Child, 'Socialization', in G. Lindzey and E. Avonson, *The Handbook of Social Psychology*, vol. 3, Addison Wesley, 1969.

[8] W. C. Becker, 'Consequences of different kinds of parental discipline' in M. L. and L. W. Hoffman (eds), *Review of Child Development Research*, New York, Russell Sage Foundation, 1962, pp. 169-208 and G. S. Lesser, *Maternal Attitudes and Practices and the Aggressive Behaviour of Children*, unpublished Doctoral Thesis, Yale University, 1952.

[9] G. S. Lesser, *Maternal Attitudes and Practices and the Aggressive Behaviour of Children*, op. cit.; A. Bandura and R. H. Walters, *Adolescent Aggression*, New York, Ronald, 1959 and *Social Learning and Personality Development*, New York, Holt, Rinehart and Winston, 1963.

[10] A. Bandura and R. H. Walters, *Social Learning and Personality Development*, op. cit.

[11] Research undertaken at St Christopher's Community Home by Dr R. V. G. Clarke and Dr I. A. C. Sinclair of the Home Office Research Unit and reported in their *Literature Survey On Aggression*, mimeograph, Home Office Research Unit, 1970.

[12] T. and P. Morris, *Pentonville: A Sociological Study of an English Prison*, London, Routledge and Kegan Paul, 1963.

[13] D. Farrington and D. West, 'A comparison between early delinquents and young aggressives', *British Journal of Criminology*, vol. XI, 1971, pp. 341-59.

[14] For example, F. McClintock and N. Avison, *Crime in England and Wales*, London, Heinemann, 1968, found that the proportions of first offenders among juveniles guilty of malicious damage, violent offences and property crimes were 83 per cent, 67 per cent and 57 per cent respectively.

[15] M. S. Folkard, *Aggressive Behaviour in Mental Hospitals*, monograph no. 1, Nethern Hospital, Surrey.

[16] R. V. G. Clarke and I. A. C. Sinclair, *Literature Survey on Aggression*, op. cit., pp. 7-8.

[17] R. G. Geen, 'The effects of frustration, attack and prior training in aggressiveness upon aggressive behaviour', *Journal of Personality and Social Psychology*, vol. IX, 1968, pp. 316-21.

[18] Those whose task it is to establish the exact dynamics of violent incidents such as lawyers or administrators in the Criminal Injuries Compensation Board, comment that it is often difficult to decide who is the assailant and who the victim when all the circumstances are reviewed.

[19] Full details of the sociometric test can be found in the report, S. Millham, R. Bullock and P. Cherrett, *A Comparative Study of Eighteen Approved Schools which Explores their Stylistic Variety and the Commitment of boys and staff*, Dartington Social Research Unit, 1972.

[20] This has been fully explored in R. Lambert and S. Millham, *The Hothouse Society*, London, Weidenfeld & Nicolson, 1968 and in R. Lambert, S. Millham and R. Bullock, *The Chance of a Lifetime*, London, Weidenfeld & Nicolson, 1975. For other examples see L. Taylor and S. Cohen, *Psychological Survival: The experience of long-term imprisonment*, Harmondsworth, Penguin, 1972 and R. Giallombardo, *Society of Women*, New York, Wiley, 1966.

[21] W. B. Miller, 'Lower class cultures, a generating milieu of gang delinquency', *Journal of Social Issues*, vol. XIV, 1958, pp. 5-19; D. Downes, *The Delinquent Solution*, London, Routledge and Kegan Paul, 1966; M. E. Wolfgang and F. Ferracuti, *The Sub-culture of Violence: Towards and Integrated Theory in Criminology*, London, Tavistock, 1967 and R. Dembo, 'A measure of aggression among working-class youths', *British Journal of Criminology*, vol. XIII, 1973, pp. 245-52.

[22] See S. Millham, R. Bullock and P. Cherrett, 'Coeducation in approved schools', *Child in Care*, vol. XI, 1971, pp. 18-28 and 20-32 in issues 3 and 4.

[23] G. Mungham and G. Pearson (eds), *Working Class Youth Culture*, London, Routledge and Kegan Paul, 1976. See especially the paper by J. Clark and T. Jefferson 'Working class youth cultures' in which they discuss the erosion of traditional outlets for youthful, working-class aggression.

[24] See R. Lambert et al., *The Hothouse Society*, op. cit.; R. Lambert, J. Hipkin and S. Stagg, *New Wine in Old Bottles*, London, Bell, 1969; R. Lambert, S. Millham and R. Bullock, *The Chance of a Lifetime?* op. cit. and U. Bronfenbrenner, *The Two Worlds of Childhood*, London, Allen & Unwin, 1971.

[25] The term anomie occurs in the writings of the French sociologist Durkheim whose work is discussed fully in S. Lukes, *Emile Durkheim: His Life and Work*, London, Allen Lane, 1973.

[26] For evidence of the increasing difficulties presented by children coming into care, see M. S. Hoghugi, *What's in a Name? Some Consequences of the 1969 Children and Young Persons' Act*, Aycliffe Studies of Problem Children, 1972.

[27] See, S. Millham et al., *After Grace - Teeth*, op. cit.

[28] See F. Strodtbeck and J. F. Short, 'Aleatory risks versus short run hedonism in explanations of gang action', *Social Problems*, vol. XII, 1964, pp. 127-40, for an illustration of the logic in seemingly impulsive acts and N. Goldman, 'A socio-psychological study of school vandalism', *Crime and Delinquency*, 1961, pp. 221-30 for a similar study of vandalism.

[29] D. Miller, *The Biology and Psychology of Juvenile Violence: Its Implications for Prediction and Treatment*, Institute of Psychiatry, Northwestern University, Chicago, 1976.

[30] Home Office Working Party on Special Units at Approved Schools, 1967.

7   Absconding

If the problems of aggressive behaviour in CHEs can be demonstrated to be exaggerated and its incidence closely related to the style of institutional life and staff professionalism, are these patterns repeated when we turn to look at absconding?

At breakfast time in England and Wales nearly a third of a million children sit down to an institutional meal. We shelter proportionately more children in boarding schools and homes than any other European country. While the majority of our children tolerate this residential situation, with greater or lesser enthusiasm, a small but increasing number do not. For example, between 1955 and 1971 the rate of absconding from CHEs increased fourfold and the same foot-loose ethos has affected other institutions, particularly special and maladjusted schools, assessment and probation hostels.[1] Although this tendency of some boys to run away is not new, it even perturbed eighteenth century child-care institutions, this recent rise has caused increasing concern to residential staff and administrators. Unlike violence in schools, careful studies of which raise doubts about its extent and significance, running away is certainly a widespread problem. Why do children run and to what extent can a place in maximum security be seen as an effective answer?

This chapter explores some of the causes and consequences of running away. Initially we shall glance at some of the studies that deal with absconding and then try to offer a number of fresh perspectives on this conduct.[2]

Absconding behaviour has always been a problem to staff in residential institutions although perspectives on its causes and significance differ widely. In CHEs, absconding by a pupil leads to anxiety among staff as it threatens the containing functions of the home, chills the institutional climate and puts the absentee at risk. But little is known about the reasons for persistent absconding and, apart from secure accommodation, few preventive experiments have been made.

In 1965 Clarke and Martin, both psychologists, began an extensive study of absconding.[3] It was in their eyes, an attractive topic for research because absconding was unambiguously defined, routinely recorded and much could be discovered about the boys and girls involved. Since absconding is prohibited in institutions, it might have something in common with delinquency in general and therefore any research could have wider applications.

Clarke and Martin's initial perspectives were those of clinical psychology. While many children abscond from residential homes, about 10 per cent persist in this disruptive behaviour over time in spite of transfer to different settings and a number of these become candidates for security. As absconding appears to be a consistent feature of the individual's behaviour, the researchers sought amongst this sub-group an explanation in terms of individual differences. All sorts of factors which might distinguish the persistent absconder from others were considered; ranging from his age and physical characteristics to aspects of his psychology, home and school experience. But an exhaustive survey established little. Comparisons of absconders with those who stayed behind revealed remarkably few differences. Indeed, the researchers found that persistent absconders were similar to a control group in every way except that they had a slightly more delinquent history and had absconded from previous residential placements. As the authors wrote, 'By this time our faith in the importance of individual characteristics was shaken'.[4] In a more recent paper, Clarke and Martin describe how this setback and the increasing realisation that the regime of the establishment was of key significance moved their ideas from an internal causation theory to an environmental learning perspective.[5]

A number of other studies, following in Clarke and Martin's footsteps, similarly failed to identify the distinguishing features of absconders. For example, Porteous and McLoughlin studying absconders from Aycliffe found 'the differences between a group of absconders and a group of non-absconders are few and on the majority of variables studied there is very little difference'.[6]

This does little more than confirm earlier findings by Brierley and Jones, who indicated that absconders were more likely than others to have started offending by the age of 10 and to have been previously to an approved school, Gunaskera who suggested that persistent absconders were likely to have been persistent thieves, Wilkins who found that absconders had more court appearances and other studies which linked absconding with numerous previous convictions and institutionalisation.[7] Indeed, this veritable correlation industry seems to suggest that only in the case of the lone persistent absconder are there any indications of personality differences, a relationship which has not been explored to date.

While the extensive survey of boys' backgrounds revealed few characteristics common to absconders, a glance at aspects of the school environment proved much more fruitful. Clarke and Martin found that not only did the *rates* of absconding differ considerably across the schools, some being five or six times greater than others despite similarities in the child intake, but also absconding was influenced by other factors such as seasonal and climatic conditions or punishments received. To link these two findings, the proneness of certain boys to run and the clear impact that school regimes have on absconding, the authors proposed a theory which emphasised learning rather than boys' backgrounds. They write:

> We believe that the main reason why boys (and girls) feel impelled to run away from the school is that they have been placed in a situation that makes them unhappy or anxious, and absconding is a way of dealing with these feelings . . .
>
> As most boys have no relevant previous experience, the likelihood that they will become absconders could depend on what they happen to experience in the school. The experience consequent upon absconding, if it occurs, will help to determine whether or not the boy will abscond again when placed in a similar position. Because previous absconding predicts more rather than less absconding, it seems likely that absconding is more often reinforced than punished . . .[8]

Of course, sociologists following in the footsteps of Goffman, Sykes and Etzioni have long emphasised the significance of institutional structures. Since Clarke and Martin's original work, a number of studies of the approved schools, Borstals and probation hostels have concluded that the ethos of the institution, that is, its values and perspectives, can override marked variations in the background of the clientele.[9] But while subsequent studies of absconding have confirmed Clarke and Martin's stress on the importance of environmental factors, they have given less support to explanations in terms of learning behaviour.

In fact, the suggestion that there is a learning component in repeated absconding is difficult to substantiate. The theory is general rather than specific and it certainly lacks a predictive quality; as the authors themselves comment, 'Absconders and non-absconders are remarkably similar groups in nearly every respect but in absconding behaviour itself and this would be very difficult to predict.'[10]

The greatest challenge to the learning theory viewpoint is, of course, that sizeable minority who cease to abscond when they are transferred to a new institution. In general, children in residential care for a long period are more likely to adopt the absconding habit the longer they stay in care but, nevertheless, many do cease to behave in this way. Indeed, both Clarke and Martin's study and a number of others show that up to one-third of persistent absconders give up the behaviour at some point during their delinquent careers.[11] If unlearning can be so frequent and haphazard, then learning theory is robbed of much of its reliability and validity.

Several of the hypotheses put forward by Clarke and Martin have also been questioned by Laverack in his study of absconding from one boys' CHE.[12] He found that the most frequent absconders did not necessarily experience poor contact with home or have greater numbers of previous court appearances; nor did they seem to be affected by hardened absconders. While boys ran away mostly during the evening, the season of the year seemed unimportant. Laverack could also find little evidence that truancy from day school was related to absconding. However, assessment reports on school absences are often unreliable and, as we shall see, this finding need not challenge the view that absconding from CHEs may be part of a long development of techniques for avoiding stress. Like the other studies, though, Laverack found that boys with a history of previous abscondings ran away from this particular home with the greatest frequency.

Generally, the evidence suggests that absconding patterns develop over time and in the case of many boys it is persistent to the point of being habitual. Learning theory has been advanced to account for the 'habitual' nature of absconding. Nevertheless, in a significant number of cases the persistent pattern of running is broken.

Absconding and recidivism

However, the implications of Clarke and Martin's research do not stop here. Schools can be demonstrated to differ greatly in their levels of absconding and we know that they also differ in their success rates with boys on release. It has been suggested that absconding and recidivism are linked. While boys are on the run their delinquent behaviour is renewed and reinforced.

Absconding has been found by both Clarke and Martin and others to correlate with failure of boys after release. Absconders, it seems, are more likely to be reconvicted once they have left their CHE. Clarke and Sinclair also found in a study of 66 boys' approved schools that high absconding rates were associated with low success rates of boys even when intelligence and boys' previous delinquencies were controlled.[13]

As Clarke and Martin and Sinclair have demonstrated that absconding rates differ widely between institutions and are independent of the nature of the pupil intake, it seems likely that high absconding could be one, but certainly not the only, index of an ineffective regime. However, it is important to stress that a strong correlation does not imply any causal relationship between running away and future persistent recidivism, a point that is frequently ignored by those working in the field.

Vital studies which could decide the question have yet to be undertaken. They would need to compare the post-release careers of absconders who commit serious offences while absconding from residential care with those who run but do not offend. What little evidence there is, such as Sinclair's findings from probation hostels, questions both the idea of a learning component in absconding and its relationship with delinquency.[14] He found that absconders who committed offences were no less successful in the long term than those who did not indulge in criminal offences while on the run.

While we cannot compare the careers of absconders who commit offences with those who do not, we can, at least, explore the characteristics of those regimes which have low absconding rates. We can relate the absconding patterns of 17 schools we studied between 1969 and 1973 to aspects of their regimes and the boys' response to them.

We found that running away from schools related to a number of indices of satisfaction with the residential experience. For example, a good pastoral care system, particularly a climate in which boys feel able to discuss their personal problems with staff, moderates absconding. Feelings of happiness and well-being within the school are also significant and an index constructed from responses to questions exploring areas of satisfaction with the regime clearly shows that high satisfaction correlates with low absconding.

When we look at other aspects of our group of schools only the differing levels of delinquency among intake and aspects of control seem to be associated with absconding. Surprisingly, factors such as the proximity of the school to home, a boy's intelligence or a school's attempts to promote good staff–pupil relationships all fail to correlate with running away.

From our analysis, it is clear that absconding rates are closely related both to features of boys' backgrounds and to certain aspects of school regimes. Schools which admit deeply delinquent boys have high absconding, but so do those schools which admitted more docile clients and exercise low levels of institutional and expressive control. The reader can look at our other publications for a fuller description of these concepts.[15] But, briefly, institutional control refers to the restrictions imposed on an individual's choice, movement and privacy which result from living in a residential setting, while expressive control measures attempts by the institution to mould and influence children's moral behaviour, beliefs and interpersonal relationships.

While all the dimensions of institutional control seem to correlate equally with absconding, in the case of expressive control, certain areas, such as the lifestyle of the institution and the expressive role of staff, seem to be more significant than others. High levels of both institutional and expressive controls are associated with low absconding. In the first case, the link is more obvious as high institutional controls must restrict freedom to run away. But institutional controls in *themselves* are not sufficient to hold children. While they provide a sense of order and security, they must also be linked with a manifestly caring, moral lifestyle which tempers for children the disadvantages of residential living.

These relationships hold even when we control for the boys' backgrounds. We might have expected that as schools which care for the most delinquent boys tend to display high institutional but low expressive controls, any established links between absconding and control could be explained by the impact of boys' backgrounds. In fact, this is not so. Absconding and control are still related even when the extent of pupils' previous delinquency is taken into consideration. As Clarke and Sinclair say from their evidence, 'Whatever the explanation of these present findings, they do not suggest that schools with low absconding rates have "easier" intakes.'[16]

What, then, can we glean from this evidence on absconding? It is clear from the extensive researches into boys' backgrounds that persistent absconding seems to relate to little else other than deep delinquency and previous absconding. There also seems to be an habitual element in the conduct in that abscondings become more likely the longer a child stays in residential care. In many cases, usually about one-third of the children, the habit is broken if they are transferred elsewhere.

There is also overriding evidence that the environment and climate of the residential setting influences absconding behaviour. Unfortunately, apart from our own material, there seems to have been very little exploration of the characteristics of regimes which display extreme absconding rates. The regimes with high absconding seem to take in very delinquent boys, exercise low levels of institutional and expressive control and achieve poor levels of pastoral care and commitment. On the other hand, regimes with low absconding rates have higher levels of control, happier boys, better pastoral care and seem to give less reinforcement to boys' delinquent aspirations so that even if some boys do run away, they commit fewer offences. Such homes are also more willing than others to take back the returning child.

We have also noted that absconding rates are related to rates for premature transfer of boys before the completion of their stay in residential care, usually because of offences committed while on the run. While this relationship held for the majority of schools, there were a number of exceptions among the schools we studied. These institutions had high absconding rates but preferred to hold on to their boys and transferred very few.

One of the surprising findings in our previous work was that schools which transferred prematurely were also those which were least successful with boys who completed their training and were released to the community.[17] These schools have high transfer rates, high absconding rates and also high failure rates. Unfortunately the majority of the schools we studied were in this category. It is because of this that we, as well as Clarke and Sinclair, find that absconding correlates with failure. In fact, it is not the *absconding* that causes the failure but the ineffective regime which produces high failure, high transfer and high absconding. When a large number of schools are analysed this general pattern will dominate, giving a correlation between absconding and failure, especially for senior schools where there are fewer exceptions to the rule. Interestingly, those schools with low transfer, high success but *high* absconding show that much is achieved by taking back absconders.

To summarise, in unsatisfactory schools boys run away and quickly get transferred. In other schools, there is less likelihood of ever running or developing a pattern of persistent absconding and in a number of 'exceptional' schools, absconders are numerous but are generally readmitted so that after release, they share in the generally high success rate of the schools. As Sinclair's study implies and these schools demonstrate, absconding does not *cause* failure.

In our previous work, we also found that in effective schools all boys, whatever their background, did better than in the bad regimes. Admittedly, individual absconders are still more prone to failure than those who never run, but a good regime can disrupt the absconding process. Indeed, from the point of view of security, only boys who persistently run away from *effective* regimes, therefore, present a serious absconding problem and this conduct needs to be identified and met early. The majority of absconders could be helped by correct transfer or, as we shall see, by providing small, open intensive care units in CHEs. Unfortunately, transfer between these homes is usually from one unsatisfactory environment to another and only very rarely is a boy lucky enough to find himself moved to a more effective setting. For example, in our sample of 17 schools there were 1,119 boys, 106 of whom had been to a previous approved school. The schools with low transfer, low absconding and high success contained 18 of these and the 'exceptional' schools (high absconding but low transfer and high success) contained 21. Of this 106, therefore, 39 had been transferred to regimes which stood a good chance of breaking the absconding habit, whereas the remaining 67, two-thirds, had been allocated to homes where failure to moderate absconding was already manifest.

We feel that these findings have considerable implications for secure provision. We noted at the outset that a child's arrival in security resulted from a process of transfer and referral. We found secure units were used more by some local authorities than others and disproportionately more by some CHEs. Studies of children's aggressive behaviour demonstrated the importance of institutional regimes in engineering conflict and turmoil. Now, once again, a careful study of absconding brings us to similar conclusions. Far from being different from other vulnerable children, the majority of absconders are like everyone else and the absconding problem is created by the institutions through which the children pass. The prospect of absconders becoming recidivists springs not from the running but from unsatisfactory residential establishments with high reconviction rates, in which vulnerable children find themselves.

Additional perspectives on absconding

It is a puzzle why some perspectives on absconding have been relentlessly explored while others are not even entertained. There are, in fact, many other dimensions on absconding which seem to have tempted few researchers and it would be useful to glance at them.

Initially the 'medical' model of disease, cause and treatment on which most research approaches to absconding are based, takes running away behaviour as given, in the same way as much research into delinquency takes the crime as a symptom. Such approaches view delinquent behaviour as a symptom or a product of an abnormality in the child which is innate or acquired early in life and which would tend to manifest itself whatever his circumstances. Therefore, interest focuses on the deviant's personality and his inner motivations, rather than on his crimes.

However, like burglary and larceny, absconding is a very complex piece of behaviour. The meanings that boys give to the act differ widely and explorations of the ways in which a boy negotiates his absence, the ways he goes alone or as part of a group, could be very rewarding. We have found that in much the same way as in group crime where boys graduate from marginal to key roles in the enterprise, so in absconding, where bounds breakers seem to move towards more conspicuous departures. The motivations for absconding vary, too. Boys are propelled by school, home or personal anxieties and these may determine whether his on-the-run offences are merely survival techniques or criminal sprees.

The following comments from persistent boy absconders should illustrate the great complexity of running away behaviour, its different motivations and institutional responses.

> I don't like coming back after home leave and begged my mum to say I am poorly or have an accident. She misses me a lot when I'm away so she knows what I feel. My dad goes mad if he knows, 'specially when my social worker comes round to see what's up.
> But this place is miles from where I live, sometimes it's like you will never see home again. If you don't get a visit or a letter you think about it all the time. Wonder if they've died or been run over. I've done a bunk four times and when you come back they say 'next time you will be off to the nick'.
>
> Boy – 13, CHE

> I don't go far but sometimes I don't want to see no one. I go and hide under the motorway, come back when it's dark. I think about my problems and

what will happen to me. But they don't kick up much and Mrs Johnston gives me a cup of tea.

Boy – 12, CHE

But some boys are group-oriented, spontaneously running because of the minor frustrations and very delinquent. They almost invite detection and retribution.

The boss said we weren't to go to the film because we had messed up his dining-room. It wasn't fair because we 'adn't been in. So we decided to bunk it, we did a couple of jobs in the village but it was pissing with rain so we hid in a hut in the park. But we got nabbed and they brought us here – I don't reckon the school will have us back.

Boy – 14, assessment centre

Some expeditions are more carefully planned and criminally sophisticated. Here a lad proffers advice to apprentice runners:

I can't remember how many times I've absconded – must be dozens. But I'm not like the rest of these divvies in here. They've no idea when it comes to doing a bunk.
For a start you don't go near roads or hang around the place like they do. Always take a few who want to go home to mum with you. Then leave 'em to get picked up. Make for some railway lines like I do and get away fast. You've got to be careful of signal boxes and stations though and you go round them. I always head it for a big town and bunk on a train . . .
Yes – going on roads is mad, you stand out like a sore thumb, especially in school clothes. You've got to get new stuff fast and the only way you can get it is by ripping if off somewhere. Sleeping rough is no good either unless you have to, because you get all messed up and then it looks pretty obvious you're on the run. Trains in railway sidings are a favourite for a kip, but you've got to watch out for the queers and winos.
Another thing, don't go home to your mum. I always let mine know that I'm OK and sometimes I visit but I always stay with one of my sisters. Last time I bunked it I got myself a job as a van lad, it gets you off the streets you see and you can pay for your keep. My mate, the driver, used to stop outside the gates of the school I'd bunked from and blow his horn. It was a right laugh. The cops are fly you see, they know you should be at school in the day and so they spot you especially an old cop, they know you're bunking it from somewhere. They usually ask where you live and what I do is give them a false address. Then they say, 'Jump in the car and we'll take you home!' – they expect you to crack then and run off, so keep cool, say 'Oh great!' then go to get in with them. If you're lucky they'll tell you to bugger off and then you know you're OK again.

Boy – 14, special unit

Unfortunately, any typology of youthful absconders simply runs into trouble because innocent attention-seeking behaviour can swiftly escalate into sophisticated criminal runs, possibly because of the reaction the initial departure engenders. This 'secondary deviance' we shall shortly explore. But the above illustrations do provide at least some glimpse of the complexity of absconding behaviour. In an interesting paper on absconding from French reform schools, Mazerol makes similar suggestions.[18] He relates different patterns of absconding to boys' motivations for running.

While Mazerol presents some evidence to support his classifications, whether renewed correlations of background variables with these different types of absconding would yield more positive results than previous less specific studies have offered, we cannot tell. It is not for the faithless to discourage such quests for the Holy Grail.

The interactionist's perspective

A further insight into the absconding process can be gleaned from recent sociological writings stressing the social aspects of interaction between individuals.[19] If we abandon the position that most deviants are quite different from other people, and much of the empirical evidence on aggressive and absconding adolescents would suggest that this is justified, we are then forced to look less at background causes, less at treatment, less at prescriptive policies for eliminating deviant behaviour and more at the ways in which children embark on unorthodox careers. In doing so, we must examine the ways in which others react to the choices that the deviant makes.

This approach leads us to ask seminal questions such as, how does a boy react to the label of 'absconder', who gives him this title and how does he realign his self-perspectives to accord with the deviant label attached to him? This realisation could shift us from a preoccupation with the absconder and turn our attention more towards the ways that institutions react to running away.

Arrival

Much interactionist literature is concerned with deviance in general and largely preoccupied with 'rule making' and 'breaking'. While, fortunately, rules are rarely posted on CHE notice boards, boys arriving at their residential placement have been sufficiently socialised by day school, assessment centre and court experiences to know that spontaneous withdrawal from the institution is not an approved activity. However, they are probably unaware of its serious consequences.

We have commented in our research study of the approved schools that boys in care tend to have a very calculative view of their residential experience.[20] In general, their stay is unwilling, and they believe that the school can only provide a few short-term instrumental benefits. Indeed, we found that deep commitment was hardly engendered in the children by the fact that nearly two-thirds of the boys in the schools had very imprecise ideas as to why they were in residential care at all. The decisions taken seemed to them arbitrary and discriminatory.

While CHEs might accept these points in theory, such awareness rarely seems to affect practice. Schools vary greatly in the reception they offer new boys and some do not give much thought to the extraordinarily complex, unfamiliar and baffling world that the residential community presents to the novice.[21]

Successful schools in our previous research were those few institutions which welcomed the children and convinced the boys that the hostile, custodial, punitive perspectives which they held were untenable. We also noted that such schools manipulated the boy's world towards a different set of expectations, aspirations and values. This perhaps is one reason why high expressive control which orients children towards moral or benign states correlates with low absconding rates.[22]

While a boy on arrival may not have departure high on the list of priorities, he certainly does not view absconding as particularly serious. Indeed, we found that boys in the old approved schools, even after several months' stay, viewed running away as a less serious and significant offence than institutional misdemeanours such as rudeness and aggressive behaviour towards staff, a poor work record or stealing within the school. They certainly did not perceive absconding as an unreasonable or particularly reprehensible act or seem able to offer any alternative strategy for coping with difficulties.

In life outside the organisation, there is no comparable rule against running away which carries with it the force of law. Thus, boys do not benefit from a degree of previous socialisation in what is, or is not, acceptable. This is in marked contrast to activities other than absconding, such as theft or aggressive behaviour. Indeed, much of a boy's outside experience, in his day school, where absence or truancy are commonplace, can run counter to the expectations of his residential school. In his big city comprehensive, considerable absences from school can be easily accomplished without uncomfortable consequences. Thus, when a boy is transferred to the residential situation, we feel it is unwise to assume prior knowledge on his part of the serious implications that staff will draw if he runs away.

Unfortunately, the child in care will usually arrive in a CHE where staff feel otherwise. Everybody *knows* that absconding is habitual and that persistent absconders will run again. Everybody *knows* that these boys commit crimes as they go and their chances of eventual success are low. Everybody *knows* that the way to break this pattern is to make special efforts to hold on to them or to transfer them to secure units. The fact that this omniscience is quite inaccurate robs it of none of its predictive force.

The new arrival is accompanied by his file, the implications of which are disturbing. A boy who absconds is expected to run again and the whole pattern of interaction between him and others in the institution is coloured by this. Staff and boys perceive him as an absconding risk and the task of coping with such a label becomes as much of a problem to the child as the more transitory anxiety of settling down or being absent from home.

Departure

The boy may settle in his CHE but, to him, the frustrations of residential life are

79

both unfamiliar and considerable. We have chronicled relentlessly elsewhere the pains of imprisonment suffered by many ordinary children in boarding schools but we know that they have been previously programmed to view this as a life-enhancing, enriching experience. This is not the case with boys 'put away' or taken into 'care'; for them the experiences seem custodial, punitive and isolating.[23]

However benevolent the institution may be, a boy in residential care faces difficulties not shared by other boarders. In his experience residential situations are reserved for the mad, bad and destitute. Thus the child in care has not fashioned any of the manipulative skills necessary to achieve gratifications in complex organisations such as schools. Many less intelligent and shattered children cannot conceive the skills that are needed for making out in a large boarding school; neither do they have the necessary stamina to succeed. One suspects that many of them run away because it is a less baffling, less disintegrating experience than staying in a complex residential situation. It is the only way in which the least adequate child can assert any degree of independence.

Particularly frustrating for a lad in residential care is the fact that the range of protest and disruptive behaviour available to him and the impact such displays can have are greatly limited because so much difficult behaviour is *expected*. Children in less specialised institutions have a wealth of weapons, such as stealing or swearing, to display hostilities, all of which are less effective when used by boys in CHEs. 'Staff understand bloody well everything, that's the trouble. Thumping someone or doing a bunk is the only thing that gets them.'

Absconding is also frequently viewed by boys as a way of 'wiping the slate clean', particularly in those schools which have a tariff system of rewards and punishments linked to home leave and privileges. Unlike ordinary schools, CHEs do not enjoy termly cycles which are broken by long intervening holidays after which boys can draw a veil over past indiscretions. Boys' continuous presence in the institution means that their sins are ever before them and, for the deviant, sins accumulate. Unlike service postings or class changes in ordinary schools, there are few ways available to boys in care of finding a fig leaf or turning over a new one.

To growing boys, even a harem can be claustrophobic and in the end someone runs away from school. Frequently, it is a marginal boy, a new arrival, one less integrated into friendship networks or less bound by pastoral relationships with staff. Sometimes it is a fisted charismatic, dragging with him reluctant disciples. But, whoever goes, the departure is news – big news to boys in isolated communities where damp breakfast cornflakes can occupy boy and staff discussions for a whole morning. The likely lads' departure for the outside world is quite something. As boys run, the attractions constructed by the school to shield children from the discomforts of enforced residence are swept away. For them all, the choice to stay or not to stay has become a conscious decision. For the boy making a coffee table for Christmas comes the attractive possibility, why not take your holiday now?

To be in an institution when the running starts is fascinating to an observer-participant and certainly merits much closer interactionist analysis than we can offer here. One can almost see the relationships between staff and boys changing, while similar shifts are manifest among the boys as well as within the staff world.

Staff scrutiny of boys increases, heads are repeatedly counted and there is a surreptitious locking of doors. Staff are abruptly summoned from class or workshop for furtive corridor whisperings, there are ringing telephones and hurried conferences behind closed doors. The deputy looks harassed, the senior assistant breaks off from organising yet another mammoth change of Saturday work routine and even the head hurries back from his conference. Within the institution the excitement gathers and there is a busyness about the place.

To the delight of eagle-eyed boys, simmering divisions increase among the staff. The trade instructors, who have gruffly forecast the collapse of Mr Trend's therapeutic house for months, smile contentedly. Teachers, smugly professional and relieved of extraneous duties, hurry away at four, murmuring about the quality of residential social workers. House staff cling to their desks with the wounded expressions of Renaissance Saint Sebastians – each 'phone call another arrow – while round the estate meanders the maintenance man, supporting a group of pathetic boys who cannot even find the gate. He has seen this many times before. At night the night duty man, stirred to sudden industry, relentlessly plods.

The boys are perturbed too, for while lip service is paid by all to the dangers of absconding, they now see that the anxieties of staff clearly reflect their role obligations. The concern of top executives focuses on the outside world. 'If you run, then run a long way and don't do a job within a 50-mile radius of this place.' House staff are seen to be more concerned with the contaminating effect of absconding on other boys rather than weeping tears for the departed. Boys note that while caring staff seem violated by children's departures, the more authoritarian staff are deeply affronted while organisational staff are merely irritated. Instructors bemoan their disrupted work schedules and deviant staff seem actually gratified, offering public comment such as, 'I don't blame the lad. Thank God he has the guts to run away. In his place I would have gone myself.' To the newly arrived boy, the reactions of the other people to absconding must seem rather contradictory and largely unrelated to his needs.

But these are minor tremors compared with the epicentred disruption that absconding initiates in the boy world.[24] As boys run, both the complex relationships and the elaborate pecking order built up in times of tranquillity disintegrate. When key figures in the leading crowd absent themselves, the boy world goes up for auction. The unofficial fruits that élite boys have culled from long and powerful residence go begging: coveted chairs before the television stand empty, beds beside warm radiators lie vacant, there is even more milk for the damp cornflakes and a halcyon chance for the underprivileged to pour it out. Established roles, nurtured over months, are gone before breakfast and high status positions are vacant. For children, this is not only very exciting but also well worth staying for. It is like Topkapi at the fall of the Sultan and provides an answer to one of the problems posed by both the interactionist and learning theories of absconding. It explains the riddle that a significant proportion of boys, who have been effectively labelled or carefully schooled as absconders, stop running. While the curve of numbers running away initially steepens in spates of absconding, it always flattens out. Many boys stay behind and some persistent absconders stay along with the rest. In spite of widespread staff fears that their school will empty, it never does: there is always a boy left to make the evening cocoa. In some ways, it is the institution's inward-looking topsy-turvy ways which finally save it. Many boys stay to enjoy those minor delights that are theirs for the asking outside. They stay because other boys have gone.

To staff, the exodus of the boys comes unheralded, as indeed does the lifting of the pestilence. But, to the boys, it is rarely a surprise. Indeed, they help to set it off.

> We always know when someone is going to bunk, you see them chatting in the tabholes or whispering in the dorms at night. So if you've got any sense you'll keep clear because the temptation to go is great.
>
> Boy – 14, CHE

Thus, there is a subtle and coordinated withdrawal of the orthodox from those to whom deviance is imputed. The lepers are forced to dance with each other and their untouchable role state is signalled.

> Everyone starts to hang on to their gear, guard your best clothes and shoes, torches, anoraks, anything you've got, because it's these they take.
>
> Boy – 13, CHE

> You must look smart when you run, school gear is recognisable so when some boys are going over the wall, I put my trousers under the pillow and shoes in the bed.
> I even eat what food I've brought back from weekend, otherwise it's gone.
>
> Boy – 14, CHE

Consequently, a munching, silent host, wearing their boots and trousers in bed, wait for the freedom fighters to take off – a vision to warm the heart of any inter-actionist!

Many departures are calculated by those that go. Friendships are tested out, alliances made and broken and the flight of a lone 'nutter' can disrupt boys' well laid plans.

> We even managed to get our weekend clothes out of lock-up and chatted up the lorry drivers at the motorway cafe, then that wet bastard, Jenkins, took off, he only hid in the school barn but it got everyone jumpy, so we jacked it in.
>
> Boy – 15, CHE

Naturally, it would be illuminating to chart the various rewards that come to absconders and the self-perspectives gathered on the run. The different receptions he will have when, and if, he reaches home must also be very significant. These interactions as much as those of the staff, will contribute to the building up of an absconding identity. But, unfortunately, space must restrict our concern to the institution.

Return

Most prodigals return to their schools but few fatted calves are killed and they have a cool welcome. The process of labelling accelerates. Those boys who return find a new informal structure among the others who remained and, in this, they must find a space. They also discover staff have revised their perspectives on them and usually not in a complimentary direction.

The return to the boy world is coloured by acrimony and reproach. Those who have stayed are blistered by endearments such as 'grass', 'arse lickers', 'time servers', 'gutless yellow bastards'. In turn, those who have run away are labelled by the law-abiding as 'thick', 'pathetic', 'big heads' or 'clueless', implying that the deviants are unable to appreciate the shining institutional truth that rewards come to the orthodox.

However, the bitterest reproaches are between paired friends or groups of mates, some of whom failed to share in the escaping enterprise. Here the acrimony is most bitter and the relationships rarely resumed. When the absconder comes back, the runner is more acceptable to those boys who have similarly returned or who view absconding in a favourable light. For some, informal status can only by maintained by going again when the signal is given. This clear reallocation of roles and accompanying self-perceptions among the boys, added to the revised estimates of staff, illustrates the ways in which some boys' deviant roles are reinforced while, in others, deviant labels wither.

Certainly, return is difficult for the absconder. His friendship patterns are shattered, his treasured roles usurped, his status dented and he has to endure a subtle chorus of reproach.

> So you're back then, well, Johnson finished the coffee table – he made a good job of it, too.

> Yes, we won the last match. Johnson scored, he's such a reliable lad.

> No, I haven't seen your training shoes, they must have gone while you were away. Ask Johnson, he's very helpful.

Sitting on his new bed, furthest from the door and window, with a gash, looted locker and clasping a handful of summons for a myriad of absconding crimes ranging from stealing a milk bottle to travelling without paying one's fare, the absconder must feel the label stick. Especially as, down below, house motherly teas and favoured expeditions grace the days of the new converts and the orthodox boys who stayed behind.

For the persistent absconder, so labelled, a number of alternatives exist, of which continuing to abscond seems from the evidence to be by far the most likely. He could, of course, adopt sackcloth and ashes and wait for the next crisis in order to return to the fold. But this is unlikely, largely because a cool analysis of the social situation is not a marked characteristic of these boys and the fold anyway is not that desirable. Many stay, some to be whimsically saved by the dynamics of the boy world just described, while others, brimming with resentment, expand their areas of deviance in the school, supplementing renewed criminality outside with a sullen hostility within. The self-fulfilling prophecy comes to fruition. He is defined as irredeemable. There is a public washing of hands and transfer is inevitable.

Evidence for the interactionist perspective

The above account suggests a process by which labels are fixed and illustrates ways in which the labelling and interaction theorist would explain absconding. But is there any actual evidence that the pattern of absconding is accelerated by the interactions so described? Do persistent absconders have a more jaundiced perception of their schools and their life chances than others? Do absconders in those schools that continue to have them back and where, presumably, attitudes towards such deviance are more tolerant, have more optimistic perspectives?

One of the problems with the interactionist perspective presented so far is the difficulty of gathering research material which tests the wealth of hypotheses presented. Indeed, the literature of interactionist sociology is a glaring example of the time lag between cumulative theoretical speculation and hard fact which supports such musings. Nevertheless, we can offer some confirmation of this interactionist process from the evidence collected during our previous researches into boys' approved schools.

When we look at the opinions of boys transferred from schools where both absconding and transfer are high, boys who are sent elsewhere seem more hostile to their schools' regime than are the boys who remain. The gap between the negative perspectives of the absconder and the favourable opinions of the orthodox is very wide in high transfer schools. But this division is much less marked in those institutions which tolerate high absconding or in schools where absconding and transfer are rare.

Hostile responses to the regime are especially marked among boys who answered our questions shortly before the breakdown in their training. In schools with high transfer and high absconding these vulnerable boys lack commitment and are unhappy. However, in tranquil schools, with little absconding or transfer, the response of rare absentees parallels that of the other boys. Even in the tolerant schools which have high absconding and low transfer, the persistent absconder is not noticeably more soured by his residential experience than the boys who stay behind.

It seems, therefore, that some effects of interaction and labelling are confirmed. In a number of schools where absconding is high but transfer is low, absconding does not appear to accompany increasing rejection of the boy or any fall in the boy's commitment. Consequently, persistent absconders remain supportive and when they are released do as well as the other boys. In schools where absconding and transfer are high, however, the pattern is different. Here, persistent absconders become disenchanted and rejected. Because low commitment tends to predict further criminal behaviour, they subsequently get into trouble and account for the statistical association between absconding and failure.

Hartnagel's study of soldiers going absent without leave is perhaps the nearest model of the kind of study that is needed to apply an interactionist perspective to absconders from CHEs.[25] He found a very radical change in soldiers' attitudes to the army after their first unofficial absence. Immediately on return, the soldiers stated that they had gone away because of legitimate family reasons and did not feel that their army careers would be hindered by this breach of discipline. Hartnagel found that punishments and measures designed to prevent further departures led soldiers to become dissatisfied and disillusioned with army life and to solve this depression by indulging in further unauthorised absences.

An ongoing study of absconding by Michel Born is yielding similar material from a Belgian reformatory school.[26] The perspectives of boys on their institutional experience changes after returning from absconding, an alienation which is increased by the use of solitary confinement as a punishment. Interestingly enough, boys scrawled 'Liberté' across many of the questionnaires exploring reasons for their departure. This whiff of the barricades should remind us that freedom is an intellectual concept for the middle class; for the working-class boy who is more autonomous at 15 than privileged boys, physical restriction is much more onerous.

It should now be clear that the interactionist approach derived from sociological theory has many parallels with Clarke and Martin's learning theory. Both are concerned with absconding itself rather than the characteristics of absconders. Both emphasise the institutional influences on absconding and both theories see running away as a response to external stress. The interactionist perspectives have moved sociologists away from their preoccupations with the wider societal constraints on deviance, such as class and delinquent sub-culture, to the more seminal questions of who is defined as deviant, how and why. In the same way, psychological preoccupation with trait or state measurement has waned.

Clarke and Martin see absconding as problem-solving and the reinforcement coming from success in reducing anxiety. In their later work, they have explored the ways in which institutional controls modify this propensity. Interactionists, on the other hand, see absconding as a problem created by the very processes of social control. The practical implications of each theory, therefore, differ. While Clarke and Martin's theories lead towards behaviour modification through manipulation of the environment, in a sense, it is still the individual who is expected to change. The interactionists, on the other hand, look not for change in the individual but much more the whole institutionalised process of ascribing deviance. It cannot be the function of a chapter such as this to explore these similarities and differences further, but it is remarkable that research workers beginning with such contrasting premises should move to so similar an explanation.

However, while there is no need for the reader to embrace wholeheartedly the interactionist approach, we believe that it should be sufficiently cogent as an argument to cause some radical thinking in residential homes and assessment centres as to the way in which absconders are labelled.

Conclusions

We have noted that the failure to discover any significant characteristics which distinguish the persistent absconder from others led researchers to look more at the institutional context. While Clarke has suggested learned behaviour might explain the persistent nature of absconding and thus graced it with the term 'habitual', we would suggest that other explanations are equally tenable.

We have demonstrated that the marked differences in the absconding rates of different schools are related not only to the delinquency of the clients but also to aspects of institutional structure such as the nature of the control process and aspects of staff–child relationships.

We have noted that a number of schools in our earlier study have high absconding yet low transfer of boys to other institutions and a high success rate with those they release. This and other evidence suggests that criminality and absconding are not causally linked. They correlate simply because high absconding, high transfer and high failure rates are the characteristics of ineffective schools. The fact that the large majority of schools in the old approved school system were ineffective means that, when a large survey is undertaken, absconding and failure correlate.

Learning theory and the resultant ideas on behaviour modification have been challenged by our suggestion that absconding lends itself equally to an interpretation through interactionist perspectives. Absconding, far from solving a frustration, creates secondary deviance. The absconder's major problem becomes people's reaction to his running away. We have offered some evidence to suggest that absconders are influenced by institutional reactions to their behaviour but we accept that much more research is needed before any of these perspectives are substantiated.

In passing we would also comment that class differences are very significant in absconding. In the case of the adolescent absconder we may be reacting to behaviour that is of long standing and has, within the boy's social group, widespread cultural approval. There are very marked differences in the sorts of avoidance behaviour adopted by different social groups and research into ordinary boarding schools, outward-bound activities, coping with debt and even going to the dentist, show consistent differences in the strategies adopted by various social groups.

However this material should diminish the almost universal concern that absconding is in itself a major problem. We would suggest that it is much more the reaction to running away than the running itself that *creates* the problem.

If institutions have a high absconding rate then it suggests that something is wrong in the institution, for children rarely run when they are happy. We have elsewhere suggested the features of effective institutions and noted that low absconding was one of their enduring characteristics. But some institutions from which children run can moderate this behaviour and allow absconders to share in their overall successes by *having them back*.

Staff in CHEs rightly emphasise the sensitive and difficult clientele that they care for but often seem to resent the disruptive behaviour manifested by such children. Children will run away and be aggressive because such testing out behaviour is often the most familiar device for exploring how much people care about them.

The institution must also scrutinise the ways in which it admits children and much more clear information should be given on arrival of what is and is not expected. All areas, such as the child's contact with home, with friends and access to the outside world, should be explained. The facilities of the institution should be explored and the way a boy gains access to them clarified. The recent moves towards more local intakes in CHEs are important here. Such changes may not immediately moderate absconding but they do reduce the risks to children while they are on the run. Not only should the way the place works be explained to the child but, also, why he is there and what the institution is trying to do for him.

If running does start, it would be wise to treat the behaviour as a serious issue and the return must be carefully negotiated. The reception must be in the hands of someone the child knows, must exclude the police and the institution must be welcoming and concerned. It would be wise to accept reversed charge telephone calls, to keep the kettle on and look pleased when the absconder comes back. The child must be guarded against a tirade of reproaches and staff should make sure that in informal areas the child has not lost *too* much. If he is to be censured, it must be seen by him to be legitimate, expressing concern rather than venting institutional wrath at organisational disruption. The aim must be to avoid the whole syndrome of secondary deviance – when the absconding label becomes more of a problem than the initial anxiety that prompted the running.

In this study of absconding we may seem to have wandered far from our major concern with secure provision. However, we have commented that the absconding issue exerted considerable pressure on the Home Office to create secure units. So our lengthy preoccupation seems justified. Admittedly, our earlier chapters and the work of Cawson and Martel have indicated that the actual decisions on security were influenced by issues of control rather than by any belief that absconding or aggressive behaviour would be permanently influenced by a period of confinement.[27] In fact, the work of Clarke and Martin appeared several years after all the secure units were in being. Nevertheless, most candidates for secure provision are still persistent absconders and research to date has been used to support its extension.

The increasing treatment orientation of the units has led protagonists to justify them on the grounds that they can make a significant contribution to the absconding problem. Supporters argue that if absconding habits are learned, then reinforcement can be prevented and, possibly, the habit broken by a spell in security. It is maintained that if running away leads to crime, then benefits accrue from preventing a boy from absconding and security ensures that he is available for treatment. But the evidence just presented should make us very cautious in accepting any of these propositions.

Neither should much confidence be placed in any treatment which the units provide. As we shall see in a subsequent chapter, treatment in secure conditions mirrors familiar CHE approaches, the efficacy of which, even with non-absconders, has hardly been reassuring. Even if we accept the hypothesis that absconding is learned behaviour, the age and absconding histories of candidates for security would suggest that persistent absentees are highly professional absconders long before they get near a closed unit. Most absconders do not begin to cause institutional alarm until late in their residential careers and by this time almost all are well beyond the age at which secure units will admit them. As in the old days, such boys go on to Borstal.

On the other hand, if we put aside the spectacles of learning theory and don those of the interactionist, then it should be very clear how secure provision can add yet another hostile label and provide a fresh arena in which the absconder's deviance is displayed. Unfortunately, the more we allow security to be seen as an answer to absconding, the more we obscure what all research demonstrates: *that it is the nature of a child's residential experience that makes him an absconder, that boys run because of the places they are in.*

Notes

[1] Details of absconding from approved schools can be found in R. V. G. Clarke and D. N. Martin, *Absconding from Approved Schools*, London, HMSO, 1971. Other personal communications with heads of residential establishments confirm this increase.

[2] A fuller account of the unit's research into absconding can be found in: S. Millham, R. Bullock, K. Hosie and R. Frankenberg, 'Absconding', *Community Home Schools Gazette*, vol. LXXI, 1977, nos. 7 and 8, pp. 280-91 and 325-37.

[3] R. V. G. Clarke and D. N. Martin, *Absconding from Approved Schools*, op. cit.

[4] See R. V. G. Clarke and D. N. Martin, 'A study of absconding and its implications for the residential treatment of delinquents' in J. Tizard, I. Sinclair and R. V. G. Clarke (eds), *Varieties of Residential Experience*, London, Routledge and Kegan Paul, 1975, pp. 249-74. Quote is from p. 254.

[5] R. V. G. Clarke and D. N. Martin, 'A study of absconding and its implications for the residential treatment of delinquents', op. cit.

[6] M. A. Porteous and C. S. McLoughlin, 'A comparison of absconders and non-absconders from an assessment centre', *Community Schools Gazette*, vol. LXVII, 1974, pp. 681-99. Extract quoted is from p. 690.

[7] H. Brierley and H. D. Jones, *The Absconding Problem*, unpublished report presented to the Home Office; M. G. S. Gunaskara, 'The problem of absconding in boys' approved schools in England and Wales', *British Journal of Criminology*, vol. IV, 1963, pp. 145-52; L. T. Wilkins, *Prediction Methods in Relation to Approved School Training*, unpublished Home Office Research

Unit report and S. G. Lubeck and L. T. Empey, 'Mediatory versus total institution: the case of the run away', *Social Problems*, vol. XVI, 1968, pp. 242-60.

[8] R. V. G. Clarke and D. N. Martin, 'A study of absconding and its implications for the residential treatment of delinquents', op. cit., pp. 259-61.

[9] See, for example, S. Millham, R. Bullock and P. Cherrett, *After Grace – Teeth. A Comparative Study of the Residential Experience of Boys in Approved Schools*. London, Human Context Books, Chaucer Publishing Company, 1975; A. E. Bottoms and F. H. McClintock, *Criminals Coming of Age*, London, Heinemann, 1973 and I. Sinclair, *Hostels for Probationers*, London, HMSO, 1971.

[10] R. V. G. Clarke and D. N. Martin, 'A study of absconding and its implications for the residential treatment of delinquents', op. cit., p. 255.

[11] See, for example, the figures given in R. V. G. Clarke and D. N. Martin, *Absconding from Approved Schools*, op. cit., p. 26 and M. A. Porteous and C. S. McLoughlin, 'A comparison of absconders and non-absconders from an assessment centre', op. cit., p. 698.

[12] K. Laverack, 'Absconding from Kneesworth House', *Community Schools Gazette*, vol. LXVIII, 1974, pp. 5-24.

[13] I. A. C. Sinclair and R. V. G. Clarke, 'Acting-out behaviour and its significance for the residential treatment of delinquents', *Journal of Child Psychology and Psychiatry*, vol. XIV, 1973, pp. 283-91.

[14] I. Sinclair, *Hostels for Probationers*, op. cit.

[15] For a discussion of these concepts, see R. Lambert, S. Millham and R. Bullock, *A Manual to the Sociology of the School*, London, Weidenfeld & Nicolson, 1970. For details of the actual measures used, see S. Millham, R. Bullock and P. Cherrett, *A Comparative Study of 18 Boys' Approved Schools which explores their Stylistic Variety and the Commitment of Boys and Staff*, report presented to the Department of Health and Social Security, 1972.

[16] I. A. C. Sinclair and R. V. G. Clarke, 'Acting-out behaviour and its significance for the residential treatment of delinquents', op. cit., p. 288.

[17] See S. Millham, et al., *After Grace – Teeth*, op. cit., chaps. 9 and 13.

[18] M.-T. Mazerol, 'Les Incidents Signifiants en internats professionnels d'education surveillée (IPES), 1 – Les Fugues en IPES', *Annales de Vaucresson*, no. 6, 1968, pp. 3-73.

[19] See, for example, H. S. Becker (ed.), *The Other Side*, New York, Free Press, 1964 and *Outsiders: Studies in the Sociology of Deviance*, New York, Free Press, 1963; D. Matza, *Becoming Deviant*, Englewood Cliffs, NJ, Prentice Hall, 1969 and E. M. Lemert, *Human Deviance: Social Problems and Social Control*, Englewood Cliffs, NJ, Prentice Hall, 1967.

[20] S. Millham et al., *After Grace – Teeth*, op. cit.

[21] See S. Millham, R. Bullock and P. Cherrett, 'Socialisation in residential communities', in J. Tizard et al. (eds), *Varieties of Residential Experience*, op. cit., pp. 225-48.

[22] For similar findings see N.S. Tutt, 'Towards reducing absconding', *Community Schools Gazette*, vol. LXV, 1971, pp. 65-8.

[23] See R. Lambert, S. Millham and R. Bullock, *The Chance of a Lifetime?*, London, Weidenfeld & Nicolson, 1975.

[24] For a discussion of informal systems in organisations, see R. Lambert, S. Millham and R. Bullock, 'The informal social system', in R. K. Brown (ed.), *Knowledge, Education and Cultural Change*, London, Tavistock, 1973, pp. 297-316.

[25] T. F. Hartnagel, 'Absent without leave: a study of the military offender', *Journal of Political and Military Sociology*, vol. II, 1974, pp. 205-20.

[26] M. Born, *La Fugue en Institution*, monograph, Department of Psychology, University of Liège.

[27] M. Martell and P. Cawson, *The Development of Closed Units in the Child Care Service*, monograph, Department of Health and Social Security, Research Division, 1975.

8 Children convicted of grave offences

The majority of clients for the secure units are persistent absconders, although aggressive behaviour, particularly in residential situations, can increase the child's chances of admission to security. We have just explored the ways in which the institutions can help to create the behaviour that they ostensibly find so distressing. But, one group of referrals to the secure units is still viewed as offering great risks if left in open society. These children are grave offenders and are not casualties of care. For some of them, the secure unit is their first residential experience.

Children who commit grave crimes and who receive sentences of detention are held under Section 53 of the Children and Young Persons' Act of 1933. This legislation has been little changed since its original enactment. Among these children will be murderers and those convicted of manslaughter or serious assaults and arson. A number will have committed spectacular driving away offences or robbery with violence. This small group of children form an interesting case. Although, after 1948, children under the age of 15 could not be given prison sentences, what exactly was done with the serious juvenile offender is very much an open question. Presumably, a number of the youngest were sheltered in the ordinary approved schools system. This was certainly the case with a boy under 15 who was party to the Standon Farm murder and with a number of other juveniles sentenced in the 1950s. However, what happened to young offenders considered to be dangerous during the period between 1948 and 1968, when they first appear in the secure units, is less clear. Very few children and young persons were sentenced under this Section during this period and, initially, they were detained in young offenders' establishments either at Aylesbury or Liverpool. There were very few girls detained under Section 53 and, apart from one who went to Redbank at the age of 11, presumably they would have gone to Borstals and then on to an adult prison.

Section 53 cases are important because a few sad children demonstrate that the care or custody conflict is irreconcilable and that finally, faced with an extreme crime, retributive and custodial perspectives dominate. We have seen that the efforts at reform have been directed towards sparing young people from the prison experience or the baffling and, possibly stigmatising experience of appearing before an adult court. While much has been done, Section 53 cases demonstrate that there is a point beyond which legal compassion will not go. A child who commits a serious offence can still receive a long sentence of detention, experience an adult trial and find his name released to the press.

Indeed, Section 53 cases have survived as a special category of child, largely untouched by increasingly benevolent child-care legislation. The sentences achieve prominence only when the offence is of sufficient notoriety to prevent any rational discussion of the long-term consequences of imprisonment for juveniles. In some ways we have not come very far for it was uncommon for young people to be long in prison or to be executed for serious offences even in the later part of the eighteenth century or in the early nineteenth. The five boys executed in 1797 after mutiny on HMS *Hermione* owe their fates to the Navy Acts rather than to common law. John Bell, hanged in 1831, at the age of 14 years, 10 months, was the last boy under 16 to be executed in Britain. He had murdered another juvenile. But all these cases engendered considerable public concern and ultimate penalties for children fell into disuse. It was not until the 1908 Children's Act that capital punishment was actually abolished for juveniles under the age of 16 and the age was raised to 18 as late as 1933.

In the Children and Young Persons' Act of 1933, Subsection 1 concerns itself with children under the age of 18 convicted of murder who must be detained during Her Majesty's Pleasure while Subsection 2 covers a much wider variety of offences committed by children and young persons between 10 and 16 years of age. These are crimes which, for an adult, may involve sentences of 14 years, 20 years or life imprisonment.

The rise in convictions for grave offences

Naturally, the sentencing of children and young persons under Section 53 is still quite unusual but the use of this legislation has shown a disturbing increase since 1969. It may be that the judiciary have found a way of making their decisions stick, feeling that the care order is insufficiently rigorous for those juveniles that seem incorrigible and a danger to the public. This suggestion is supported by the fact that the increase has been confined to Subsection 2 of Section 53 where there is greater scope for judicial discretion. It is also probable that the judiciary are aware of the rapid decrease in the length of time that boys spend in Borstal which has resulted from the increasing pressure of numbers. In addition, the general increase in juvenile crime may be reflected in this rise in the number of children convicted of grave offences. Whatever the reasons, Section 53 cases are clearly increasing (see Table 8.1). On average seven young people between 14 and 16 years were sentenced annually under Section 53 until 1971, but since then, 34 young people a year have been sentenced in this way.[1]

Table 8.1

Number of young persons aged 14–16 years convicted under both Subsections of Section 53 received under sentence by Home Office establishments

1966	1967	1968	1969	1970	1971	1972	1973	1974	1975
6	4	7	7	11	7	21	46	25	42

It is also noteworthy that this increase in the number of young persons sentenced under Section 53 means that there is a rapid accumulation of young people between 14 and 16 years held in prison establishments on long sentences, although very few of these are likely to be 14-year-olds. Much current concern, quite under-standably, has been directed at the increasing number of young persons remanded to prison on unruly certificates to await trial, particularly as the majority of these do not, on conviction, receive a custodial sentence. Whatever the deficiencies of such a system, most juveniles on remand do not stay in prison department establish-ments very long. Unfortunately, their plight has quite overshadowed the much more serious problems of those young people sentenced to long terms of detention who actually serve a considerable part of their sentences.

It is difficult to estimate the number of young people contained at the moment but, between the beginning of 1972 and the end of 1975, 134 boys and girls between the ages of 14 and 16 were convicted under both Subsections of Section 53. Of these young people, 23 were accepted by the DHSS for shelter in child-care establishments.[2] The remainder, more than 100 young persons, must have spent some considerable period in prison during this time and the length of their deten-tion suggests that, at any given moment, an increasingly large number are in prison serving long sentences. Of the 134 young people sentenced between 1972 and 1975 under this legislation, 20 had indeterminate sentences (Her Majesty's Pleasure in lieu of life imprisonment), 72 were to be detained for up to four years, 39 were to be detained from four to 10 years and three were to be detained for over 10 years. We have no precise indication of the length of time these young people stay in prison because the Home Secretary's discretion can override any sentencing. But it seems likely that, with some exceptions, the same procedures apply to juveniles as to adult prisoners, that is, one-third of the period of detention must be com-pleted before parole is considered. If this is the case and the use of Section 53 continues to increase, the total number of young persons in prison detained for long periods of time must rise.

The statistical tables presented on the numbers of young people sentenced under Section 53 may underestimate the true figure. This is because the annual reports on the work of the prison department do not give any indication of the number of 17-year-olds who receive sentences under Section 53. It may be because at this age a wider number of disposals exist for people convicted of serious offences, that the courts do not use Section 53 legislation.

It is also clear that Section 53 cases are putting considerable pressure on the limited number of secure places in the CHE system. It is the policy of the Home Office to offer to the DHSS those Section 53 cases that they feel would benefit from shelter in child-care establishments. Presumably tender age is the guiding factor influencing both Home Office applications and DHSS acceptance of candi-dates. But is is clear from the small numbers of Section 53 cases, an average of five a year, taken into CHEs that the majority of serious offenders stay in Home Office establishments.[2]

The policy adopted by the DHSS towards these young people convicted of serious crimes is also a matter of interest. As the number of juveniles convicted of serious crimes has increased, so more young people have been offered to the DHSS and the number of Section 53 cases sheltered in child-care establishments has grown.

For example, at the end of 1970 there were four Section 53 cases in CHEs but, at the end of 1975, there were 16 such young people in local authority institutions. Naturally, the accumulation of young offenders with long sentences in institutions where the stay of children is relatively short causes problems, a point that we shall explore later. Maintaining some balance between various categories of troublesome children is one of the skills of institutional management and care has to be taken that the concentrations of certain types of child do not change the nature of the prevailing regime. Thus, while more young persons are being presented by the Home Office, they are being increasingly rejected by the DHSS for these and other quite legitimate reasons. For example, seven could not be found a place in child-care establishments in 1975.[2]

It was not the task of this research to look at security for children in Northern Ireland. Much of the present concern over the serious offences committed by children in Ulster is, we hope, transitory. However, in comparison with England and Wales, in Northern Ireland the number of young persons convicted under Section 73 of the Children and Young Persons' Act (NI) 1968 has shown an alarming rise in recent years (in Northern Ireland, Section 73 corresponds to Section 53 of the Children and Young Persons' Act 1933).[3] The number of young people serving long prison sentences is particularly disturbing as the figures in Table 8.2 indicate. The rate of Section 73 sentences between 1972 and 1975 for young persons under 16, expressed as a proportion of the total juvenile population, is approximately 13 times the rate for England and Wales. For Subsection 1 of the Act, the rate is 22 times this rate.

In the same way, while Scotland may be proud of its juvenile panel system for young offenders, there seems to less reason to rejoice when the number of young people convicted of serious offences is studied. Grounds for comparison between English and Scottish figures are difficult. While Subsection 1 of Section 206 of the Criminal Procedure (Scotland) Act corresponds with Subsection 1 of England's Section 53, Subsection 2 of the Scottish act is less comparable as, characteristically, the Scots equate the seriousness of the crime with the values of the property involved.

Conviction under Section 206 (Subsections 1 and 2) of the Criminal Procedure (Scotland) Act 1975 legislation is approximately 11 times the rate for England and Wales. For example, a total of 50 young people were detained under this legislation in 1975, of whom 41 were 16 years of age or under on conviction and an average daily population of between 72 and 74 young persons were contained in Scottish prison establishments between 1973 and 1975.[4] Table 8.3 gives details.

It is also important to note that from 1973 to 1975, 24 young people in Scotland were held under Section 206(1), which is usually applied in cases of murder, compared with nine held under its equivalent in England and Wales.

Table 8.2

Young persons detained under the provisions of the Children and Young Persons' Act (Northern Ireland) 1968

Year	Number committed: Age on committal under sentence					Total		Initial placement			Released on licence		In custody at end of year	
	14	15	16	17	18	73(1)	73(2)	Prison	Borstal[1]	Training School	73(1)	73(2)	73(1)	73(2)
1971	-	-	-	-	-	-	-	-	-	-	-	-	-	1
1972	-	1	1	1	-	1	2	2	1	-	-	1	1	2
1973	-	-	5	-	-	-	5	3	2	-	-	-	1	7
1974	-	3	19	3	1	3	23	19	5	2	-	-	4	30
1975	-	6	23	4	10	16	27	29	7	7	-	2	20	55
1976[2]	1	1	4	5	7	11	7	17[3]	-	1[3]	-	36	31	26

Notes: [1] In 1975, 13 Section 73(2) cases who were initially placed in a Borstal institution were transferred to a special unit for young offenders at HM Prison, Maze.

[2] Up until 29 November.

[3] Of the 17 in prison, 2 are under assessment as is the person placed in the training school.

Table 8.3

Prison receptions of young persons detained under Section 206
(Subsections 1 and 2) of the Criminal Procedure (Scotland) Act 1975

	1973		1974		1975	
	M.	F.	M.	F.	M.	F.
206 (1)	10	–	5	–	8	1
206 (2)	27	1	18	–	17	–
Total	37	1	23	–	25	–

Characteristics of young persons convicted of grave offences

This research cannot offer much insight into the characteristics of young people who commit grave offences. We do not know in what ways the prosecutions of these young people differ according to social class, intelligence or age; neither do we know how many young persons are dealt with in other ways, such as by care orders, admission to special schools or adolescent units in mental hospitals. We can only make some comment on those few young people (about one-fifth of all Section 53 cases) who are offered by the Home Office for shelter in child-care establishments and for whom the DHSS accepts responsibility. Clearly, we are concerned with an atypical sample of cases and how they have been selected, apart from tender age, is quite unknown to us.

We have looked at the background and careers of 14 Section 53 cases admitted to the secure units since 1965. Two other young people who have committed violent crimes and were admitted on care orders have also been considered but those three boys under 15 recently given long sentences for burglary or robbery with violence have been excluded. It is unlikely that these three young people would have been given sentences under Section 53 (Subsection 2) before the 1969 Children and Young Persons' Act came into force.

In spite of the concern that some of these juvenile offenders arouse, very little research seems to have been undertaken into them. Indeed, in the planning of the original secure units, we have already noted that these cases were not mentioned and one suspects that their existence was quite forgotten. Even in the USA where the number of juveniles convicted of homicide in a single year (just under 2,000 in 1973) provide a sufficient number of cases for elaborate research studies, little material has been produced.[5] In a situation where very little is known apart from a few limited studies and clearly more inquiry is needed, these brief comments may excite other research workers to explore further. Even if the comments are very superficial on the sorts of children that commit serious offences, at least they describe the grave offenders who find their way into special units.

Almost all the grave offenders whom we have studied display the characteristics of other grossly deprived children. They have usually had very disrupted family lives and have often been reared in poverty with frequent changes of home, parent figures and support agencies. Their mothers were particularly problematic, being either over-dominant or preoccupied with many children from an early age or suffering from physical or mental illness which prevented them from providing consistent care for their children. As with the background of many other boys and girls in CHEs, fathers are more frequently absent from home than mothers and other members of the family show signs of disturbance, distress or delinquency. Frequently the households have been violent and Section 53 cases have often witnessed fights between parents and older siblings from an early age. The young people themselves have displayed since infancy symptoms of serious disturbance, such as wandering from home, but tend to have more cooperative personalities than other children found guilty of less serious offences.

However, there are many difficulties in trying to generalise from case histories. As so much of the material available in children's files has been culled after a serious or horrific crime, little that is complimentary to them or 'irrelevant' is allowed to appear. The rather naïve, psychological approach found in assessment files means that we know very little of these young people's educational performance, peer group and broader social history. Because faulty parental relationships are considered the key to every large or small deviation in the child, material is inevitably presented from this perspective. But, in spite of the inadequacies of such background material, boys seem to be much more influenced by peers, by status and instrumental considerations than girls. Boys' violence is often for gain, for peer group esteem or sexual gratification and, frequently, they have responded in a disproportionately violent way to minor frustrations, fears or challenges.

While much of boys' violent behaviour is unpremeditated, spontaneous and situational, offences of arson are much more calculated. Arson is frequently threatened beforehand and directed against something hated such as the day school, the children's home or the youth club. Only occasionally is it used to disguise a burglary or other offences. Girls, on the other hand, seem to commit violent crimes more as a part of persistent attention-seeking behaviour. They frequently invite detection in a way that is less usual in boys. Far fewer girls commit grave offences than boys and their crimes are more situational, such as the killing of irritating infants whom they have been left to supervise.

While it is clear that children who commit grave crimes appreciate that their behaviour is proscribed, the significance and consequences of committing such serious offences seem far less appreciated. These grave offenders when charged frequently comment, 'I won't do it again, I promise', and, at the outset, even the implications of their life in secure institutions are less than understood. 'If my life in prison is more tough than it is at Redbank then I shan't stay, I will run away', volunteered one juvenile murderer and another commented after his first few days at Redhill, 'When I get fed up with this place, I'll write to my dad and ask him to take me out of here'.

We are not qualified to comment on the assessments provided by psychiatrists in the cases of juveniles convicted of serious crimes, but we have seen during our studies that the influence of their diagnoses can be considerable. Psychiatrists do seem to pay attention to what the young people actually say and seem particularly resistant to the whimsically gathered material that makes up a typical social case history. Almost all grave offenders are assessed by psychiatrists as having a serious personality disorder and there is usually a long history of disturbed behaviour preceding the spectacular offence to confirm this, even though previous violence is rarely in evidence. The degree of the child's disorder, however, is not usually sufficient to merit a hospital order even though three boys among the Section 53 cases we studied were subsequently transferred from secure units to closed mental hospitals on a psychiatrist's recommendation. A number of other young people in secure units have been similarly moved because of a deterioration in their behaviour.

From all the evidence, it seems that children convicted of grave offences do not differ in any marked way from the many thousands of other very deprived children sheltered by the local authorities. As is the case with other candidates for security, the needs of Section 53 cases have not been diagnosed or met early enough to prevent the final crisis. Within the institution, grave offenders do not present themselves as particularly violent or as a dangerous threat to the public. Usually they are sad and withdrawn children held in a limbo of uncertainty. 'I just live each day as it comes and hope something good, at last, will turn up', said a young boy at Redbank. Naturally, this unhappy situation does not escape the notice of staff. A special unit principal commented, 'I have lived with this lad for nearly four years. If it wasn't for his file and 'phone calls from Whitehall I couldn't believe him to be a killer. I often think they have made some dreadful mistake'.

We shall shortly explore the impact that these serious young offenders have on the daily life of secure units but it is worth discussing here the uses made of the assessment material on these children. When one lives in a special unit, one rapidly sees that assessment reports, case conferences and the lengthy negotiations with the external, prestigious figures at Queen Anne's Gate seem to have little to do with the treatment of grave offenders. In fact, the function of all this activity is clearly to prevent the process of 'normalisation' of deviance which, with these children, is a constant, almost irresistible, temptation to staff. It is easy for young offenders to be exonerated from their crime in a closed unit which offers a treatment approach which stresses deep relationships and a universal feeling of compassion for these tragic young people. The ritual of the case conference serves to keep the 'bad image' of the offender ever before staff, preserving social distance, sterilising the relationships and keeping observations clinical and objective. This process staves off staff guilt and deviance, both of which could not only be considerable in such situations, but would also be highly disruptive.

Effects of serious offenders on institutional life

The Section 53 cases raise important questions about the wider functions of the secure units and the constant presence of serious offenders influences the daily life of the establishments in a number of ways. Without pre-empting a subsequent chapter on the style of life within the closed units, it is useful to note the specific problems posed by Section 53 cases.

It is clear that the sentences which grave offenders receive are extremely difficult to reconcile with the treatment philosophies that secure units have developed and the presence of such a group makes it difficult for staff to establish a viable regime. Some of the sentences boys receive are long and have to be completed either in Borstals or prisons. Staff in the units often find it difficult to understand why security has been assumed to be necessary for the majority of Section 53 cases. As the Home Secretary is allowed the widest discretion in his placements, staff frequently suggest that many of these young people could be successfully sheltered in open child-care establishments. After all, hardly any of these grave offenders have been difficult in previous residential settings and many have never been in residential care before so there is much to support this opinion, especially as, before 1965, young Section 53 cases would have been placed in open approved schools.

There are also more serious objections to the treatment of grave offenders in closed conditions. Even if assessment centres were able to devise a suitable approach to the problems of this group, it is very doubtful whether, in practice, the special units could implement these recommendations. For example, Redbank, which has sheltered more Section 53 cases than any other unit, functioned for a long period without the support of a visiting psychiatrist and, during interviews, staff in the secure units could offer few suggestions on any treatment suitable for these children. St Charles youth treatment centre perhaps offers more hope of developing long-term treatment models but even there staff are very cautious in their estimates of success.

Our interviews with psychiatrists working with adolescents would also suggest that, although they disagree on many issues, they unanimously stress that long stays in security are detrimental to an adolescent's emotional development. It seems that decisions on the placement and the need for security of Section 53 cases are taken mainly on the grounds of age, vacancy and seriousness of offence, but the psychiatrist Derek Miller would argue that more sophisticated criteria do exist which enable us to distinguish the dangerous child from those unlikely to offend again and so minimise the damage of lengthy incarceration.[6] He notes that professionals, even fellow psychiatrists, are not particularly successful at predicting the future behaviour of violent offenders.

Miller suggests that our response to violence, which is usually one of retaliation or rejection, actually reinforces the personality maladjustment in young people because, during adolescence, personality development is most influenced by social pathology. Much of our defeat in treating young violent offenders springs from our failure to distinguish between different kinds of aggression. We tend to view the majority of violent offenders as possessing the 'cold/killer' characteristics of the rare, predatory aggressor rather than those of the affective aggressor whose attacks are situationally determined. We fail, Miller maintains, because punitive responses to violent behaviour actually reinforce the likelihood of further aggression by treating the inmate in a less than human way. We enhance the possibility of future aggression because, in turn, our action legitimises the violent offender's dehumanisation of others.

We would hasten to add that we do not view the regimes in the secure units which we studied as 'dehumanising' and Miller probably had in mind the large penal establishments for young offenders found in some American states. Nevertheless, his paper does suggest that for most violent offenders, security offers nothing positive and is likely to be harmful. If the majority of Section 53 cases are low-risk, affective aggressors whose offences are largely situational and, from their psychiatric reports, this seems likely, then we must consider the view that it is not the security that protects society but the high staff ratios, the warm relationships within the units and the clever manipulation by staff of social interactions. If Miller is correct, one is concerned less for those Section 53 cases in the special units and youth treatment centres and more for those grave offenders who find their way to Aylesbury prison or to Rampton or Broadmoor, institutions where in spite of valiant attempts of staff there is far less scope for concealing the retributive nature of intervention.

Section 53 cases not only raise treatment problems within the units; they also affect radically the day-to-day running of a secure establishment. Security has to have high priority within the units as the outside world views these young offenders as highly dangerous and there is high-level official scrutiny of these children's progress. Thus, boys' crimes and their consequences are a constant talking point among both staff and children. 'Because of what you've done, you're different and you know it. We all stick together because you don't know when you'll get out', said one Section 53 boy. Staff label in other ways, particularly in their anxiety to stress the good points of this group.

> In some ways the unit has brought out the best in him, he gives the other boys a lot of support. He is probably going on to prison and he knows it, so do the rest of the boys. What he says carries weight.
>
> Teacher, secure unit

This labelling is reinforced by the different approach inevitably accorded to these young people within the unit. The long stay of Section 53 cases and the desire of staff to ease the pains of imprisonment mean that close and reciprocated relationships develop. But restrictions have to apply to these serious offenders in a way that thrusts staff into policeman roles and puts great strains on the relationships that are created.

The serious offenders are also labelled in other ways. Much to our surprise, visits outside security and home leaves were very much part of most boys' lives in the units. Indeed, one child, wise in the ways of institutions, confided to us that he preferred secure unit life to that in open CHEs, 'because you go out more'. We shall explore these oddities in more detail later but it should be swiftly apparent that home leaves are less easily accorded to Section 53 cases and that, initially for this group, the sampling of liberty must be very restricted. These serious offenders cannot bargain for freedom nor can they be rewarded for conciliatory behaviour in the same way as other special unit pupils. Indeed, in one unit, boys made a contract with staff and sealed it with a formal handshake in which they pledged cooperative conduct in exchange for guarantees. Within a week, it was possible for boys to gain five points for good conduct. Forty points qualified them for a visit outside the unit, 60 points for a home leave and 100 points gained release. Naturally this tariff was subject to a good deal of manipulation by staff and an external observer might wonder how such specific encouragements for boys to 'work the system' could be reconciled with treatment pretensions. Nevertheless, it was a game in which the Section 53 children could not participate, for even when brief liberty is given to a child convicted of a grave offence, it seems to be fraught with considerable anxiety. One new member of staff was advised, 'If you have two kids outside and someone runs, whatever you do, grab the 53'. Similarly, their special status is not lost on the children themselves. A juvenile murderer, taken to a seaside resort for the afternoon, almost collided with the Prime Minister hurrying to his Party Conference. The child turned to the principal of the unit, who was providing the escort, and commented, 'He'd've had a fit if he knew I was here – and you wouldn't have lasted long either.'

The presence of Section 53 cases whose crimes and sentences are well known keeps all in the units mindful of its prime function, that of security. It means that in special units, the oscillation between care and custody, which we and others have highlighted in the ordinary CHEs, is greatly increased. A structure and routine has to be developed in which constant scrutiny of the children is maintained and autonomy largely denied them. Bureaucracy grows to organise every moment of the day and busy staff strive to create employment for themselves and the children. Lists are made and changed, reports written and read, case conferences sat through but as one housemaster said, 'Sometimes at the end of the day it hits you, you are a screw – a nice, fatherly, kindly screw.' Another commented, 'You have to keep busy because otherwise you think a lot about the children, particularly those with a long time to go and that doesn't help.'

The differences between Section 53 cases and other boys are demonstrated in many other ways. For example, parents have to see their children by visiting the unit. This causes the boys considerable anxiety, as one commented, 'They come for the whole day 'cos it's a long way and you just have nothing to talk about after the first hour. Nothing seems to have happened to you.' Letters from parents to staff in the secure units also suggest that they find visits something of a strain. 'We are very worried about him. He seems a stranger to us when we come. It's like talking to some neighbour's boy.' Naturally, the perspectives of staff on parents are not always wildly enthusiastic and there seems very little real contact between the units and the boys' families in spite of the social worker attached to the unit staff. This situation parallels the distancing and boundary maintenance which all residential staff seem to need in order to justify their 'usurper' role with the children.

Further difficulties arise from the tendency for Section 53 cases to be older than other boys in the units and their stay is also much longer. Consequently, they are far less attention-seeking and hyperactive than the younger children. This age gap, which is frequently a problem in any group of adolescents, creates considerable difficulties. The Section 53 cases find the endless, wearying taunts and provocation of younger boys exasperating:

> You just want to be by yourself to get away from them but you don't ask to go up to your room, because you are locked in and someone has to keep an eye on you. Besides, it is put down in the book and might be used against you when staff have their talks.
>
> Section 53 case, aged 14

Sometimes the strain on boys can be considerable:

> You just want to slam some of these little kids, they drive you mad. But you daren't because you have so much to lose – my chance of getting parole.

Unfortunately, parole needs more than a good recommendation from the unit, but sometimes the boys do explode:

> I got hold of Smith, he'd asked for it, but two staff jumped me and took me off to my room. I was locked in and lost my privileges, now Smith keeps whispering to me, 'I'm not your second murder'.

The Section 53 cases also challenge the ethos of the security in other ways. While there is a general consensus on the parts of staff and children that most boys in the units 'deserve' or need to be there, this is not the case for many Section 53 cases. In many ways a deprived child's vulnerability to prosecution and the known inequalities in court sentencing are brought home to everyone in the special units in a way that is rare in other child-care establishments. There is a widespread feeling that they neither need nor deserve to be in the units and certainly not in security for long periods. Frequently, boys' long sentences are viewed by staff as unjust and, in contrast to the other children, they have no scope for bargaining over their detention. One persistent absconder summed up the situation by saying, 'I've had a good run for my money before I got in here, about fifty good runs, so it's fair, but Mick will be years in the nick just because a policeman snuffed it – and he didn't even mean to kill him.'

It is no one's fault that Section 53 cases exist. They are a residual group of young offenders bypassed by the increasingly liberal legislation of the last 50 years. They have symbolic functions demonstrating that 'in extremis' no one is exempt from the law. However, who rejoices in this symbolism or who is actually deterred by these children's awesome fate is rather difficult to determine. It is clear from the voluminous correspondence between the units and the central authorities that both the Home Office and the DHSS are particularly sensitive to the plight of these young people but, unfortunately, their freedom of manoeuvre is greatly circumscribed by these boys' legal status. Indeed, much that is benevolent is accorded to Section 53 cases because those with the immediate responsibility for the children in the units choose to accept the risks of a scandal which an abuse of opportunities for liberty would involve.

More important, the presence of these young people in the units greatly increases the pressures on staff who work with them. They cannot agree that their task, in the words of the governor of a remand centre, 'is to prepare these boys for prison, not to give than unrealistic ideas of early release'. Inevitably, relationships are built up over three or four years and gains are encouraged in their boys' educational, emotional, social and spiritual states. Not only are these relationships very difficult to sever but in the days when grave offenders were abruptly removed to prison, staff used to feel that their efforts were being mocked. It is a relief that this pattern of departure seems to have been modified in the past two years, particularly at Redbank which shelters a group of Section 53 cases. Those young people recently allocated to the unit have moved on to open situations. However, any abrupt removal of cherished children is to be regretted; it defeats staff, damages the boys and puts unnecessary stress on everyone.

Conclusions

This chapter has added yet another hot pepper to the curry of secure provision. We have seen that Section 53 cases call into question the functions of the units in both a theoretical and practical way. A small residual category of offenders convicted of grave crimes illustrates the contradictions of both the care and custody arguments. As the number of serious juvenile offenders increases, so the issue of young people under lock and key will become more pressing and the unsuitability of the present placement procedure will become more obvious. Within the units, we have seen that Section 53 children raise other problems, those of management, staff and child morale and legitimacy.

The contradiction, essentially, is that the units were designed for children whose behaviour in other residential situations had been problematic. For such children, security seemed an answer and, at least, it protected them from themselves. In recent years, some secure units have increasingly sheltered a number of Section 53 cases, children whose behaviour, apart from their grave offences, has been less problematic and many of whom have not been previously in residential care. For the original group security can be viewed as a regrettable and transitory means to a therapeutic end, but for Section 53 cases, it is an end in itself. Indeed, if we accept Miller's suggestion and the opinions of other psychiatrists, then security actually works against the rehabilitation of violent adolescent offenders.

We know very little of the different ways in which these serious offenders come before the court or the various methods by which they are disposed. Although for serious crimes the law seems awesome and immutable, our evidence suggests that with children, a serious offence has to be linked with other social or psychological handicaps before a Section 53 order is made. This may be quite fair but, once sentenced, the decisions on a boy's actual placement seem shrouded in unnecessary mystery and, if his arrival in security is mysterious, his departure from detention is even more obscure. Why is security so essential for the majority? On what basis are children offered by the Home Office and accepted or rejected by the DHSS? The gaining of a secure place should not be a matter of luck, chance vacancy or depend on unit tranquillity and policy. It should be a careful decision and part of a care programme. The consequences of a young person going either to an open CHE, a secure unit or to prison are very different in terms of the actual experience, the self-perceptions it engenders and the prospects for eventual release.

Unlike adult offenders enduring a long conviction, Section 53 children have few rights and what rights exist are well beyond their comprehension. Their parents are similarly disadvantaged carrying much of the onus for the crime. While others are mindful of these children's vulnerable situation, it would be a brave social worker that would take on the holy alliance of Home Office and DHSS. Thus, the agencies that imprison the child or young person also have to act *in loco parentis*. In many ways, this is unsatisfactory. If young people have to be locked up for long periods, they should enjoy very clear rights in much the same way as adult prisoners and they should be continuously visited by external and powerful legal representatives. The onus should be on the authorities to justify repeatedly the child's continuing detention. This is, of course, an issue with all juveniles placed in security. It is not that we have any evidence that official decisions are actually being taken contrary to the interests of the child, but it is the very lack of explanation, the absence of external independent scrutiny and the ease with which hostile decisions could be taken that make us uneasy.[7]

Notes

[1] Statistics taken from annual reports on the work of the prison department.

[2] Evidence supplied by DHSS, social work service.

[3] Evidence supplied by the Northern Ireland Office.

[4] Evidence supplied by social work service, Scottish Office.

[5] See P. Wilson, *Children who Kill*, London, Michael Joseph, 1973; M. Gardiner, *The Deadly Innocents*, London, Hogarth Press, 1976; K. S. Walshe-Brennan, 'A socio-psychological investigation of young murderers', *British Journal of Criminology*, vol. XVII, 1977, pp. 58–63; J. M. Sorrells, 'Child murderers', *Crime and Delinquency*, vol. XXIII, 1977, p. 312, J. McCreadie, *Characteristics of Grave Offenders in Special Units*, thesis for advanced course in residential social work, University of Newcastle, 1974 and A. Hyatt-Williams, 'Adolescent Murderers', *Proceedings of the International Conference on Adolescents*, Association for the Psychiatric Study of Adolescents, 1976.

[6] D. Miller, *The Biology and Psychology of Juvenile Violence*, Institute of Psychiatry, Northwestern University, Chicago, 1976.

[7] It is encouraging to note that the 1976 figures released by the DHSS indicate a significant change in policy regarding the placement of Section 53 cases. In 1976, there were 19 referrals to the DHSS from the Home Office for advice concerning placement. This is a considerable increase on the 1975 figure but,

nevertheless, 15 were placed in either a CHE or a youth treatment centre. Two were refused as being inappropriate and two were still under negotiation at the time of our research. It is also encouraging to note that the decision-making processes with regard to the daily oversight of these children is being reviewed and will, we hope, be simplified and made more sensitive.

Part IV
Security in operation

9 The differing styles of secure units

For the majority of people outside the child-care system, secure provision implies one thing – locking up. We saw that even social services departments stress in their applications the need for maximum security and very few of the requests discuss at length the treatment or the educational and social provision which the child needs. But, in spite of this stress on containment, it is surprising to find, from our investigations, such a wide variety of secure settings for children. Some secure units are isolated and self-contained while others form part of a wider, open CHE. Some units are adaptations, frequently done in haste, of existing structures while others have been purpose-built. In the same way, the sizes of the units vary from one or two locked rooms to the provision of 35 places in a separate building. The length of time for which a child may be confined also varies from six hours in some units to as much as two years elsewhere. Something of the heterogeneity and geographical distribution of secure provision can be gathered from Table 9.1.[1]

We can see from the table that, by the end of 1976, in England and Wales there were 198 secure places within the community home system, 61 (31 per cent) of which could be used for girls. This is a slight underestimate of the actual provision for it excludes the secure separation rooms that exist in some CHEs and assessment centres, facilities which vary considerably in the extent to which they are used. More closed accommodation is scheduled to become available by the late 1970s but despite this expansion, there were still 56 vacancies, representing 28 per cent of the places available when the survey was made. The smaller units in particular had many empty rooms.

Two major differences between the units are the variations in size and the length of time which children stay in them. The ways in which provision differs can be laid out as in Figure 9.1.

The secure accommodation available at the end of 1976 is laid out below but, as we shall see, the range of styles included in this provision varies widely.

	Long Stay	Short Stay
Large	Special units Youth treatment centre	Secure remand facilities
Small	Intensive care units	Secure rooms or suites

Fig. 9.1   Types of security

Table 9.1
Secure accommodation available in November 1976

Regional planning area	Name of home	Total number of places in secure unit	Number usable by girls	Number usable by boys	Vacancies as at 5 November 1976
Area 1	Aycliffe	14	4	14	–
	Benton Grange	4	4	–	4
Area 2	Rosehead	2	2	2	2
	Spring Cottage	3	3	3	3
	Springhead Park	3	3	–	–
Area 3	Burford	4	4	–	4
	Redbank	30	–	30	5
	Blackbrook House	5	5	–	–
	Meadowcroft	7	7	–	7
Area 4	Tennal	7	–	7	–
	Rowley Hall	3	3	–	1
	Knowle Hill	4	4	–	4
Area 5	Saxon House	3	–	3	–
Area 6	Boyles Court	6	–	6	4
Area 7	Thornbury House	5	–	5	5
	Crouchfield	12	–	12	5
Area 8	Cumberlow Lodge	6	6	–	–
	Redhill	28	–	28	1
	Stamford House	10	–	10	–
	Duncroft	4	4	–	4
Area 11	Farringdon House	6	6	–	4
	Sedbury Park	6	–	6	–
	Kingswood	20	–	20	1
	The Crescent	6	6	–	2

But of course, in addition to these patterns there are also considerable differences in the *functions* which secure units serve. Each type of security should have a specific role in the wider child-care system. At least five distinct functions can be observed among the present provision. These are: assessing the child's needs and his future placement; remanding a child while awaiting further decisions; separating a child from others or moderating his crisis behaviour; treating a serious handicap or behaviour disorder; and, finally, placing the child in a benign setting that offers protection to the general public. It is vital to appreciate these differences in the functions served by secure provision because the concern about the general lack of places expressed by magistrates, politicians, police and others frequently refers to the need for one rather than for all of these functions. These differences should be kept closely in mind for later, in Chapter 12, where we explore alternatives to security, these functions will be important.

Short-stay security

We have not investigated many short-stay facilities as our main preoccupation has been with secure provision that either has treatment pretensions or assists the normal workings of the child-care system. Neither have we been concerned with security as a device for ensuring that children appear before the courts, important though this is and for which there seems, from the number of unruly certificates made, to be some case for an increase. Neither does this survey offer a comprehensive review of the need for secure assessment facilities. Nevertheless, we did visit in the course of our researches, the remand wings of prisons, a number of remand centres and some secure accommodation in observation and assessment centres. It is an area which needs research scrutiny as the conditions under which children are detained seem to differ widely. For example, at Aycliffe the secure remand facility was a coeducational setting in which homeliness was emphasised. Other remand situations for juveniles, however, seemed to differ little from prison. Here children may wait for a period either before a court appearance or for a transfer elsewhere. There is also some pressure put on these facilities to take children that cannot be placed elsewhere. The mixture of children found in secure remand situations seems to be extreme and several children, particularly girls, can find themselves stranded in remand provision which has no long-term care programme. [2]

Secure withdrawal rooms

Locking up recalcitrant children has a healthy pedigree and a large number of CHEs have long had secure rooms for punishment or temporary withdrawal rooms. The development of secure separation rooms, 'coolers' as they are affectionately known to the adolescents, was encouraged by the recommendations of the Durand report which stressed the need in the approved schools for detention rooms suitable for difficult children. We have noted that a number of schools already had these facilities although it is difficult to estimate how much they were used before 1966. Certainly the use of security was not uncommon in the girls' schools at that time and was generally employed in holding overnight absconders returned to the schools or those awaiting a court appearance. For absconding boys, devices such as spending the day in shorts, underclothes or pyjamas added a bizarre supplement to the controls exerted by security.

Today, the use of these withdrawal rooms in CHEs can vary considerably, as can the length of time children spend in them. For the majority of children the sojourn is brief, a few hours pondering on an institutional sin, but for others the stay can be longer and, subject to external approval, they may spend several days inside. Thankfully, boys seem to have ceased to parade in Y-fronts as a deterrent to absconding. There have also been other changes. The conditions covering the detaining of children in security have become more stringent. They are elaborate and provide considerable safeguards for the child. For example, in some authorities the director

111

of social services has to be personally informed when any secure place available in CHEs is put to use and serious consequences for the authorities can ensue from even minor infringements of the regulations.

While external scrutiny on the use of security is careful and benign, a punitive inheritance still seems to influence the style of secure accommodation provided. Frequently, the rooms have bars at the window, they are small and cell-like with the minimum of sturdy furniture, the bed is firmly anchored to the floor and a bare table and chair are provided. A peephole enables staff to glance regularly at the captive. We feel that a number of these secure rooms fall short of the recommendations of the DHSS which suggest that 'accommodation should be as light and airy as possible and decorated and furnished in a style that children recognise as homely'. [3]

On entry to the secure room, the child is usually searched for matches and weapons. This is particularly important for children who are suicidal or prone to self-mutilation. Although frequent visiting by staff is obligatory, the experience for the child is lonely and frustrating. In some cases a radio is permitted and approved reading material or pastimes are always encouraged. Usually a secure room is discreetly located at the end of a corridor or in the administration block of the institution, well beyond the range of visitors and children. However, an acute observer can frequently identify an occupied secure room by an extensive pile of institutional *bric-à-brac* near the door. Hurriedly moved debris of old floor polishers and tired squeegees can be observed, the cell's customary and less protesting tenants.

We feel that the use of such accommodation may, in rare cases, be justified particularly in the case of an hysterical or suicidal child who needs close staff supervision. But these secure rooms have no treatment pretensions and provide no education or social experiences. The response of the children to our questions suggests that they view the provision with considerable unease. This is re-emphasised by the isolation of children in security from their friends in the main school. Outside visitors are discouraged, even when there is no threat to the control function of security. Indeed, 'continuous effective control', in the words of the DHSS circular, [4] 'is the first priority' and this is the guiding preoccupation in the use of these secure separation rooms. The 'coolers' hover symbolically, reminding everyone that care and treatment in a planned environment is obligatory. The fact that some institutions with difficult children have managed to operate for years without this facility casts some doubts on the needs of others for the provision.

The longer-stay small secure units

Some of the small secure units are quite different from those we have just described. Although they are still small, they are more treatment-oriented and their clientele is expected to stay for some months. These units usually have about six places and are part of a wider institution such as a CHE. They are generously and professionally staffed and there is little overlap of staff roles with the main school. In organisation and external relationships these units have a considerable degree of autonomy.

112

Unlike the withdrawal rooms where inconvenient behaviour in the parent institution commands a place in security, the criteria for entry into the longer-stay units are more heterogeneous and ill-defined. In fact, entry to the units shares all the weaknesses of the selection process that were apparent in our opening chapters. In most cases the boys and girls will have been unresponsive to open provision in a variety of ways but the occasional remand or medical problem can also appear. The units are particularly likely to be left with a child whom social workers find impossible to place. They have also to face the additional difficulty that applications for security come from the same regional authorities that have provided the facility. Thus, there is always a risk that these units will take on a riot shield function either for the larger institutions of which they are a part or for the wider geographical region. Usually these units are expected to do little more than hold the situation and modify the acute symptoms of the child's distress. Their small size and lack of facilities means that they can do little else.

The units are usually located in a wing or outbuilding of the main institution and because of considerable local pressures for their provision, they have often been hurriedly converted from less prestigious accommodation. They are often graced with the euphemism 'intensive care units' which thinly disguises past splendours or, more usually, disasters. For example, at one unit passing cows hover outside the barred windows of their erstwhile milking parlour while at another, an escape hole in the ceiling had been creatively covered by an abstract, flaking mobile. Even when they are purpose-built, some remarkable planning errors seem inevitable. One unit squeezed all the windows of the teaching block high above everyone's head to hinder escape attempts and to prevent the children peering out of security or their more fortunate colleagues from looking in. The resulting claustrophobia was so intense that nobody could either teach or learn. Another plan omitted windows altogether from several important rooms which certainly made security easier but unfortunately breached an international convention on human rights for prisoners and, at considerable expense, windows had to be inserted. We feel that in all the units, both large and small, the need for careful planning is very apparent, if only to minimise the amount of locking and unlocking that seems to take place and, of course, the risk of fire.

In these units, a number of secure rooms cluster round a central core of facilities which are used for teaching, recreation and taking meals. The staff attempt to run a relaxed, flexible and homely regime in which individual attention can be given to each child. As staff provision is usually generous, several of the units approach this ideal successfully. Some smaller intensive care units have attempted to develop a treatment programme, such as the 'bridge unit' at Sedbury Park, a CHE for boys. Children selected for this type of small, long-stay unit are those whom the local assessment centre and a psychiatrist defined as needing both intensive care and security. These are not necessarily the most difficult or criminal of children in open settings. Indeed, most of these small units strenuously resist admitting those disruptive children whom other CHEs wish to load on to them. Frequently, the units shelter adolescents who are identical with those outside but staff maintain that as the treatment programme makes more demands on the child selected for intensive care, security is necessary to prevent absconding.

Staff and psychiatrists maintain that two groups of children can best be helped by this provision. The first group are those who display acute neurotic symptoms and attempt to abscond when confronted with difficulty or pressure. The second group who benefit from this provision are those children who are isolated and unexpressive. We know that there are many such deprived children in care who need intensive support but clearly only a few of these need security. Most intensive care units within the CHE system are in open environments such as that at Headlands which we shall describe later. These open units are quite effective for both the neurotic absconder and the very deprived and greatly moderate their presenting behaviour. Unfortunately, a lack of intensive care places in many regions seems to encourage the use of security to provide a level of care which is unavailable outside. Any candidate for security should demonstrate that he cannot be held in open intensive care facilities and when security is used, a cogent case must be made for it. Again, the care advantages of security should always be weighed against its disadvantages. The small size of the units greatly restricts the educational, social and recreational opportunities of the children who are contained by them. Even in the best of units, all these are sacrificed to the advantages of a close relationship with staff and the largely unproven benefits of psychotherapy.

The stability of these small units poses serious problems for local authorities. They are subject to vicissitude and crisis. For example, it is clear that these units can only be successful when they are added to an open, viable establishment. The wider institutional climate must itself be stable and free from serious problems of control before it can accommodate a secure or even an open intensive care unit. There should be a widespread consensus among staff in both the main institution and the units on aims and strategies. Pupil commitment to the main institution should be high and this good morale should be demonstrated through low rates of absconding and of premature transfer. It is unwise to build small secure units to solve the problems of the parent institution.

It is also clear that the small secure unit must have a specific function, otherwise it will accumulate children with varying difficulties, such as the aggressive adolescent or the Section 53 case. It may be useful, therefore, in the early days of a new unit, to select children from the open parts of the establishment and to discourage all admissions who have not first been tried in a benign setting. Direct entry from the courts in particular should be discouraged because judicial perceptions on the control needed may not correspond with the type of secure provision that is available. Care must also be taken that the existence of a secure unit does not lead to a rapid change in the sorts of adolescents being admitted to the parent institution. Once a facility is in being, there is a clear tendency for all sorts of misfits to be allocated to the parent school because it is such a short walk from an open to a closed environment.

The recruitment and selection of staff also raises considerable difficulties for the small secure unit attached to an open CHE. It is never an easy task for the head of the institution to integrate the unit staff into the wider world of the campus. We shall see later that working in secure units puts a severe strain on staff and when the unit is small and isolated from the main school, these stresses multiply. There is little variety in the daily routine to stimulate them and maintain their interest. It is, therefore, important that people working in such situations should be stable, free from external anxieties and given considerable support from the parent institution. A number of studies have demonstrated how general anxieties of staff, concerns over status and conflicting personalities can greatly influence the behaviour of the children who are sheltered by the units. [5] In a large institution, unease, anxiety and conflict can be accommodated but smaller units have fewer resources to divert tension and it is difficult for both staff and children to fashion any avoidance of each other.

Unfortunately, there is a dearth of evaluative material on the effects of intensive care for children. [6] What little we do know of the impact of care in these small secure units is not very encouraging. For example, in one follow-up study of some 50 boys who passed through such care provision, four-fifths of them went on to Borstal very rapidly after release. The unit had to close after a serious disturbance and it was found that while boys made good progress within the unit, particularly in their education and relationship skills, intensive care had little effect on their persistent recidivist behaviour. However, we shall explore more fully in a later chapter the consequences for children of a period spent in security. We would suggest that small, secure, intensive care units can provide an additional resource to a good open CHE but their claustrophobic conditions engender tensions in staff and the threat of crisis is constant. Above all, a belief in the benefits of intensive care should not allow children to remain in secure accommodation after the need for the lock has gone.

The larger units

Three long-stay secure units, Kingswood, Redbank and Redhill, have provided much of the evidence offered in this study of secure provision. The pressures leading to their creation and their development over time are easier to approach than the smaller intensive care units which are less enduring and where documentation is poor. Consequently, we have already been able to see why the larger secure units were opened and the sorts of child that have been admitted to them over the years.

The special units were purpose-built and shelter about 26 boys each. They were attached to the campus of regional classifying schools in order that they might share facilities and use the nearby training school as a release or preparation institution. Not all the classifying schools accepted from the Home Office the proffered secure accommodation. Aycliffe, mindful of earlier difficulties, declined and Stamford House, which had previously developed secure remand provision, felt that they had done enough.

Considering that the three units were designed within a short time to meet the needs of almost identical clients, the physical plants differ remarkably. Kingswood is the most cramped of the three with its bedrooms downstairs in a claustrophobic flat that feels as if it is below ground level. Redbank is more open, while Redhill surrounds a large courtyard which is used for boys' exercise and recreation. All the units tend to look inward, both physically and socially for in spite of the facilities available on the wider campus, the units are virtually self-sufficient. Considering the small number of children sheltered, the educational, social and recreational provision is generous. There is usually a gymnasium, a large exercise yard and, in one case, an extensive garden to occupy the children. Use is also made of the campus swimming pool. Boys are taken for their swim by mini-bus already changed and return, dripping slightly, later.

We have noted that the origins of the units were specifically custodial and that the planned regimes were punitive; for this reason, the larger units contain boys, not girls. The style of the early days was much influenced by the detention centre programmes which, at the time of the units' creation, commanded high hopes. During the first months, the units admitted a number of boys in their late teens who had been extremely difficult in open schools and who fulfilled everyone's expectations of intransigence, belligerence and non-cooperation. Because of the teaching and control emphasis of the old approved school system to which the units were a supplement, educational ends were highly prized and still are. Teachers dominated the staff and, in association with a large number of prison staff who were employed early on, they set the ethos and pattern of a secure school. Thus, the units were hierarchically structured and allowed little autonomy to staff and less to the children. Because of the complicated shift systems for staff, the units tended to be organisationally very inflexible.

We have noted in earlier chapters that over the years, boys admitted to the units have become younger while the range of problems they present has grown wider though not necessarily more severe. The units have also increased their child-care emphasis so that nowadays the new arrival will experience a relatively benign regime. But the units still present a curious combination of intensive care and security. Indeed, the extent to which custody is viewed as paramount may surprise the outside observer who has been wooed by the language of treatment. Security is still prized and the amount of locking and unlocking doors is very noticeable. Boys are never out of sight; several members of staff scrutinise every moment from waking to bedtime and at night, the sleeper is glanced at every half-hour. Management is concerned with containing, moving and occupying groups of children as quietly and smoothly as possible.

The juxtaposition of care and custody can also be seen in many other areas. Naturally, one expects to see bars in a secure unit. One also expects to hear the jangle of keys, but one prison feature we did not hope to find was the unlovely practice of slopping out. The units can offer no better symbol of the punitive and degrading perspectives that hovered at their birth than the morning row of chamber pots. After all, plumbing had achieved a modest degree of sophistication in 1965 and slopping out has since been deliberately avoided at two of the most recent secure units. It seems incredible that regimes which seem to involve large numbers of staff for case conferences on boys' welfare cannot, on the other hand, offer sufficient night supervision for boys to go to the lavatory in a civilised way. Curiously enough, one of the units has added a sumptuous open extension to its secure section, yet the practice of slopping out proceeds quite unnoticed less than 30 yards away. Indeed, efforts to prevent the development of prison language among the boys seem rather pointless at the sight of a number of children, each clasping a potty, drifting to the latrines in the mornings. Here, indeed, are new vistas of socialisation.

It would be wearisome to go through many other examples of the ways in which the prison model coexists with care provision. The scrutiny of mail, the careful restriction on telephone calls, the list of approved girl friends, the censoring of literature, the frequent searching of boys and their accommodation and the unnecessary restrictions on parental and friends' visiting all remind us of where we are and we feel that little of this has much relevance to intensive care. As a set of custodial regulations, they seem merely to provide people with something to do.

Many elements of this prison style are quite absurd. The adolescents are not all potential escapees and anyone bent on departure would only have to wait for an outing or weekend leave to absent themselves. It is unnecessary to scrutinise the majority of children in a way that is possibly necessary for new entrants or Section 53 cases. To treat everyone as a potential suicide risk or fire-raiser constantly raises these possibilities in the minds of impressionable children. Most of the major concerns in the dreariest units have yet to be demonstrated to have any relevance to the adolescent's disturbance or any effects on his antisocial behaviour which, after all, is what the units are supposed to be about.

Linked to this somewhat restrictive approach is a boarding school routine. All the boys spend much of their daytime hours in the classroom and, benefiting from regular attendance, sufficient sleep and physical care, the children make rapid advances in educational skills. Remedial teaching is a strong feature of the provision. Some boys may increase their attainments, particularly in reading, by several years while they are in the units. Naturally those children who stay the longest make the greatest educational gains. Some Section 53 cases, who are not necessarily among the most backward on arrival, will be taking 'O' levels before they leave. As in the open schools, these are considerable benefits and do much to engender a positive response from the children towards the secure regime.

While the educational provision is generous in terms of the numbers of children to be taught, the width of the stimulation is inevitably restricted. This, of course, is even more a problem in the smaller intensive care units just described where teachers are frequently hard pushed to teach even the basic skills. But educational opportunity is still restricted in these larger units. For example, the lack of any laboratory space means that science teaching or project work in integrated studies is very difficult to organise. In some units expressive subjects such as music, the plastic arts and drama are scarcely developed. Similarly, any child who had sporting potential would be much disadvantaged in the units as there are few possibilities for team games and competitions. In fairness, it is not easy to generalise, for Kingswood has some very impressive facilities and Redbank had an excellent art department. But the units cannot achieve this excellence in all such activities and the quality of provision seems dependent on a particularly lucky appointment or the special interests of staff.

It is easy to be complacent about what we offer difficult adolescents or to be dazzled by certain aspects of provision in these units. We often forget that the individual's liberty has been removed and that if prison perspectives are really to be cast aside, an extensive range of stimulation needs to be provided. It may be rather whimsical to note that had not Renaissance Italy had slightly more expressive perspectives than our own, Michelangelo and Caravaggio would probably have spent their infancy and formative years in security. It is very unlikely that either of them would have been released. But, because we cannot envisage the Sistine ceiling being nurtured in a secure unit, we act accordingly. Creativity in the arts is frequently linked with aggression and maladjustment but in most CHEs and special units adolescents are provided with few vehicles for such expression.

In such environments, the intensive care which the units now advance as their *raison d'être* is inevitably diminished. We shall explore later in our consideration of staff–child relationships the difficulties of undertaking psychotherapy but, in general, the organisational priorities of security and the educational emphasis seem to elbow care areas aside. The status inadequacies and lack of training of the residential social workers in closed units and their general lack of child-care experience mean that they are ill placed to advocate a less evaluative and more child-care-centred regime. Written instructions to the staff at one of the units makes this point very clearly, showing that not only do the custodial concepts on which the units are based enjoy considerable antiquity but also the school ethos has nostalgic whiffs of the past.

Particular note should be taken in the following extract of the ways in which counselling and pastoral support are displaced – 'for reasons of time-tabling these can only take place during breaks and evening activities'. It is also interesting that the way in which ultimate isolation in a cell, even in a unit of maximum security, becomes the final sanction. The conflict between care and custody is nowhere more apparent than where we persuade children that they are behind one set of locks for intensive care while we employ another set in an explicitly punitive way. Part of the instructions to staff in one of the units went as follows:

> Bedtimes will be staggered according to the degree of privilege allowed:
>
> Grade 1 – 8.35 p.m.
>
> Grade 2 – 8.45 p.m.
>
> Grade 3 – 9.05 p.m.

All staff will be allocated 2 boys whom they will counsel, advise and support. Generally they will follow their boys' case histories and contact and discuss their roles with the psychiatrist and psychologist. Much of this approach can for reasons of time-tabling only take place during breaks and in evening activities. The counsellor involved will be expected to keep an incident log for his own boys and should accept a measure of responsibility in ensuring that other members of staff make their contribution to each of these logs. Staff counsellors will prepare notes for the monthly reports and be prepared to take part in case conferences about their boys. Their logs should be available for typing weekly.

At all times, staff counsellors should seek the discretion of their Senior Man or the Warden.

Discipline and Sanctions in the Unit

What we expect of our boys: Boys are expected to be clean, tidy, and properly dressed. The boys will be responsible for the condition of their clothes, bedspaces and rooms. Boys will be expected on all occasions to stand or move about smartly (without their hands in their pockets) and generally to offer a positive appearance. Comics, unless recommended educationally, will not be allowed in the Unit.

Boys will be expected to control their language, and prison vernacular should be discouraged.

While much of the day is positively organised on our time-table certain periods have been deliberately set aside when boys will be in their unlocked rooms. During these periods boys will need advice and guidance over using this time to themselves, in the hope that they will become self-sufficient as individuals (a further function for counsellors). Many of these boys may later in life be obliged to take lodgings and it seems vital to encourage them in activities and entertainments which do not require group support.

For minor difficulties during group work and activity the teacher and housemaster have the sanctions of the pay card, and the behaviour grading. If these sanctions prove inadequate in any situation after talking to the boy, his case may immediately be referred to the Senior Man on the shift who may reprimand or exclude the boy from a group situation. The Senior Man may decide to reduce the boy's privileges or even order him to do general fatigues for the benefit of the Unit. (It is important that all jobs in the Unit should be obviously purposeful.) If this should still fail, the Warden may intervene and the boy may be placed in isolation with a further loss of privileges. Staff should not hold on to a difficult situation any longer than necessary before ringing for the Duty Officer or Senior Man.

It should be stressed that this set of instructions can be found not in the most restrictive of the secure environments but in a unit which had developed the most coherent treatment programme of any we visited. Naturally, the attitude which readers will adopt towards the regime illustrated above will depend on their particular philosophies of education or, more precisely, what they feel schools should be about. However, reading the comments on comics, one feels the work of Bernstein has yet to have much influence in this establishment. On the other hand, those interested in the functions of schools, that is the way in which they prepare children for adult roles and sensitise them to particular cultures, will treasure the phrase, 'obliged to take lodgings later in life'. Similarly, disciples of philosophers such as Leach and Marcuse, who have long argued that education is one of the most potent forms of social control, will be delighted by the above programme of delicately balanced restrictions.

It is clear that in addition to the difficulties of selecting that minority of children who will benefit from a period in security, the style of long-term secure provision has many contradictions. Its punitive conception and its association with the ailing approved school system seems to have left its mark in a carefully regulated and scrutinised educational programme and in the creation of a secure boarding school environment. In this situation, intensive care is expected to find a place. At best, such care is an ill-defined concept which does not seem to differ from what any children's home should provide as a matter of course or from what all vulnerable children need. Unfortunately, unconditional love withers in a secure school.

The research studies of the Tizards have established a link between the regimentation of children and a lack of autonomy for staff. [7] Hargreaves's studies and the work of Kushlick show that when school and hospital models are rigidly adhered to in contrast to the accepting stance of child care, an adverse impact is made on children. [8] Rutter and Bartak's studies have measured the ways in which certain differences in goal emphasis, particularly in special schools, can affect the language and stance of staff towards the children with significant results for pupils' progress and well-being. [9] Several of our studies have emphasised how a confusion of institutional aims and unresolved conflicts between them can reduce the effectiveness of the school. [10] Unfortunately, in spite of this accumulating wealth of research evidence, knowledge still seems to have little impact on the ways in which institutions are run.

The conflicts between custody, school and care models are not just theoretical problems. Their impact is immediate and considerable. For example, Redbank, which contained among the most difficult of all the children in security, completed its treatment programme in an average of six months, while Redhill took nine months and Kingswood spent 18 months doing the same task. The youth treatment centres, which we shall shortly consider, can have a treatment programme lasting several years. When they are released to the outside world, the consequences for the children of such varying lengths of stay do not seem to differ in any appreciable manner. Such a simple finding characterises the confusion surrounding the concept of 'treatment'. But this is also an expensive confusion for if all the longer-stay units achieved the throughput of Redbank, we could double the amount of secure provision available in the child-care system without any appreciable increase in expenditure.

The youth treatment centres

We have noted that the secure units from their first days were called upon to cope with a wide variety of difficult children. The first admissions to Kingswood were problematic and one had even been considered at a very early age for admission to Broadmoor. Thus, before the secure units were functioning, it was clear that the needs of psychotic and neurotic juveniles were unlikely to be adequately met. A short period under a brisk regime in a unit designed primarily to help the approved schools function was certainly no answer to the problems of very difficult children.

However, there were differences of opinion between the Home Office and the Health Service as to which department could support these children most effectively. [11] The Health Service maintained that some of these children were unlikely to respond to hospital treatment and that in any case most of them did not require full medical facilities. Understandably the Home Office felt that very disturbed children needed the specialist care of the medical authorities. Hence a compromise was reached in that the Home Office decided to make provision for these children although, where appropriate, children could still be placed in mental hospitals under the existing legislation. Thus, in June 1968, the Home Secretary was able to moderate increasing public concern that no appropriate provision for the younger disturbed child existed by announcing the creation of new facilities.

It was also clear, reading the report of the working party which was then set up to plan these new establishments, that girls were causing increasing concern. It is a noticeable feature in the development of all care and educational facilities that girls are viewed very differently from boys. Although girls are probably more disruptive in residential situations than boys, the reluctance of the working party deliberating secure provision to include girls in the scope of their inquiries is clear. Possibly, this hesitation was understandable as girls' absconding behaviour did not usually involve offences and the majority of these children had been taken into care for protection and control rather than for persistent delinquency. However, it is worth noting that girls, on both treatment needs and exposure to risks while absconding, are probably stronger candidates for security than boys, especially as the range of possible residential placements is smaller.

The working party reported in the summer of 1969 and recommended that the new centres were to do the following things. They were to provide long-term care, in graduations of security for seriously disturbed children, either those committed on care orders or Section 53 cases. The units were to attempt to arrest deterioration in children's behaviour, to prevent further personality damage and to increase the understanding of severe disturbance in juveniles. They were to explore treatment possibilities, to evaluate them and report to the wider child-care audience. The units were to offer staff training facilities to those in relevant fields.

St Charles youth treatment centre was opened in the spring of 1971 with a medical director and a generous number of specialist staff. Located in a recently completed community home at Brentwood in Essex, it has three houses, one of which is secure. The children stay usually for more than a year and are admitted at an average age of 13. However, the variation in ages on reception and in lengths of stay is greater than in most other secure units. There are more girls accommodated than boys and the treatment approach was originally intended to be sequential, that is, the young people began in the secure house and, with increasing maturity, moved on to open conditions.

Although we visited St Charles, our opportunities for research were severely restricted. We talked to a number of senior staff but were unable to visit any of the houses and could not mount any investigation of children's backgrounds or the process of selection. This was a severe handicap to our studies because, at that time, St Charles youth treatment centre was the only large institution which sheltered girls in security for any length of time. The youth treatment centres are also important in other ways for they represent a logical development of the 'treatment' philosophy that is so influential in child care. Unfortunately, as with all treatment, there seems to be more consensus on what not to do with difficult children than any agreement on what constitutes effective therapy. Thus, the centre experienced very severe difficulties in its early years. Indeed, had not the responsibility for it rested with the DHSS it is doubtful whether it would have survived. The original secure unit was unable to contain the young people, the strains on staff were extreme and there has been a succession of crises. It re-emphasises how fraught a task it is to initiate and develop special facilities for difficult children, particularly when security is involved.

These difficulties not only led to a change in leadership but also to a change in style. The consultant psychiatrist was replaced by an approved school headmaster who had considerable experience in handling crises of control. While this displacement of the psychotherapeutic stance of St Charles by the more custodial perspectives of the approved school has proved to be largely symbolic, it is important. We have noted that secure units find it very difficult, because of external pressures, internal vicissitudes and developing philosophies, to maintain their original intentions. When complex organisations come under stress, organisational goals, particularly those of control and external public relations, rapidly achieve priority.

The sequential pattern of treatment for children, beginning in security and moving out to open situations, has also been much modified. Ostensibly this is because movement through the system depends on suitable vacancies existing in the open houses. Some children lingered long in security blocking the flow and the practice was for some time adopted of admitting children direct to the open units. In some ways this has diminished the importance of security in the overall treatment programme. But, whatever the reasons for the change, it is noticeable that all the secure units originally had the intention of releasing their children rapidly to an open training school situation. This did not develop and there are indications that some of the recently established small intensive care units are developing similar isolations from their parent institutions. In these cases, the 'blockage' arguments of St Charles do not apply. We suspect that, in fact, this hesitation to transfer is more the result of boundary maintenance within the institution and the development of embracing treatment rationales rather than any difficulties of organisation. It is noticeable, for example, how independent the three long-stay secure units have become from their parent institutions. At St Charles, the house units also have a singular degree of autonomy which has created management problems. Small units seem to find it difficult to pass on their 'successes' for others possibly to damage – a reluctant *aubade* that is familiar to anyone who knows ordinary primary and preparatory schools.

It is also clear that the attitudes to security have been somewhat revised at the youth treatment centre. The working party considered it as providing only a small part of the treatment programme at St Charles and certainly did not view it as the most important component. In contrast, Birmingham youth treatment centre which has recently opened offers 54 places, all of which are secure. This again represents a major shift in the philosophy guiding the development of the youth treatment centres.

Social workers find it difficult to be dispassionate about St Charles. At one level it is the apotheosis of institutional care for children – complex, highly staffed and extremely expensive. At another level, those who believe that treatment is largely illusory, particularly in a residential context, and have high hopes of improving community services, find the 'Homes and Gardens' ambience at Brentwood particularly infuriating. Where resources in the social services are scarce, the generosity of the provision naturally arouses external criticism. In addition, the youth treatment centre began with a rather superior stance towards the other secure units and entertained rather pretentious notions about treatment. The trauma of its early days has inevitably brought humility and realism. The staff now seem to approach the children's problems in a pragmatic and experimental way; much of its work is pioneering, particularly with regard to family casework and its efforts with extremely difficult girls. It is to be hoped that the centre will eventually tell us much about the contribution residential care can make to the minority of very disturbed, high-risk children.

Conclusions

In this chapter we have attempted to describe the wide variety of provision that can be called secure. Not only do the units differ very markedly in their approach to children who present very similar problems but containment in the child-care system seems to bear little relationship to security provided elsewhere, by Borstals, remand centres and mental hospitals. Presumably the needs of some children and some problems are best met in one environment than another, so any regional provision should have regard to the variety of ways in which these needs can be fulfilled. Even at the most simple level there seem to be unjustifiable differences, particularly from the children's point of view, between secure unit experiences. There are marked differences in the degree of security provided, in the time children stay in the secure units, in their access to the outside world, in contact with and provision for their parents and, of course, in the daily control and regulation children experience. These contrasts exist even before the perennial debate begins over what constitutes treatment. The punitive heritage of the units and the multiplicity of functions thrust upon them merely increases this confusion. Therefore the response of those working in security is to approach the most accessible of the children's difficulties, their physical needs, their educational deficiencies and their lack of social skills. Unfortunately, the conflict between the stance of secure boarding schools and the requirements of intensive care diminishes the support the child actually receives. As we turn to aspects of the staff world we will see the difficulties of treatment within security do not only spring from contrasting models of intervention.

Notes

[1] For a guide to planning and a discussion of the range of styles for secure accommodation within the CHE system see, *Development of Secure Provision in Community Homes*, Development Group, DHSS, 1974.

[2] One study of admissions to a secure assessment facility is M. Hoghugi and S. Nethercott, *Troubled and Troublesome*, Aycliffe Studies of Problem Children, 1977.

[3] DHSS, local authority circular (75) 1, para. 12.

[4] DHSS, local authority circular (75) 1, para. 10.

[5] See the papers by B. Tizard and I. Sinclair in J. Tizard, I. Sinclair and R. Clarke, *Varieties of Residential Experience*, London, Routledge and Kegan Paul, 1975, pp. 102-21 and 122-40.

[6] A survey of these facilities is being undertaken by J. McCreadie as part of a Cropwood Fellowship at the Institute of Criminology, Cambridge.

[7] See the papers by J. Tizard and B. Tizard in J. Tizard et al., *Varieties of Residential Experience*, op. cit., pp. 52-68 and 102-21.

[8] See D. Hargreaves, *Social Relations in a Secondary School*, London, Routledge and Kegan Paul, 1967 and *Deviance in the Classroom*, London, Routledge and Kegan Paul, 1976. See also K. Heal and P. Cawson, 'Organisation and change in children's institutions', in J. Tizard et al., *Varieties of Residential Experience*, op. cit., p. 69-101.

[9] See L. Bartak and M. Rutter, 'The Measurement of staff–child interaction in three units for autistic children', in J. Tizard, I. Sinclair and R. Clarke, *Varieties of Residential Experience*, London, Routledge and Kegan Paul, 1975, pp. 171-202.

[10] See S. Millham, R. Bullock and P. Cherrett, *After Grace - Teeth*, London, Human Context Books, Chaucer Publishing Company, 1975 and R. Lambert, S. Millham and R. Bullock, *The Chance of a Lifetime?*, London, Weidenfeld & Nicolson, 1975.

[11] See, for example, the *Report of a Specialist Working Party on Severely Disturbed Children and Young Persons in Approved Schools*, unpublished report, Home Office, 1969. See also P. Cawson, *The Development of Closed Units and its Research Implications*, Research Division, DHSS, 1975.

10   The staff world

Sociologists have been so preoccupied with the residents of closed institutions that residential staff have attracted comparatively little interest.[1] Many studies of prisons, mental hospitals and schools explore the inmate world and its response to the pains of imprisonment almost to the exclusion of the equally important world of staff. The works of Taylor and Cohen at Durham or Goffman's *Asylums* well illustrate this partial stance.[2] Possibly it springs from the reformist intention of some research and the radical, 'underdog' orientation of much sociology but, whatever the reason, these perspectives inevitably cast residential staff into uncomplimentary stereotypes.

In our studies of CHEs and ordinary boarding schools, we have always tried to redress this balance and in this case, a careful look at staff in secure units is rewarding both practically and theoretically. It is, for example, particularly interesting to note the shifting relationships in secure units between staff and child worlds and the ways in which the strengths of the latter seem to affect the institution as well as to have personal consequences for the staff. It is also surprising, considering the specialised nature of these places, to see just how much the recruitment and staffing structures reflect the system in which secure accommodation developed. The hierarchical distribution of power, the clearly defined roles of staff, the routines and shift systems and, above all, the perspectives that staff have of their task, are all very reminiscent of the old approved schools.

As might be expected, the secure units are more generously staffed than are most open CHEs. The need for constant scrutiny of the children both night and day and the individualisation of teaching and pastoral care within the units, means that a larger number of staff is required. Yet, there seems no particular reason for the wide divergences between the units in areas such as staffing ratios and in the proportions of men to women. For example, at the time of our research, the Rossie Farm unit was running with fewer staff than any other whereas St Charles youth treatment centre was generously staffed with, for example, 15 night duty staff. There were also as many women care staff looking after the 12 children in the secure house at this establishment as in all of the other large secure units put together. Overall, less than 10 per cent of teachers in the units are women and none of these hold senior posts which is surprising in view of the fact that women can be particularly effective in dealing with difficult and disruptive boys.[3] If the tasks of the units are similar one would not have expected to find the difference illustrated in Table 10.1.

Because all the units are relatively new, there is far less variation in the length of time that staff stay than is common in other residential homes and schools. Staff serve, in general, for about three years before moving on and their average age is only 33. Their youth and their desire for increased responsibility means that movement is much more rapid than in most other CHEs and even among the senior staff, few have worked in the units for more than five years.

Table 10.1
Ratios of teachers and housemasters per shift per child

	Sedbury ICU	Redbank	Redhill	Kingswood	Rossie Farm	St Charles YTC House 1
	1 : 1	1 : 2·9	1 : 3·6	1 : 2·4*	1 : 7	1 : 0·7
Number of children	6	25	29	26	36	12

* Not a two-shift system

The staffing structures of the larger units which we visited were all very similar with an hierarchical structure of authority passing from the head, via the deputy, senior assistants, care and teaching staff, case workers and domestics to the pupils. Part-time psychiatrists and psychologists were also employed but there had been periods when some of these posts were not filled. Elsewhere, the patterns varied. At the time of our research, Kingswood had just developed an 'open' section to its secure unit, so its staffing structure was beginning to deviate slightly from the others and at St Charles, the generous staff provision had allowed a federal structure to develop with considerable autonomy among the component units.

Although the maintenance of security requires more staff than would be necessary in open homes, it is also clear that the numbers of staff employed increase the more the units stress a treatment orientation. But this does not mean that custodial perspectives are automatically depressed, because in secure units it is not always easy to decide exactly where control ends and treatment begins. None of the units we visited had an effectively secure perimeter and control is generally maintained by the constant scrutiny of each child, by the fragmentation of his friendship groups and by individualised teaching. Thus, much that the units perceive as treatment has clear control implications.

These generous staff–child ratios are also something of a mixed blessing as they create an entirely new management problem. The units find that large numbers of staff can create as many problems as having too few. One head commented, 'My worry and concern is making sure that everyone has got a job'. Much of the time, for example when children are watching television or being taught, there can be a considerable underemployment of staff. This diminishes job satisfaction and leads to the creation of artificial tasks and the laying out of petty territories. For instance, in one of the units, the selection and duration of the TV programmes had almost become a jealously guarded staff office.

Teachers were the predominant professional group in most of the secure units and their perspectives were, therefore, particularly influential in determining practice. Of the professional staff employed in the three large units in 1975, only

126

11 per cent from Redbank, 44 per cent from Redhill and 26 per cent from Kingswood had previous experience of the CHE system and none of them had ever worked in a children's home. This preponderance of teachers reflects both the origins of the units and the rather uneasy perspectives on security that are generally entertained by residential social workers. Tables 10.2 and 10.3 illustrate the previous occupations and qualifications of teachers and care staff at three of the larger units for boys.

Table 10.2

Previous occupational experience of teachers and housemasters, including senior assistants (figures are percentages)

	Redbank	Redhill	Kingswood
Day school teaching	53	39	52
Industrial	11	39	22
Clerical	5	22	4
Forces	5	11	0
CHEs	11	44	26
Penal establishments	5	6	4
Youth work	0	11	0
Children's homes	0	0	0
Other	0	6	9
N =	19	18	23

Table 10.3

Educational and professional qualifications of teachers and house staff, including senior assistants (figures are percentages)

	Redbank	Redhill	Kingswood
Teaching Certificate	74	39	52
BEd	21	0	13
Youth work	0	6	4
City & Guilds	21	17	9
NC & HNC	5	6	9
Social work	5	6	4
Residential Child Care Certificate	16	7	26
Degrees	11	0	9
Diplomas	5	11	30
N =	19	18	23

Most of the teachers working in the units said that they were initially attracted to work in a secure setting because of the good salaries offered. They had not usually heard of the units before seeing the advertisement and knew little about this type of work. But, all the staff we talked to stressed that the financial benefit was no longer the force that kept them there. As one teacher explained, 'Once you get here, although the money's important, that's not the reason why you stay – you stay because you get involved with kids'.

We have already noted that in planning the secure units, the Home Office had few models on which to base their new institutions. Naturally, they leaned heavily on the experience of their newly developing detention centres and well-established Borstals. If they had looked to Scotland, the early difficulties experienced there would have produced little guidance except to suggest that more staff, skilled in prison management, were probably necessary. Similarly, Kingswood's brave attempt in 1964 to reject custodial perspectives ran into early problems, not so much because of the therapeutic stance that was initially adopted but more because of the early clients. As the first unit to open in England, Kingswood had to act as pioneer with a number of very difficult boys who had long been stored in the approved schools system and, inevitably, its pioneering role took on a frontier-like pattern.

During the 1960s, all this encouraged the recruitment of Borstal and prison staff to work in the units and this helped over time to nurture unsympathetic perspectives on the role of security in the approved school system. When they first opened, Redbank and Redhill employed quite a high proportion of prison officers and a number of these still remain. (Redhill, in fact, has employed a total of 14 prison and Borstal staff since it opened in 1965.) But it is only fair to stress that the strong-armed, authoritarian stereotype of the prison officer is probably as far from reality as are popular notions about the dangerous boys they supervise. Possibly, it is the more 'liberal' officers who move out of the prison system into related tasks which offer them more job fulfilment. But, whatever the reasons, the prison officers whom we interviewed in the secure units or CHEs were most certainly not insensitive to the vulnerability and problems of the children. These early recruitment patterns, combined with the 'dustbin' function of the units and the enhanced 'treatment' image of the approved schools as they became CHEs, resulted in a dearth of applications from staff in other children's establishments for jobs in secure units. [4]

It is also clear that in some cases, the actual recruitment policy militates against the selection of child-care staff for the units. Some senior staff doubt whether CHE teachers or housemasters are those best suited for this work. Indeed, at Redbank it was once almost an explicit policy to exclude them. It is argued, not without reason, that staff who are familiar with difficult and demanding children in open conditions might rapidly come to doubt the need for security. It seems that staff with no previous child-care experience adapt more easily to the demands of the task, particularly because they accept more readily ideas that the children are difficult and dangerous and that security is essential.

The 'low status' of secure unit work in the eyes of other child-care workers

seriously affects staff self-perceptions. They tend to feel misunderstood, stig.
and disadvantaged. But, contrary to this widespread belief that work in sec.
goes unrewarded, experience in closed units does confer on staff considerable care.
advantages. Of the staff who have left Redbank special unit, for example, 35 were
promoted and three are now heads or deputy heads of CHEs, a pattern similar at
Kingswood and Redhill.

The bulk of the responsibility for running the units falls on the principal or headmaster. He is the chief link between the unit and his local authority social services
departments and is also responsible to the Home Office, through the DHSS, for any
Section 53 cases that he may choose to accept. He is also finally responsible for the
selection of children to the unit but takes decisions on applicants in consultation
with other senior staff. He has to be present at all case conferences on children and
is finally responsible for the decision about whether a child is ready to leave security.

All the principals we talked with had previously been on the teaching staff of
secure units, frequently in senior positions and they usually had extensive teaching
experience in ordinary day schools. In the case of the first youth treatment centre,
the initial policy of giving a psychiatrist overall responsibility for the institution
proved unsatisfactory and he was later replaced by an experienced headmaster
from the CHE system.

In spite of the obligation to hold the children under their care in some form of
security, the heads of special units have considerable autonomy and, with some
exceptions in the case of Section 53 children, they can interpret the degree of
security needed and implement treatment programmes for children without much
external reference. It seems that provided the units fulfil the Home Office or DHSS
expectations of containing the children, all seems to be well. In the early days, the
main concern seemed to be an unwritten understanding that the children should
not cause trouble and, as far as possible, remain unnoticed by the outside world,
but recent efforts by the DHSS, particularly in the case of Section 53 children,
seem more concerned with promoting the long-term welfare of the child.

All the important decisions regarding secure unit children are negotiated between
the principal and the external authorities. The rest of his staff have very limited
decision-making responsibility. But the frequent case conferences and staff meetings
do give junior staff a semblance of power and the deputy heads and senior assistants
take responsibility for the day-to-day running of the units and the internal administration. For example, they prepare timetables, write reports, ensure that the staff
keep children's files up to date and maintain both internal and external security.
They also manage the team structures, ironing out various personal and organisational problems that staff present to them.

The clearly defined roles of teacher and house staff that now exist in open
CHEs are less delineated in special units. One housemaster stated his position
succinctly and, at the same time, highlighted one of the chief causes of friction in
the units: 'The only real difference between teachers and housemasters here is that
teachers get more money'. Naturally, because roles overlap so much there is considerable role conflict. People do not surrender their professional roles lightly and,

tends to be an over-involvement in the daily tasks that staff
care staff in the secure units often find that the caring roles which
open CHEs are much more widely shared and that as academic,
work are usually undertaken by specialists, they find themselves
ring the day. The less specialised concept of the group worker
Treatment Centres may well have important implications for
secure units in the near future.

The establishment of territorial boundaries and rights is not only of concern to care staff but is also important to all members of the secure units, whether adults or children. Indeed, little colonies are constructed as staff struggle against the surrender of autonomy inherent in the team approach. The staff find that their work as team members can violate their private and professional identities. Not only is this situation unfamiliar but it also presents problems similar to those experienced by the teachers in day schools when team teaching and integrated studies are developed.[5] Particularly problematic is having to work continuously in public. As one teacher commented: 'The most difficult thing on arrival, funnily enough, was not the boys but being on show all the time. In outside teaching your performance is private, the classroom is yours and you can do largely what you like'.

It is the care staff who express most concern about their conflicting roles of pastoral father and prison officer. They refer frequently in interviews to some of their more unenviable tasks, such as body and room searching which teachers tend to avoid. The majority of housemasters, nevertheless, feel that the relationships they enjoy with boys are not greatly affected by their dual roles, at least, not after the first few months of a boy's stay. However, those few house staff who have been professionally trained stress that they can see little relationship between their training and the tasks they face in the units and, generally, experience a much greater unease about their roles.

Teachers, on the whole, experience fewer problems in reconciling their warder role with that of enriching and stimulating the children intellectually. They tend to be largely shielded from many of the security tasks and teachers' normal controlling roles with children mean that they perceive less conflict than untrained staff. Teachers, in fact, believe themselves to hold the units together. In addition, because they come from outside the child-care system and, consequently, have little experience of difficult children, teachers find it easier to maintain stereotypes about the extreme threat to society that secure unit children pose. Teachers generally find it easy to conjure their children into anarchists, possibly to strengthen their professional position and, generally, we found that the teachers in both secure units and CHEs not only have less complimentary perspectives on the children but are also more authoritarian in their approach.

However, it was clear from our interviews that, at deeper levels, all staff find it difficult to come to terms with the demands of security. They experience considerable guilt at locking up children, an unease which varies with their backgrounds, training and the ethos of the particular units in which they worked. Naturally, the Section 53 cases become the catalysts of the deepest misgivings and it is interesting that Redbank, which contained more Section 53 cases than anywhere else, has become the most open of all the large units. Not only did the children go out more frequently than elsewhere, but they also visited the private houses of staff. This had little to do with the stated treatment programme of the unit but seemed to be the way in which staff atoned for their guilt.

Staff in all the units stress the importance of close cooperation with colleagues. They put great emphasis on the team approach although the actual organisation of this varies widely. At Redbank, Redhill and St Charles, for example, a two-team approach is operative while at Kingswood, staff rotate their working hours in a more individual way.

As many of the staff who join the units have little or no experience of the sorts of behaviour problems that the children present, the team system is particularly effective in providing initial support for the young, inexperienced member of staff during the difficult and testing period of initiation.

But, like any other system, the team approach has its disadvantages and close cooperation within one group often leads to overt antagonism towards the team that follows. Frequently, the regime of the unit alters perceptibly as teams change and the children adapt their behaviour to suit the situation. This often increases staff friction even though the development of a child's skill in reacting to different demands and personalities should be a vital part of the care programme. It is sometimes forgotten that the shift system is an institutional concept and contrasts sharply with life outside. It must remind children continuously that they are in less than a family.

Staff commitment

In our visits to the three secure units all the available staff were interviewed about their views on the work of the units and their job satisfaction.

There are clear contrasts between the perceptions of different groups of staff. Teachers, for example, are particularly concerned with the improvement of children's basic skills. They show themselves to be highly committed to all academic and control areas and feel, if anything, that the stress on these aims should be increased. Indeed, many teachers are concerned about the limited nature of the educational provision in the units and the way in which security inhibits project work and a child's independent exploration of interests. Few teachers have much previous experience of the severe educational difficulties of children and are quite unfamiliar with the low attainments and retardation in basic skills that special unit boys display. Several teachers recollect that on arrival they were shocked at the boys' backwardness and feel that this was an area in which they could make a vital contribution. Indeed, the dominant position of teachers in the units and their understandable concern with educational standards reinforces the organisational emphasis that, inevitably, strict security imposes.

Because teachers come almost entirely from non-residential backgrounds, they offer little criticism of the care provision in the institutions. They feel that the physical, emotional and spiritual care of the children is adequate, although some are uneasy about the single-sex nature of the institutions. Teachers are committed to the custodial aspect of the units, such as protecting the public and maintaining security but they do not embrace punitive perspectives on the children.

Care staff, on the other hand, tend to be much less enthusiastic about the units' contribution to the children's welfare. They resent the academic and control domination of the units which they feel puts care areas at a discount. In spite of the units' stated therapeutic orientation, care staff maintain that the daily 'school routine' hinders the development of relationships and does not really meet the primary needs of the children. They feel that the preoccupation with educational skills in the units allows others to ignore the wider, external social difficulties of the children. They maintain that the emphasis on education and control tends to justify and reinforce the hierarchical distribution of power and influence within the units.

Residential social workers are also perturbed by the relationships which the units have developed with children's parents and the imprecise criteria for the entry and release of boys, where everything tends to be judged in predominantly behavioural terms. As a group, the care staff are far less committed to the custodial stance of the units and less concerned with public safety. The older the residential worker or the more training he has received, the greater his disenchantment.

These contrasting perspectives between the care-oriented child-care workers and the educational concerns of teachers remind us of the situation that we found in the old approved schools during the late 1960s. Yet, even though both groups of staff seek in their different ways to enhance the welfare of the child, we found in our previous research that the scope of the interaction between adults and children was severely limited by a variety of constraints. Secure units are no exception to the pattern and it is not easy for staff working in such environments to develop close relationships with the children. Some of the controls over the interaction spring from the nature of residential social work itself while others spring from caring for deprived young people in a small, closed institution. In open situations, children and adults can withdraw from each other's company or, at least, distance themselves. We have, therefore, to explore these forces in much greater detail as they have clear implications for effective social work practice.

Ostensibly, the residential situation might be expected to encourage in staff a sense of well-being. Frequently they live on a campus of amenity, are generously housed, have security of tenure and enjoy precise terms of employment which should be the envy of those working with children in other residential situations. Yet many residential staff feel insecure and it is worth exploring some of the reasons.

We have noted that many of the child-care staff lack professional training. In the secure units, the domination of the teachers springs not only from their clear professionalism but also from the jaundiced view among residential social workers of education and teacher colleagues. As one care staff pithily commented, 'When we were all in school, they were at the top of the class and we were at the bottom.

They don't let you forget it either'.

If at one level the differences between care staff and others can be sharply drawn, at another, all those who work in secure units share, to a greater or less extent, a number of common problems. For example, the material benefits that accrue from residential living often have long-term disadvantages. Staff in tied houses often have large families and it means that if they buy property, they do so late on the ever-rising market. Their lifestyle is tied to the job and they are caught fast in much the same way as service families. If staff in the unit move, then they are forced to move within the residential care system, not only to maintain their living standards but because they are in a less competitive position *vis-à-vis* the outside world. Both field social workers and teachers in day schools are usually better qualified and have a width of experience which residential staff, particularly those in the special units, lack.

The special unit children also increase the sense of insecurity and failure among staff. Deprived adolescents are manipulative, attention-seeking and emotionally exhausting. As children, they give little back to those who care for them and they are extremely dependent on staff yet, at the same time, seem indifferent to them. For the adults, disappointment is built into the situation. Much that staff have to do in the special units is rejecting and custodial, relationships are difficult to establish and, in the long term, almost all the children break down and enter other institutions. Staff have to distance themselves from the children in order to survive emotionally. We know very little about providing care for deprived children in any residential situation but looking after adolescents in security is a very difficult task about which we know almost nothing. It makes utterly different demands on staff and is without the immense satisfactions that brim in other residential caring and teaching situations. Staff have not only to survive as individuals but they also have to provide treatment.

The techniques of social interaction that staff adopt in the units are those widely used in psychotherapy. Ideally, staff attempt to express a warm, accepting, uncritical attitude of interested concern in the child. Anxieties and conflicts are discussed and previous experiences are explored. It is hoped that the sharing of these feelings with an adult will relieve the child of anxiety, particularly as the adult's reaction is uncensorious and encouraging. Staff try to appreciate the child's point of view and to give him insights into his behaviour and, it is hoped, bring about change. New ways of facing difficulties and engendering committed, active participation from the child are suggested and his passive acceptance of situations is discouraged. Staff may give therapy in groups or in individual counselling and their efforts are frequently supplemented with psychiatric advice and support.

In spite of fierce allegiance to various forms of therapy across a wide range of child-care institutions, it is likely that the success with children is less related to the actual techniques of psychotherapy and more to the personalities of those offering care. Recovery is most rapid when care is provided by staff who are warm and tolerant and who can listen and empathise with the child. Indeed, a number of studies would suggest that briefly trained students and non-qualified psychotherapists are as successful as those who are more highly trained. [6] In the same way, Martin's unpublished paper on St Charles youth treatment centre demonstrates that children's behaviour is markedly affected by the operation of different staff teams. [7] Similarly, in a rather different context, success with new recruits in the armed forces seems very closely related to the personalities of their class supervisors. [8] This would suggest that the selection of staff for secure units on criteria of ability to control and teaching capabilities, rather than experience of, or preliminary training in child care, militates against the treatment aims of the units.

This form of 'treatment' arouses the strictures of sociologists and radical social workers and the reasons for this seem to us somewhat curious. [9] Presumably, furore is engendered because so much of the approach focuses on the personality development of the child and ignores the social and cultural constraints which can influence conduct. Critics would argue that difficult behaviour has to be defined as deviant and, as the meaning to the actor may be quite logical, the definition is negotiable. It may be that the theoretical basis of the treatment philosophy within child-care establishments is questionable but, when linked with improved educational opportunities and help outside, with family, friends and employment, any harm to the child is difficult to prove. Within CHEs or the secure units, the discussion of personal problems and the cultivation of relationships may have long-term benefits and, after all, these things are a widespread preoccupation of most of us at liberty. Admittedly, the child eventually emerges from the institution with perspectives that differ from radical criminologists but in this, he may be fortunate as he is more likely to be in accord with the retributive and conservative perspectives of his own social group.

Staff working with difficult children have to put their faith in some doctrine and if the religious beliefs which supported them in the early days of Redhill and Kingswood have given way to psychologically based treatment ideas, little contribution is made by research which destroys these ideas without offering viable alternatives. Recollection of the problems of the Section 53 cases should bring some hesitation to those who imagine that fixed sentences for juveniles and the abandonment of the welfare ethic would achieve so much more. Indeed, the unintended consequences of emphasising the legal rights of juveniles in the USA has led to many children staying longer in prison than would otherwise have been the case. [10]

But treatment in the units is hindered by much more critical factors than a doubtful theoretical base. As in other residential institutions, the relationship between the staff and the child world diminishes the impact of therapy. We have noted in a number of other studies that the informal norms of staff limit the nature of their contacts with the children. [11] In the case of the deprived and delinquent child, staff resist deep involvements because of the anxiety and disappointment that most of these relationships inevitably arouse. The children in the special units are, almost by definition, those with whom anything more than a superficial involvement is likely to invite considerable future hurt. But in a secure setting, deep involvements are difficult as the public nature of any interaction with the children creates a scene that is artificial and highly charged. It requires a skilled social psychologist to analyse the patterns of interaction that security thrusts on staff and children but some general facts should be noted.

Initially, the process of bargaining rewards and satisfactions as a friendship proceeds is even more one-sided in the secure units than is usual in other adult–child relationships. In the old approved schools, the stress on stimulating activities or on trade situations encouraged rapid sharing of values and interests inherent in the task and there was a tendency for these shared values between staff and children to expand into other areas. In the secure units, this is difficult because teaching is individually programmed and rather specialised and trade training plays a very small part in the units. The noteworthy success of the printing press and the very active model club in one of the units sprang from the shared activities that boys enjoyed with highly committed staff.

The negotiation of relationships is also difficult in secure settings because it has to take place in public. The way in which staff and children develop mutual relationships in a residential situation is for both parties to signal preferences for one another. In turn, each one demonstrates that they do not quite match their respective stereotypes. Inevitably, this process involves a private breaking of unofficial rules and norms of behaviour and, in some cases, even the breaching of formal edicts, such as turning a blind eye or offering an unofficial warning. All these negotiations are very delicate and require careful synchronisation. For example, consider the significance in timing, context and expectations of the move from surname to Christian name, particularly in interactions between adults and children, between those with power and those without. This is especially important in establishments with a strong formal order such as public schools, warships, prisons and monasteries. Indeed, the ways in which formal and informal worlds meet in residential institutions and the manner in which members present themselves are enormously subtle and one of the few enduring delights of residential life. [12]

Relationships may begin with little more than an exploratory conversation which fixes areas of mutual interest. The interaction will then move on to situations where each seeks the company of the other and to demonstrations of mutual partiality. This development leads to the exchange of ideas and feelings, many of which may be quite contrary to the official ideology. Public fronts become relaxed in the presence of what is cherished and signals are exchanged to indicate that this relationship is of a different sort. Indeed in residential institutions with a really explicit and elaborate formal order, avenues of making relationships are also informally signposted and are as clear as most aspects of the formal system. In such institutions, watching the progress of others and covering your own tracks preoccupies almost everyone.

Contrary to popular belief and to much sociological and social work writing, one is inclined to maintain that the more total the institution and the more differentiated the structures of power and status within it, the deeper the relationships between members of the organisation. In such situations, deviance is more pervasive and capable of infinite gradation. As deviance is frequently shared and relies on the discretion of others, the consequences of apprehension can be calamitous, hence in these conditions, trust is usually real. Above all, in such institutions relationships between high- and low-status figures, between officers and men, child and staff and, of course, between the inmates themselves are private, partial and based on mutual confidence. In the case of the secure units where everything is public, any demonstration of partiality is difficult and the selective violation of group norms in order to build up confidence is quite impossible. It means, therefore, that the relationships within the units have a curiously artificial quality.

We have little understanding of the ways in which adolescent children negotiate their relationships with each other. Frequently their conversations are distasteful to adults in phraseology, content and implications and again, much of the orientation of the child world is to gain amusement at the adults' expense. Unfortunately, in the special units, it is difficult to call into doubt the parentage of your teacher, the shape of his wife or the possibilities of his daughter if he and his colleagues are ever with you. Similarly, much that is contraband is also denied. Cigarettes, improper books, love letters, gear, all of which furnish a currency in the children's exchange system, are banned. Consequently, the shared risk-taking and cooperative defiance of the formal order that cements friendships in a wide range of other institutions cannot really develop in the secure units.

Now this may be very proper and entirely justifiable on many grounds, but it makes for extreme boredom, a boredom which is increased by the small size of the institution for not only are the children's friendship choices greatly restricted but the whole range of events is greatly limited. Secure institutions are antiseptic and lack the rich underworld that makes life tolerable for children in other open residential institutions. Indeed, the secure units could be awarded the wooden spoon across a hundred institutions for interest. Because of their small size, unrelieved scrutiny and invariable orthodoxy, they are extremely dull places either to work in or in which to be a resident child.

Deviant subcultures may be inconvenient in institutions, particularly when they manifest themselves in some spectacular way – such as a drug scandal or the elopement of the under-matron with the rugby captain – but such subcultures are highly functional for an institution's well-being and, for this reason, are largely tolerated by the formal order. So, one of the reasons why staff find work in the units frustrating and move on rapidly may be the lack of stimulation provided by working in secure units. Life in other residential institutions is often extraordinarily funny. It might be miserable or infuriating for adults but for adolescents, residence is rarely dull.

It is inevitable, therefore, that therapeutic relationships are hindered by the scrutiny and control that goes with security. The actual process of locking up boys in cells creates considerable guilt in the staff because, as an action, it violates the trusting relationships so carefully nurtured elsewhere. This is particularly the case when the children have to be locked in their rooms at night. There is an immediate denial of the relationship when the door is closed and, in many cases, the child's reaction is to beat on the door with his fists as the key is turned. Similar patterns of behaviour can be witnessed in other secure institutions such as Borstals and staff in these places stress that particular care always has to be taken not to violate inmates' territory.

Staff find the actual locking up of children extremely difficult to get used to and find it particularly embarrassing when they are showing visitors round the unit. As the deputy principal of a secure unit confessed, 'I often nip back and lock the door once visitors have moved on a bit. I don't like to remind them that they are in a maximum security place'. We suspect that the children in the units find this locking up similarly violating for, unlike children in other institutions, getting up in the morning is a sepulchral experience. The chatter, noise and high spirits of ordinary children as they wash in the early light or celebrate breakfast is just not found in secure settings. As one perspicacious housefather remarked, 'I don't think you can really achieve much with them, it's as if each day you have to start your relationship anew'.

At home, a child's departure to bed is an elaborate ritual, a parting which is protracted in its negotiation, elaborately signposted and where parents soften the ultimate rejection, particularly with younger children, by leaving doors open, lights burning and making more audible life downstairs. While parents control, albeit with difficulty, departures to bed, the child is more autonomous in getting up. Indeed, young children have an elaborate strategy of resuming relationships in the morning. Distant movement is supplemented by song and monologue, by the discreet opening of doors and a moving closer and closer to the still recumbent parent. Now, few institutions can mirror this interaction for staff control both evening rejection and morning return. But the secure units emphasise the difference with the lock. It is interesting that even in our own homes, in the security of our closest relationships, we negotiate our absences and take care to emphasise to our children that their departure is not a rejection. Of course, sending to bed without these overtures is widely used by parents as a rejecting and controlling device.

Naturally, for some staff, the guilt is more easily encompassed than for others. Indeed, the extent of the security and the necessary janitor roles come as a moment of truth for newly arrived staff. Many say that they are so rushed to keep up with everything, that the moment of locking boys away goes in a flash. 'It's like jumping in the deep end of the swimming pool or off the top board, if you thought about it, you couldn't' said one senior assistant. From a sociological viewpoint, this locking up takes on a labelling significance comparable with that crystallisation of role experienced by newly appointed therapists in a massage parlour. [13] A number of staff swiftly resign once the full implications of their job become clear and their worry is very rarely due to any incapacity and unsuitability for the task. The confusion of new staff about their roles is greatly increased by the fact that they are usually interviewed outside the unit and the extensive use of euphemisms such as 'intensive care units', 'secure suites', 'bedrooms' and 'treatment centres' not only shelters incumbent staff from reality but also baffles the uninitiated.

If new staff are somewhat confused about the implications of an intensive care unit, the children are not. Indeed, staff are often thrust into custodial roles by the children and even reminded of their custodial functions. As one housemaster commented, 'The boys are funny, if I forget to lock their doors, they peer out and say, "Watch it, you'll soon be out of a job,".' The early history of the units demonstrates that the first boy arrivals had very clear perceptions of what maximum security should be like and what their role was to be. They created a gaol and it has taken very considerable efforts by staff over the years to woo the boys into a more benign position.

The early histories of the units, when difficult boys thrust staff into an embattled position, have certainly left a legacy. Children in the units are still represented by staff as offering a potential threat. Adolescents still have to be managed, to be endlessly scrutinised and occupied and there is a constant concern about 'cover'. All this involves the constant use of as many staff as possible. Much of this scrutiny and herd management gives the claims of intensive care a hollow ring. For example, in spite of the very generous staffing ratios in the units, group management is still very much a feature of the institutional style. Everyone rises, washes and eats, even goes to the lavatory, at the same time. This is actually quite unnecessary considering the proliferation of staff, and makes rather absurd the claims that treatment in the units is individualised. Providing the children with much more choice in all these activities would not threaten institutional tranquillity because there are enough staff for almost individual attention. But it is when submerged in the group that both staff and children feel the safest.

The children are so institutionalised and so familiar with the severance of relationships that will come sooner or later, that they seem to insist on a superficial style of interaction. Indeed, much of the time, even the communication of 'problems' between children and staff and the interchanges on which the whole treatment philosophy rests, appear to have a tired, ritualistic air about them. After all, these things are what staff expect. They keep them happy and demonstrate 'progress'. Getting out naturally preoccupies most adolescents in the units and 'openness' to staff and conciliatory behaviour are, therefore, the best ways of working this system. Such a situation may lead to tranquillity in the units but the rapid disintegration of most children after release questions the depth of any conversion while in security.

In the early days, then, children were very hostile to staff on arrival at the units. They set a style of interaction which was very difficult to break down. As a principal, familiar with Kingswood in its early days, said, 'Boys really didn't give us a chance, years in other institutions had soured them. It was heartbreaking. They seemed happiest when you shouted at them. It was what they wanted'. Unfortunately, many elements of the structures developed to cope with these older, difficult boys still survive and remind us just how critical are the relationships set between staff and children in the initial stages. For example, quite unnecessarily, one unit still locked its boys in cells for an hour after lunch to provide staff with a pre-afternoon breather. At another unit, the norms of child hostility to staff were set early on by a group of intransigent girls. It has taken six years to moderate these difficulties. As a member of staff commented: 'It was extraordinary, the children arrived and everything went well for a couple of days. Then, I was off for the weekend. When I got back on Monday morning, it was us and them from the moment I got in'.

The influencing of the informal world of inmates in institutions is a difficult and subtle task but the secure units and youth treatment centres have had problems which are quite out of the ordinary. Unfortunately, these experiences begin with a difficult population and staff have to approach them without the fund of experience that accumulates over time, either individually or as a tradition within the institution as a whole. In the case of special units, the clients have become easier as the staff have grown more sophisticated. It would perhaps be wise when initiating new ventures to start with a number of less problematic adolescents. They would provide a stable and relatively benevolent informal world into which disruptive children could then be absorbed. By starting the other way round, as have all the secure units, a disruptive, hostile phalanx of adolescents, soured by repeated failures in residential care, are well placed to exploit the initial staff tensions and inexperience.

We have only a superficial knowledge about the ways in which the informal worlds of children and staff relate to each other in residential settings. In some institutions, the staff penetrate, fragment and manipulate the inmate world to mirror their own values. Such practice is best exemplified in the English public schools or in religious communities and training establishments for commissioned officers. In such places, the relationship between the holders and seekers of power is eased by the prior commitment of the novice, the status conferred by his membership and the integration of his role into wider sectional interests such as social class or particular élites. Even so, these institutions have been involved in this process for a long time and even their early histories are not without considerable vicissitudes.

In residential child-care institutions, particularly the CHEs, the task faced by staff is infinitely more difficult. The adolescent world is much more cohesive and certain values are deeply pervasive and resistant to change. It is not that the children are anti-staff or that they actually reject the values and attitudes purveyed to them; but they fail to internalise them. To obey the instructions of staff and to echo their beliefs is an effective way of getting by in the situation in which these young people find themselves. But, despite this conformity, adolescents do not covet staff roles; neither do they subscribe to staff values. They find much that is offered to them quite irrelevant to their previous experience. Staff in the CHEs, therefore, have extreme difficulties in making much impact on children's behaviour and, in the secure units, their tasks are doubly difficult.

In all the secure units, and even those smaller structures attached to open CHEs, the stress on staff in early years seems to be extreme. Staff in the end are victims of the same treatment philosophy as are the children. If staff fail something must be lacking in them. As with the children, it is rarely entertained that the institutional structure might be presenting staff with insoluble problems.

Finally, the stress on staff is greatly increased by the unsympathetic stance of those who are outside, who are opposed to security or to the approach of the youth treatment centres. Opposition may be quite justified and no doubt much in this book will add ammunition to the conflict on both sides, but the units contain some very damaged children and good staff have to be attracted to stay and work with them. It is one of the least rewarding of child-care occupations and, as such, staff engaged in it deserve maximum support. Admittedly, in some cases the 'hubris' of the arrogant claims to be providing effective treatment when everyone else was simply marking time, meant that the institutions got more than their just reward. But generally staff in all the units felt that those outside cared little about the difficulties they faced and few understood the problems peculiar to working in secure settings. Professions are not built merely by the creation of qualifications; they are also based on a sharing of values and principles and a sense of fellow feeling for colleagues. This sense of corporate identity should certainly encompass staff working in the secure units or youth treatment centres.

Working in the units is an unenviable task. It is easy from a safe distance to highlight the deficiencies in staffing patterns and failure in relationships but more difficult to provide something constructive. However, we would stress that the need for training of all staff working in secure units is particularly pressing. Attendance on training courses which have little expertise in security is less important than giving staff the widest experience possible of other institutions which deal with difficult adolescents. They need particularly to visit the open adolescent units of mental hospitals, drug addiction centres and the adolescent unit at places like Broadmoor. They ought also to spend a number of placements in local remand centres and Borstals and a visit to a youth treatment centre would also be very beneficial. This would do much to diminish their anxiety and lead to less scrutiny in their regimes. [14]

The units at the moment are very isolated, inward-looking and they inevitably feel beleaguered. We should remember that the units are as much a product of the child-care system as are its candidates. Staff are trying to advance our knowledge and practice with some difficult children and they should receive support and encouragement from the system as a whole.

Notes

[1] For a full discussion of the studies which have been undertaken see S. Millham, R. Bullock and P. Cherrett, *After Grace – Teeth*, London, Human Context Books, Chaucer Publishing Company, 1975, chap. 11. See also R. Lambert, S. Millham and R. Bullock, 'The informal social system', in R. K. Brown (ed.), *Knowledge, Education and Cultural Change*, London, Tavistock, 1973, pp. 297-316.

[2] T. and P. Morris, *Pentonville*, London, Routledge and Kegan Paul, 1963; S. Cohen and L. Taylor, *Psychological Survival*, Harmondsworth, Penguin, 1972 and E. Goffman, *Asylums*, New York, Doubleday, 1961.

[3] S. Millham, R. Bullock and K. Hosie, 'On violence in community homes', in N. Tutt (ed.), *Violence*, London, HMSO, 1976, pp. 126-65.

[4] See discussion in *Financial Incentives for Staff of Special Units*, Kingswood Special Unit, Sept. 1969.

[5] See, for example, M. D. Shipman, 'Innovation in schools' in J. Walton (ed.), *Curriculum Organization and Design*, London, Ward Lock Educational, 1971 and 'The role of the teacher in selected innovative schools', in *The Changing Role of the Teacher and its Implications*, Paris, Organisation for Economic Cooperation and Development, 1972.

[6] See M. Argyle, *The Psychology of Interpersonal Behaviour*, Harmondsworth, Penguin, 1967.

[7] Unpublished paper by Dr D. N. Martin, clinical psychologist.

[8] Personal communication with officers at HMS *Raleigh* about survey undertaken there.

[9] See, for example, P. Bean, *Rehabilitation and Deviance*, London, Routledge and Kegan Paul, 1976.

[10] See cases quoted by Bean in *Rehabilitation and Deviance*, op. cit.

[11] See S. Millham et al., *After Grace – Teeth*, op. cit.

[12] See discussion in R. Lambert et al., 'The informal social system', op. cit.

[13] See A. J. Verlade, 'Becoming prostituted', *British Journal of Criminology*, vol. XV, 1975, pp. 251–63.

[14] For a full discussion of models of staff support, see M. Hoghugi and S. Nethercott, *Troubled and Troublesome*, Aycliffe Studies of Problem Children, 1977, pp. 59–60.

11   The effects of security

Earlier in this book, we noted that secure provision was originally set up as a safety valve for other schools, an unenviable task thrust upon it by enduring and complex pressures from within the residential child-care system. But grand titles help to conceal doubtful origins and most secure units have increasingly presented themselves as offering intensive care facilities. Can these claims be justified and what sort of an impact does a stay in security have on children?

Because of the small number of girls in security and the difficulties of doing research at the youth treatment centre, we cannot discuss the effects of security on girls. Neither have we much evidence on the consequences of short stays for boys and girls in small secure units or lock-ups. However, we can explore the impact of a long stay in security on boys in a number of ways. These are: the commitment they display towards institutional aims, the psychological consequences of isolation, the social and educational benefits of security and, particularly important, what happens to them after release.

Boys' responses to security

An investigation into the attitudes of children in security is not an easy task. Boys in the special units are highly volatile; some are anxious to answer everything in record time, others more inclined to make paper aeroplanes while one or two dictated aloud the answers for all to hear. The conditions were not ideal for objective data collection. In addition, one or two of the boys in the unit were in a highly distressed condition at the time of our visit and their answers were clearly coloured by this.

The small number of respondents also prevents any rigorous statistical analysis of the data, particularly as the replies of new arrivals or others in a distressed state had to be excluded. There was also the additional problem that boys were institutionally experienced and familiar with form filling. Any questions would savour of yet another assessment and the results that we might have obtained would probably reflect a façade which boys felt it wise to present. But, as we intended to stay in the units for a considerable period, we would be able to talk with each boy quite frequently, both on his own and in a group.

Whatever the merits of this approach, we obtained results which corresponded closely with the replies offered us at Kingswood in 1969 when we had to use a more systematic approach. [1] The boys at two of the units were, generally, highly committed and saw the help which they were being offered as tangible and useful. They spoke favourably about their relations with adults. At a third establishment, however, the boys were more critical.

142

It can be maintained that there is little value in exploring boys' expressed opinions about their residential experience. Critics would suggest that the things boys say in interviews are only secondary institutional responses and these are often symptomatic of much deeper personality problems.[2] For example, deprived children may be conciliatory on the surface but this hides considerable anger, isolation, fear and suspicion. Nevertheless, the commitment expressed by boys to us seemed genuine and, if nothing else, it was real to them. This is, at least, a reward for the considerable efforts of staff.

The task of research is to be critical and often the recipients of sociological inquiry find it negative and so react accordingly. But any investigation should recognise the achievements of residential care when they are manifest. To gain any degree of commitment and a positive response from the unpromising material that arrives in the special units is a considerable achievement. As with the better schools in the old approved school system, boys' failure after release was not due to any lack of staff efforts with them within the institution.

There is some danger in making *a priori* assumptions that security will alienate young people more than open environments and we need to be much more open-minded and accept that children's commitment to security will vary in much the same way as it does to open CHEs. If security is linked with a caring ethos which the child accepts as beneficial, then the secure units will win high commitment from inmates. If, on the other hand, security does little more than conceal problems and offer boys very little in exchange for the deprivations of liberty then the situation, as we saw in the opening chapters, can be explosive.

Our comments are based on the replies of 58 boys who had already been at Redbank, Redhill and Kingswood special units for over two months at the time of our visit. This figure includes 10 who have committed grave offences and who stay for longer periods than the rest. Methodologically, the approach has weaknesses and the further away one sits from boys in secure units, the easier it is to see its faults.

There is little doubt that the majority of boys, 65 per cent, were fearful of the future when arriving at the special units. Only 8 per cent expected anything pleasant and most of these were at Kingswood. The boys who had committed grave offences were particularly gloomy about their future prospects (see Table 11.1).

Table 11.1
Boys' recollections of their initial expectations (figures are percentages)

	Ordinary admissions	Grave offenders
Unfavourable	65	90
Indifferent	27	10
Favourable	8	0
	N = 48	10

The majority of boys were distressed by the prospect of being denied freedom for several months. While almost all the boys we talked with said the experience of being locked up depressed them, their fearful expectations of the units were soon dispelled by the efforts of staff to befriend them. Many boys said that staff concern helped them during the early period when weeks dragged by and the first leave seemed a mirage. Throughout their stay, few boys claimed to have received much support from other boys, a pattern which echoes in a more pronounced way the general isolation from peers which characterises the deprived child. A general indifference to other boys seems to be the rule in the inmate world although clear exceptions are noticeable. For example, the coloured boys at one unit formed a distinct sub-group as did the grave offenders at another. When we asked boys what they had gained from their stay in the units, 'relations with adults' were viewed as far more significant than friendship with other young people. Boys' perceptions of the benefits covered a wide range of provision including the teaching, sport and activities, care and the opportunity to sort themselves out, although the long-stay offenders did not echo this last opinion. Unexpectedly, boys also frequently mentioned the greater 'freedom' offered by the units once they had settled in and earned privileges. These results are shown in Table 11.2.

Table 11.2
Boys' assessments of benefits gained from their experience (figures are percentages)

	Ordinary admissions	Grave offenders
Relations with adults	75	80
Relations with peers	31	60
Teaching, instruction	69	80
Activities, sport	54	70
Clear of trouble, worry	69	30
Greater freedom	58	30
	N = 48	10

Just over 40 per cent of the boys informed us that they had enjoyed the whole of their stay in the units. They said that they had made progress and had, at last, arrived in a place that cared for them and offered them something useful. Only a quarter expressed an unqualified dislike of their experience, although this proportion is considerably higher at some units than others. The remainder oscillated in their views, mentioning periods of enjoyment following weeks of depression and despair. The grave offenders were more hesitant than the others and at the time of our visits, half were discontented. It seemed to be their long sojourn in an ambience where the turnover of other children is rapid that upset them rather than the actual regime of the unit. Boys' replies can be summarised as in Table 11.3.

Boys' views on their unit experiences vary. But, generally, the main areas for boys' complaints are the extent of time spent alone, long periods in the classroom, insufficient home leaves and a lack of visits from family and friends. They perceive the experience as custodial but not particularly punitive and feel that they are progressing educationally as well as receiving adequate pastoral care.

Table 11.3
Boys' enjoyment of their stay (figures are percentages)

	Ordinary admissions	Grave offenders
Unqualified enjoyment	44	10
Happy now but not initially	8	40
Increasingly unhappy	15	20
Indifferent, bearable	6	10
Unqualified unhappiness	27	20
	N = 48	10

Our material suggests that boys make considerable improvements in basic educational skills. Naturally, gains in educational attainment depend on the extent of boys' backwardness on arrival and the length of time they stayed in the units but in a context where boys are physically very well cared for and where they are obliged to be in class daily, they do make rapid improvement in basic educational skills. Whether this educational emphasis militates against improvement in other areas, hinders treatment or, at wider theoretical levels, is of any use, cannot be explored here and some comments on these issues have already been made in the preceding chapter.

However, a number of criticisms still apply in much the same way as they did in the old approved schools. If efforts in basic educational skills are considerable in the units, the range of educational experience made available to the children is very limited. No unit can provide the variety of educational stimulation that is available in a good comprehensive school. The suggestion that these boys, as persistent truants, never used good facilities when they were available does not justify present deprivations. Indeed, a number of boys in the units have good day school records, particularly some Section 53 cases. If Dartmoor prison can act as a leading adult education centre and Wakefield can provide the stimulation of Open University courses, the secure units should also be saying something significant from an educational point of view, particularly when this contribution seems to be so highly prized by the majority of staff. It is, in many ways, a reproach to the system as a whole, particularly the old approved schools and their successors, the CHEs, that they offer so little of educational interest. In spite of the many thousands of backward boys that have passed through the system and in spite of the struggle to maintain the nomenclature 'schools', those wishing to see remedial education at its best still have to visit the army.

While the adolescents are in the care of the unit, their difficult behaviour is moderated. Few of the boys manage to break out of the units and in a relatively short time, about two months, the majority are able to cope with journeys outside or visits home without untoward incident. Success is the most rapid with the neurotic absconder; these boys quieten down once they are unable to run away from difficulties and cannot avoid contact with others. It is very unlikely that their problems could be approached in unsatisfactory CHEs because these neurotic children refuse to stay. Aggressive boys and those subject to extreme changes of mood, on the other hand, seem to fare less well. While outbursts and conflicts are rare in secure units, this control is only achieved as a result of skilled manipulation by staff of potentially threatening situations. Violent boys may, therefore, be counselled and jollied along but their deeper difficulties remain unsolved. Indeed, the positive responses of children which we have noted, such as the educational and social gains boys make during their stay in security, may mask deeper difficulties.

Psychological effects of security

There is a considerable debate over the psychological effects of living for long periods in maximum security. Cohen and Taylor's book, *Psychological Survival*, which describes life in 'A' wing of Durham prison (the maximum security wing) aroused a variety of responses. [3] It was greeted with euphoria by the sociologists, scepticism by the inmates of secure wings and understandable hostility by the Home Office.

The work follows the familiar paths trod by Clemmer, Sykes and Cressey, parallels much of the work on total institutions, such as asylums and concentration camps, and illustrates its argument with a wealth of personal recollections from people faced with extreme deprivation. Although Cohen and Taylor's writing is acknowledged to be partial, unsympathetic to the controlling authorities and iconoclastic, we have found some of its insights very relevant to children in security. Naturally, the situation of boys in the secure units is less extreme than that of adult prisoners under close confinement at Durham.

Taylor and Cohen make much of the problems of coping with passing time in an environment where all the signposts familiar in the outside world are removed. This was discernible among the children in the secure units who seemed to find it very difficult to recollect how long they had been in the unit, what season of the year they arrived and who entertained unrealistic ideas of when and how they would emerge. The authors of *Psychological Survival* also explore in detail the problems of making friends in an environment where there is little choice of companions and where the negotiations of friendship are much inhibited. They argue that companionship remains superficial because prisoners protect themselves from the hurt inflicted on them by the abrupt severance of close relationships. There is a policy in prison of moving long-term prisoners at regular intervals. We have already commented elsewhere that this characterises many of the relationships between children in the units and between children and the staff that shelter them.

Taylor and Cohen explore in greater detail the consequences of public living. Using the concepts of Westin, they distinguished four states of privacy: solitude, intimacy, anonymity and reserve. These writers and many others argue that all these elements of privacy are important for psychological health. The writers define 'solitude' as the state of being alone or unobserved. 'Intimacy' refers to the type of privacy sought by two or more people who wish to achieve maximum personal affinity. 'Anonymity' refers to the seeking and achievement of freedom from identification and observation in public places, while 'reserve' is defined as a person's ability not to reveal certain aspects of himself that are intimate or shameful. Now it is clear that the demands of maximum security violate all these needs. Despite the benevolence of the regimes exercised in the special units, in this respect the child in security experiences as much control and deprivation as the inmates of Durham gaol. In fact, because of the expressive involvements of staff which we have noted elsewhere in this study, there are even fewer areas of privacy accorded to the children in the units than are enjoyed by adult prisoners. For example, in prison the officers are not concerned with the moral and spiritual states of detainees; neither are they preoccupied with their sexual proclivities or their deviant aspirations. But with the children in the special units a conformity to staff values and the adoption of conciliatory behaviour in a wide range of areas is demanded in a way that would be most unfamiliar to inmates of an adult prison. Neither in prison are ostensible demonstrations of commitment and 'progress' linked with chances of parole. However, there is far less evidence among boys in the special units that this constant invasion of privacy leads to the bizarre behaviour, to the mysticism and extreme withdrawal that Cohen and Taylor document for adult offenders.

If we remind ourselves of the wide variety of backgrounds and presenting behaviour of the children in the units, then of particular interest is Cohen and Taylor's finding that serious offenders, when isolated in a claustrophobic wing, greatly fear contamination from other prisoners. Inmates at Durham are particularly careful about association with those convicted of crimes of extreme violence or of a sexual nature. We have already noticed the tendency of Section 53 cases to cluster together, but it may be less the result of fellow feeling than their general unacceptability to other boys in the units. It is also true that, in turn, Section 53 boys reject the younger and more immature children in the unit as 'little nutters'. Much of this fragmentation of the inmate world into competing interest groups is noted by Taylor and Cohen. It leads them to share our questioning of the cohesion and hostile orientation of the inmate social system in penal establishments – doubts which are amply supported by the positive disposition of boys to the aims of the units just described.

Naturally, much of Taylor and Cohen's material could only have been gained by a very long association with adult prisoners, by their overt identification with them and by a ruthless manipulation of the privileged situation in which they found themselves. We could not duplicate these advantages and therefore cannot share their sensitive insights into the deeper anxieties of long-term prisoners. For example, we know little of boys' increasing sense of isolation, their sense of unreality of the outside world, the relentless destruction of identity and the severe sexual anxieties that, it is suggested, long-term prisoners experience.

But, of course, Taylor and Cohen's findings are not left undisputed. The sweep of their perspectives inevitably means that the empirical brushwork is open to question. It is difficult to reconcile their vivid descriptions of deprivation with the findings of clinical psychologists who worked as part of their team, for a careful study by Bolton, Smith, Heskin and Bannister of the effects of security on long-term prisoners reached conclusions that were by no means as alarming.[4] The tests administered, described fully in a number of papers, measured changes in the intelligence, the abilities, personality and attitudes of the men during long stays in security. Analysis revealed no evidence of psychological deterioration. On the contrary, verbal intelligence showed a significant increase between first and second tests and there was a marked reduction in inmate hostility. These improvements were associated with increasing emotional maturity. The psychologists state in summary:

> The results of the longitudinal analysis offer little support for the ideas that long-term imprisonment is associated with psychological deterioration, as assessed by a large battery of psychometric tests. Intelligence remained intact and hostility declines over the test–retest period. These results ... suggest that imprisonment may sometimes be associated with beneficial effects which are rarely, if ever, discussed.

If at adult levels the effects of security are still a matter of academic dispute, in spite of careful and contrasting studies, it is impossible for us to be more specific about the consequences of a spell in security for children. Our research brief was wider and more concerned with the process of arrival in security. The above studies, however, should make us extremely cautious in chronicling too readily the deleterious effects of imprisonment. However, in fairness to Cohen and Taylor, they have attempted the much more difficult task of exploring the effects of imprisonment in areas which are very resistant to careful testing by psychologists. The authors would also maintain that a prisoner's psychological deterioration is not so important as his *belief* that it is happening.

However, in the case of boys in the secure units we can only repeat the general consensus of those working with them and of the five psychiatrists that frequently visit the units. In addition, the effects of security on adolescents were discussed at a conference of the Association for the Psychiatric Study of Adolescents where there was a general agreement among many psychiatrists on the psychological consequences of security for young people.[5]

It is generally agreed that for boys who stay for a short period in security, that is up to six months, the psychological effects are minimal. Indeed, the constraints put upon a boy's disruptive behaviour may lessen his anxiety and his acceptance by sympathetic adults may improve his self-image and diminish his feelings of rejection and isolation. Also, we have already noted that boys respond positively to the education and caring efforts of staff.

However, there is also general agreement that the deleterious effects of security increase markedly with time. Boys who spend long periods in security run the risk of institutionalisation, of overdependence on particular adults and of a withdrawal from the outside world. For example, a homeless boy was encouraged to spend his summer leave from the unit at a nearby children's home. On his first morning he did not come down to breakfast and the matron presumed that he was sleeping in. When finally she looked in on him towards lunchtime, he was lying fully clothed on the bed. He had been waiting for hours in his unlocked room to be released and given orders to come out. Staff also comment that boys' behaviour remains immature because they are isolated from models provided by older adolescents. Naturally, the definition of what constitutes a 'long period' in security differs considerably. For example, Redhill and Redbank would suggest that anything in excess of nine months to a year was detrimental to a child, while at Kingswood and St Charles 18 months to two years in security is viewed with equanimity. But there is unanimity in that staff and psychiatrists maintain the long stays in security of Section 53 cases, some of whom remain three or four years in the units before moving on to prison, must do damage. In fact it is the boys who linger long in security who cause the staff gravest anxiety. As one housemaster said, 'I am worried when I see a 16-year-old playing with soldiers and happily bargaining with young-sters for sweets. They stay little kids longer in here'. A principal, also, echoed his fears:

> I don't know much about child development but I feel these boys are really missing out. There are no girls, no discos, no Saturday nights, no chip shops and, for some lads, this is going to last a long time. After all, men in prison have something to look back on and their identities are pretty well established. But these boys are still trying to make it in every way, shutting them up for long terms can't help.

So far these findings are encouraging. The majority of the boys in the secure units are not hostile to their experience. The units confer some physical and edu-cational benefits and some of the boys' more extreme patterns of behaviour, such as compulsive absconding and extreme withdrawal, are modified. It is also likely that a short stay in security does little psychological damage, with the reservation that some Section 53 cases probably stay too long in the units for psychological health. In the short term, the units also succeed in the tasks for which they were designed. They contain the disruptive boy and control his aggression and running away. They protect some children from themselves, particularly the suicidal or sexually vulnerable and, above all, restore something of their faith in adults and in the care they exercise. Can the units do more? Is there any evidence that they have any lasting effect on the difficult child?

Effects of security on boys' post-release careers

The ability of residential institutions to modify boys' delinquent behaviour is still a much debated issue. While our own studies, along with those of Tutt and Sinclair, leave little doubt that boys' behaviour *within* the residential setting is much influenced by the prevailing social climate, the *long-term* effects on subsequent behaviour in the outside world are less clear. [6] It is not difficult to establish differences in the success of various treatment approaches but such findings frequently lose their significance when the nature of the clientele is accounted for. Some institutions shelter more difficult clients than others and their success will be influenced accordingly.

The most recent exercise by Clarke and Cornish is unduly pessimistic. When discussing their research at Kingswood, they maintain that whatever the experience, residential care has no measurable effects on delinquency. [7] Our own studies and those of Dunlop are less categoric. [8] Although no dramatic variations in the long-term effectiveness of different approaches were found, small and significant effects were established. It is clear, for example, that in a community home a delinquent boy with few convictions stands less chance of being in further trouble than his contemporary with a large number of convictions. However, although the odds are good for him, the chances of such a boy being still out of trouble 12 months after release from school still varied from 42 per cent in schools P, M, N and G to 62 per cent in other schools (Q, K, F and E) in our previous study. It would be unwise to claim dramatic results for residential treatment but we would reject the suggestion that residential experiences are completely ineffective. Indeed, in the context of normal education, we have demonstrated the considerable benefits that can accrue to children from a boarding experience.

The boys in the special units are, as we have shown, not among the best candidates for long-term behaviour modification. We saw that they display characteristics of high risk adolescents in that they have usually been delinquent since an early age and come from home backgrounds where there was considerable dislocation. Their chequered histories in previous institutions also increase their vulnerability. We have noted that many boys arriving in the secure units are already well experienced in residential living and a number are quite familiar with life in secure establishments such as those run by the prison department. While only a few of the boys are institutionalised in the clinical sense of displaying pathological neuroses, nearly all of them are institutionally experienced and in most cases their absconding and allied offences have established a delinquent identity. They have also developed effective techniques for avoiding stress. One would not, therefore, expect great changes in behaviour to follow a stay in a secure unit.

When we undertake a follow-up study of boys selected for the three large special units, we find that the results can be used to justify almost any point of view, depending on how success is defined. Many boys, for example, are transferred direct from the units to other establishments such as open schools or special hospitals. Thus, the units may claim considerable 'success' in helping boys mature, an improvement which facilitates such a move. On the other hand, some of these transfers are unintended and follow serious misbehaviour either while the boy is on leave or inside the unit. Thus 'success', never an easy concept to define with young offenders, becomes even more controversial in any discussions of the effects of security.

During our research at Redhill and Kingswood we were able to follow through all the boys who had been released from the units but, at Redbank, the resources available only permitted us to study our 1971–72 sample of 47 boys. Fortunately, the careers of the first 91 boys admitted between October 1966 and July 1969 had been investigated by David Martin and his figures in combination with our own provide a study group of nearly 55 per cent of all boys who have passed through this unit. [9] The subsequent histories of all these boys in the two years following their release from the units were as shown in Figure 11.1

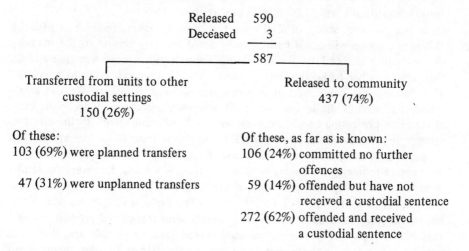

Released   590
Deceased   3

—————————— 587 ——————————

Transferred from units to other custodial settings
150 (26%)

Released to community
437 (74%)

Of these:
103 (69%) were planned transfers

47 (31%) were unplanned transfers

Of these, as far as is known:
106 (24%) committed no further offences
59 (14%) offended but have not received a custodial sentence
272 (62%) offended and received a custodial sentence

Fig. 11.1   Subsequent histories of boys following release from secure units

We can see immediately that 26 per cent of the boys are transferred direct from special units to other residential institutions such as open CHEs, Borstals and mental hospitals. The figure is particularly high at Redhill (32 per cent), contrasting with only 16 per cent at Kingswood. Two-thirds of these transfers are planned, in the sense that the transfer is deliberate and said to be in the boy's interest, whereas the remaining cases consist of boys who abscond on leave or break out of the unit and commit offences. This last group can be said to have been lost prematurely, that is, before the time of their intended release. Kingswood is something of an exception, however, transferring fewer boys than Redbank or Redhill and only ever having lost one boy prematurely, a pattern which may reflect the longer stay experienced by boys at Kingswood.

Estimates of the 'success' of special units will, of course, be influenced by this group of transfers. They offer a good example of the dubious nature of simple statistics when applied to high-risk children. If we view transfer as due to an inability on the part of the institution to hold on to a client or ameliorate his situation, then the figures just provided increase the gloom. However, if we adopt a more medical perspective and view these boys as graduating to further treatment, we can accept that they have been successfully handled in the initial stages. Depending on the reader's perspective, this sizeable contingent will influence his interpretation of success rates.

While such statistical manipulation can create a little dust, it fails to obscure the view displayed in these figures. Clearly, few of the boys released to the outside world stay clear of trouble and the majority undergo a further spell of residential care, usually in a Borstal. About 25 per cent of those discharged stay out of trouble for at least two years while over 60 per cent go quickly to renewed institutional experiences. Of this 60 per cent, we found that four-fifths were inside another custodial institution within 24 months of leaving.

In our previous study of CHEs we identified the characteristics of high-risk children, a group which we have already noted are very similar to the majority of secure unit clients. [10] We found that these high-risk boys were more likely than others either to be transferred prematurely or to break down after release. This pattern was more marked in some schools than in others. We also established that schools displaying high staff and pupil commitment were the most effective in preventing recidivism even with high-risk adolescents. In the effective schools, 7 per cent of the most vulnerable boys were transferred prematurely and 42 per cent of leavers were not convicted of any further offences during the two-year period following their release. In the ineffective schools, however, the results were worse. Twenty-two per cent of the high-risk boys were transferred and only 23 per cent did not offend after leaving. The findings that 26 per cent of the boys who have been admitted to closed units were transferred prematurely and that only 24 per cent of those released stayed clear of trouble are, therefore, important, for they indicate that secure accommodation is no more successful in modifying the behaviour of high-risk children than were the CHEs of our earlier study. This does not mean that secure units are completely ineffective as 28 per cent of the group studied did not undergo a further custodial experience. But this evidence gives little support to the notion that a spell in security will diminish criminal behaviour.

A stable, happy unit will achieve transfer and reconviction rates that are similar to those obtained with high-risk children by open CHEs. However, evidence from Kingswood, Rossie, Sedbury and St Charles suggest that in times of crisis, the reconviction and transfer rates of secure units soar, so confirming our earlier suggestions that the regime of the establishment is by no means insignificant in influencing boys' behaviour, even if in the end the majority fail.

Conclusion

In this chapter we have looked at the impact on adolescents of a stay in security. In spite of the survival of many custodial elements in the regimes of secure units, the boys are not hostile to or deeply alienated from the efforts of staff. Indeed, they are comparatively responsive to the provision. We have commented briefly on some of the educational and expressive contributions of the units. The psychological consequences of a period in security do not seem deleterious, at least in the short term. While these advantages should not be underestimated, the rapid return to custody of the majority of boys released provides little comfort. Security offers an expensive and very short respite from the age-old problems presented by high-risk boys. It certainly offers no solution.

Notes

[1] See S. Millham, R. Bullock and P. Cherrett, *A Comparative Study of Eighteen Boys' Approved Schools which Compares their Stylistic Variety and the Commitment of Boys and Staff*, Dartington Social Research Unit, 1972 for the 1969 Kingswood figures.

[2] See, for example, R. Balbernie's introduction to S. Millham, R. Bullock and P. Cherrett, *After Grace – Teeth*, London, Human Context Books, Chaucer Publishing Company, 1975.

[3] S. Cohen and L. Taylor, *Psychological Survival*, Harmondsworth, Penguin, 1972.

[4] N. Bolton, F. V. Smith, K. J. Heskin and P. A. Bannister, 'Psychological correlates of long-term imprisonment', *British Journal of Criminology*, vol. XVI, 1976, pp. 38–47. Other articles by these authors on this theme are found in the same journal, vol. XIII, 1973, pp. 312–31; vol. XIV, 1974, pp. 150–7 and 359–68. Quote is from the first article, p. 46.

[5] See Proceedings of the 1976 Conference at Edinburgh.

[6] S. Millham et al., *After Grace – Teeth*, op. cit., I. Sinclair, *Hostels for Probationers*, London, HMSO, 1971 and N. Tutt, 'Recommitals of juvenile offenders', *British Journal of Criminology*, vol. XVI, 1976, pp. 385–8.

[7] D. B. Cornish and R. V. G. Clarke, *Residential Treatment and its Effects*, London, HMSO, 1975.

[8] S. Millham et al., *After Grace – Teeth*, op. cit. and A. Dunlop, *The Approved School Experience*, London, HMSO, 1975.

[9] *Statistics to 31.7.69*, Redbank special unit, 1969.

[10] S. Millham et al., *After Grace – Teeth*, op. cit.

**Part V
Other considerations**

Part V
Other Considerations

12 Alternatives to security

Is maximum security the only answer to the persistently disruptive child? We have traced the ways in which present ideas on security have developed. We have illustrated the difficulties in selecting children for security and suggested that other perspectives on their difficult behaviour should be entertained. It is also clear that alternatives to secure provision would have little difficulty in matching the success rates of boys released from the special units. But can such alternatives be found?

Initially, the most important alternative to secure provision is to improve the services we already have. This is not the cliché it sounds for it is quite clear that almost all the candidates for secure places are casualties of the care system. This is also true of many Section 53 cases who have demonstrated distress from an early age. If social work services would only acquaint themselves with the considerable research consensus that exists on what creates a difficult child and what maintains his problem career, then our preventive efforts in child care would be more sophisticated. In the long term, the demands for security would diminish.

Our knowledge of child maladjustment is not sparse. We know that the early onset of criminality and its frequency have very important prognosis implications for the child. We also know that high-risk children are identifiable almost in infancy. The consequences of early separation are well documented. We know that a proportion of children in residential establishments could be cared for by providing the appropriate resources in the community and that the needs of the majority of children in CHEs make the care of the very difficult minority impossible. We are also aware that taking into residential care is fraught with long-term consequences for children. Once the child has been taken into a residential institution we know that the transfer of highly vulnerable children from one placement to another is likely to be detrimental. Our earlier studies of the approved schools system and more recently a number of CHEs, linked with the evidence from the secure units, clearly suggests that accepting back the prodigal provides more effective treatment than transferring him. A more general awareness among social workers of these simple facts would eventually do much to diminish the demand for secure places.

This emphasis on improved social work practice, both field and residential, as an alternative to security should be linked with something much more difficult, that is, the need to change our attitudes towards the deviant behaviour of children. We should, at least, entertain the possibility that children's persistently difficult conduct is a reflection of the stresses put on them by our care programmes. Unfortunately, people find it very difficult to accept that our interventions may actually create the very problems we struggle manfully to modify.

The resistance to these ideas is strengthened by an intellectual inheritance which is heavily weighted with specious notions of original sin. There is an irresistible continuity of perspective from the religious and biological explanations of offending behaviour and present psychological preoccupations. The relentless chase of personality traits and states in the child and the identification of his deeper needs allow those engaged in rehabilitation and liberal reform conveniently to forget that deviance is socially defined. Our welfare preoccupations need raise no questions about children's rights or the criminal law, except possibly the Section 53 cases, or even be particularly interested in the child's crime itself, as it can be viewed as a symptom. However, our studies of aggression and absconding have tried to suggest that the definitions of this behaviour are negotiable and that complex patterns of social interaction can provide as adequate an explanation of the deviance as more orthodox investigations into the children's background and personality.

As we seek alternatives to security for problematic children, we should also remind ourselves that institutions, irrespective of their clientele, differ markedly in the difficult behaviour they experience and the ways in which it is approached. Unfortunately, residential establishments are extremely resistant to the idea that success rates on release, absconding and violence, premature transfer rates and the low commitment of children to institutional aims have anything to do with the regimes they run. But such a realisation would do much to provide an alternative to secure accommodation, particularly when the local authority social services department realises that each application for security is likely to be an indictment of the care already provided.

We are certainly not alone in hopefully lighting candles at the shrine of improved child care. But some must work while others pray and we have to ask whether there are practical alternatives to the various forms of security which we have laid out in Chapter 9. Several establishments shelter in open conditions candidates already earmarked for maximum security or attempt to help young people removed from custody. We shall illustrate these alternative approaches to the difficult and persistent offender by briefly glancing at some of them.

The approaches we shall describe are alternatives to the long-stay secure treatment settings which have been the main focus of this book. The five examples will fall into two distinct groups: those which seek to prevent a deterioration of the child's status and those which provide a theoretically based treatment programme. By status deterioration we mean the familiar Rake's Progress through a series of increasingly custodial and punitive settings. Theoretically based treatment programmes, on the other hand, include approaches based on a coherent theory of behaviour modification such as a therapeutic community or various types of therapy.

First, let us describe a project designed to improve the care of persistent absconders at Headlands School, Penarth, a CHE for junior boys. A grey, crumbling hotel has passed, by way of a sea school, to house 45 very deprived and delinquent boys from the South Wales towns. The National Children's home, a charity organisation, now treasures as a school a relic of an ambitious Victorian seaside resort that unfortunately forgot the need for a beach.

The school had kindly cooperated in our research into the approved schools and is one of a group of junior schools referred to in *After Grace - Teeth*. [1] When we visited it in 1969 and 1971, it ran a benign regime, closely following the family group style and was slightly above average in its success with boys after release. However, the school suffered from a high absconding rate and consequently transferred a number of boys early to other approved schools. Since the Act of 1969 and the raising of the school leaving age a little later, the upper age limit of the school has risen from 15 to 16 years.

Although absconding from Headlands had always been high, it reached a peak in the early 1970s when the school endured one major absconding epidemic after another. Although quite a number of children, about two a year, had been transferred to secure units, the philosophy of the National Children's Home made the idea of locking up difficult children unpalatable. The school tried hard to contain its disruptive children without much success, and clearly something had to be done. The immediate neighbourhood is an exclusive residential area, allowing executives and administrators a refuge from Cardiff on the one side, without having to embrace the candyfloss horrors of Barry Island on the other. But the boys, as they embarked for a run to Splott and Tiger Bay, found ample provision for their safari by plundering the cavernous villas overlooking the sea. Thus, the local reputation of the school, like the foreshore, was at rock bottom.

A secure unit at the school was put forward as a solution to the problems but discussion with staff and the National Children's Home ruled out the possibility of such provision. As the principal commented:

> It was clear that whatever we set up, it would have to be non-secure because locking up children would be contrary to the policy of the National Children's Home and because having secure accommodation would make us very liable to the responsibilities and problems that we are not prepared to accept. We just haven't the skilled staff needed to run a small secure unit.

On 30 June 1975, a group of boys were admitted to an open intensive care unit called Uppercliff. Located in a block some 300 yards from the main school, the building was originally intended as a working boys' hostel. With its own catering facilities, recreation space and classroom, it was well suited to the task of sheltering very vulnerable children. It was intended to have seven care staff and one teacher, but it took longer than expected to build up a suitable staffing pattern.

So far the new unit has admitted 20 children; it takes a maximum of 8 at any one time. Of the 12 who have left, 5 have been successful, returning either to the main school or to home. Another 6 have been transferred to CHEs, all of which are open. The remaining boy was transferred to St Charles youth treatment centre for, although his absconding pattern was greatly modified, his bizarre offences suggested that he needed specialised care.

The average age of boys in the unit is 12 years one month (they range in age from 11 to 14 years). This is rather younger than the closed unit boys. However, the average IQ is 84, ranging from 66 to 105 and this is noticeably lower than for boys in the special units. The ages at which boys at Uppercliff were committed to care ranged from 6 years to 12 years and the care histories of the boys display the familiar pattern of persistent running away from home or school, with associated motoring offences, and violent outbursts in other institutions.

The average number of previous placements for Uppercliff boys is five. The children tend to have as many children's home placements as do special unit boys but, naturally, have spent less time in CHEs. Because boys arrive at a younger age than those entering closed units, they have not travelled so far along institutional corridors. Similarly, the Uppercliff children have fewer offences and court appearances. Many have, in fact, committed a large number of offences, often while absconding from children's homes, but because of their age, few of these crimes have been dealt with by juvenile courts. Family backgrounds share in all cases the characteristics of other deprived children's home circumstances. For example, only three out of ten boys lived with both natural parents. But all these disadvantages have been exacerbated by the boys' refusal to settle in a range of care settings and all have long histories of absconding.

Uppercliff provides intensive care by means of a few obvious devices. It has a generous staff complement which enables children to be held by close relationships with adults. The children frequently go out with staff which gives them a semblance of freedom. Many staff live cheek by jowl with these difficult boys in a way that is not a feature of the secure units and is, in fact, fast disappearing in all CHEs. The boys play with the children of staff, eat with them and are casual visitors to their homes. Uppercliff boys are isolated from the pressures of the main school, particularly from older boys who, staff and children maintain, do much to precipitate their absconding. Little boys are either bullied into running or tempted by older boys to accompany them.

This isolation from the main school allows considerable flexibility in the unit. Children go to bed at a wide variety of hours, are continually moving about, go to the pictures or along the cliffs and any excuse is seized upon by staff for diversion. They frequently go shopping with adults or on other expeditions. Indeed, the boys seem to need a lot of physical movement and a high level of distraction. Possibly it replaces the fantasy element which figures large in young boys' absconding. Whatever the reasons, the boys run away less frequently than before.

Table 12.1 overleaf shows the number of times boys released from Uppercliff absconded before and after their transfer to the unit. The majority were located in the main school at Headlands on arrival but their tendency to run away made them early candidates for the unit. Subsequently they ran away less. Whatever else it does, Uppercliff seems to be successful in reducing boys' propensity to run away.

Interestingly enough, when we recollect our interactionist description of absconding, the creation of the intensive care unit at Uppercliff also had a marked effect on absconding and bounds breaking in the main school, as the figures in Table 12.2 confirm.

As these figures show, there is a significant decrease in the number of abscondings per month across the whole school. There is an even larger decrease in the number of bounds breakings and this, taken in conjunction with the general fall in absconding,

160

indicates a quite dramatic change in the school as a whole in the numbers of boys running away.

Table 12.1
Number of abscondings before and after transfer to unit at Uppercliff

	Abscondings/month, main school	Abscondings/month, Uppercliff
Boy 1	1·1 (21 mths)	0 (12 mths)
Boy 2	1·5 (23 mths)	0·5 (11 mths)
Boy 3	0·2 (22 mths)	0
Boy 4	7·0 (4 mths)	2·0 (16 mths)
Boy 5	0·4 (11 mths)	0 (12 mths)
Boy 6	0·6 (17 mths)	0·1 (8 mths)
Boy 7	5·0 (1 mth)	1·2 (5 mths)
Average:	2·2	0·54

The number of boys involved in the experiment is, so far, very low, so any firm conclusions about Uppercliff must be reserved but if present trends continue, something very interesting is taking place. As the boys have displayed difficult behaviour from an early age, have offended as young children and, when taken into care, have been disruptive, have run away and have been liable to frequent transfers, they are very clearly embryonic candidates for secure accommodation. If their absconding had not been reduced by the Uppercliff experiment they would no doubt have been once more transferred and continued that trek towards security on which they were already well embarked.

Table 12.2
Abscondings from whole school (including Uppercliff)

	Abscondings per month	Bounds breakings per month
Before Uppercliff opened July 1973 – June 1975	11·5	9·0
After Uppercliff opened July 1975 – June 1976	9·7	3·0

Note: Bounds breakings are defined as absence followed by return by midnight on the day of leaving. Absconding occurs when the absence extends beyond midnight.

Another example of beneficial changes at an open CHE caring for vulnerable adolescents can be seen at Risley Hall. Here a traditional block approved school has been rebuilt as a CHE for 60 boys along the lines laid out in *Care and Treatment in a Planned Environment*.[2] A combination of care in small groups, low staff-boy ratios and a fostering of close links between home and school has greatly modified both the actual levels of and staff concern about problematic behaviour. Boys are rarely together more than 10 at a time and there are 20 care staff and eight teachers.

In the late 1960s the statistics from Risley Hall prepared for the Home Office reveal rates of absconding around the 100 per cent level, indicating that each boy ran away on average once a year. This dropped as change was introduced and since the occupation of the new buildings early in 1975, both absconding and violence have become uncommon. After 1976 Christmas leave, for example, the incidence of boys returning late from weekend leave, with the usual excuses of missed buses or sudden illness, is barely 1 per cent.

These reforms must not be taken as a panacea, for there is still difficult behaviour at Risley Hall. It does have some absconding and occasional violence. However, the important point is that staff are less anxious about these problems and, consequently, when difficulties do arise, they can be dealt with in a relaxed and professional manner. Boys do regress, break down and commit offences and it is perhaps fair to state that during the last two years there has been one intractable case.

The developments at Risley Hall demonstrated that, as at Uppercliff, modifications in regime can reduce boys' antisocial behaviour within the school. Our own survey of the intake to this CHE in 1974 revealed an agglomeration of deprived, delinquent and difficult adolescents from a heavily populated industrial region and many boys were potentially long-term recidivists.[3] There was very little hope for much change in their behaviour. The old Risley approved school clearly failed to meet boys' needs but the recent changes, particularly the high staff ratios, have produced an environment where boys' commitment to all aspects of school experience has increased. There has been a consequent reduction in the behaviour that puts demands on the region's scarce secure places.

For older offenders, an interesting alternative to security is offered by the Bristol new careers project. Here is an attempt to apply the American 'new careers' concept to a group of lads who would otherwise have been in Borstal. Our two previous examples have concerned themselves with hindering the downward spiral of situations, but here there is a deliberate attempt to reverse the pattern, by status enhancement rather than deterioration.

The concept of 'new careers' developed in North America during the 1960s and includes a wide variety of projects which seek to provide socially useful careers in health, education and social services for talented people who had been unskilled and without regular work.[4] Particularly influential in this field were the projects of Joan and Douglas Grant at Vacaville, California, which employed young offenders in community work.[5] In Britain, particular interest was displayed by NACRO – the National Association for the Care and Resettlement of Offenders – and they decided to initiate a new careers project for the older teenage offenders in Borstal.

NACRO were successful in persuading the central authorities to accept a radical project, for the residential base was to have elements of freedom unusual in a probation hostel. The responsibility for managing the project passed to the Bristol region of NACRO who owned a property suitable for the scheme. An ex-probation hostel was converted to take 12 boys and 3 resident group leaders, and the first offenders were admitted in May 1973.

While the aims of the scheme were very complex and open to varied interpretations by different participants, it was agreed that the 'new careers' concept should be applied to a group of young men aged 17 to 21 who would otherwise have been in Borstal. Sentenced at crown court to a 24-month probation order with a condition of residence, it was envisaged that these boys would spend a year in the hostel. During this time they would be trained in social and community work skills as well as pursuing educational courses and group exercises aimed at fostering personal development. During the day, the students were to work in a range of placements, such as hospitals or play groups, with the eventual hope that they would be admitted to this work as full-time trainees. Clearly, not all Borstal receptions were suitable for such a demanding programme and preference was, therefore, given to the intelligent, aggressive and extrovert rather than the less able and withdrawn.

The hostel is administered by two non-resident social workers. However, the main responsibilities for the daily running of the hostel and students' training programmes rests with resident group leaders, all of whom are serious ex-offenders. Although the daily routine is rigorous, the hostel is completely open and students travel around the city freely.

It is not relevant here to discuss the success of the application of the 'new careers' idea and the experiences of this experiment have been documented elsewhere. [6] However, the hostel and its operation have considerable significance for secure provision. It is clear that although the project selected their intake from the larger Borstal population, many of the boys admitted to the scheme were highly institutionalised, deeply criminal and seriously disturbed. By January 1976, 29 students had been accepted and when we applied the scales of probable need for security employed in our next chapter on the Borstal population, 21 displayed characteristics which would *probably* necessitate placement in secure settings. The problematic characteristics of the intake are also confirmed by the fate of seven boys who in 1975 were accepted for the project but who were refused permission to participate by the judge at their trial and sentenced to considerable terms in custody. Five of these were given prison sentences and two went to closed Borstals. Clearly, then, the residents at the new careers hostel would otherwise have been destined for secure institutions had not the opportunities for community work been presented to them.

It is inevitable that a hostel which cares for such vulnerable young offenders in an open setting will experience many vicissitudes. The new careers hostel has had good and bad spells and these variations have been reflected in the levels of boys' abscondings and acting-out behaviour which tend to increase when things are difficult. But, despite these problems, the hostel has never ceased to operate and the overall experience confirms that it is possible for such offenders to live in an open environment.

By January 1976, 23 boys had been through the project. Eight left on completion of training and 15 left early either to take up employment or because their probation order had to be breached. Table 12.3 gives details of boys' histories.

Table 12.3
Subsequent histories of boys passing through new careers hostel

Number of boys passing through project = 23

Subsequent custodial experiences
  4 absconded from hostel
  4 went to Borstal
  8 went to prison or detention centre

Subsequent employment
  6 went on to social work jobs

Time spent in hostel
  7 stayed in the hostel for more than 9 months
  8 stayed in the hostel for less than 3 months
  Mean length of stay = 6·0 months (SD = 3·8)

It would be unwise to offer many comments about the effectiveness of the hostel from 23 cases. But even if the results appear disappointing – 17 per cent of admissions abscond and 63 per cent of the boys released go back into custody – these figures do not compare unfavourably with the poor success rates of Borstals where 63 per cent of trainees released in 1972 were reconvicted within two years, a figure that rises to 79 per cent for boys aged under 17 on reception.[7] There is no evidence to suggest that in terms of reconviction the open hostel was any less successful than the secure Borstals for which these boys were otherwise destined.

The greatest success of the project lies in the freedom and status offered to adolescent offenders who otherwise would have been in maximum security. Costs, too, are reduced and the average expenditure on each student is about 15 per cent below the expense of maintaining a trainee in Borstal. It demonstrates the willingness of many interested parties, often cast into less than complimentary stereotypes, to participate. The local neighbourhood, police, probation and social work services cooperated while the courts, remand centres and prison authorities were encouraging. The Home Office financed, and still continues to support, the scheme. Its success not only demonstrates that alternatives to security can exist but also, equally important, that attitudes to the young offender are less retributive than is frequently argued.

While Uppercliff, Risley and New Careers are concerned predominantly with maintaining the inmate's status, there are some other institutions which aim to do more than this and offer a clear treatment programme. It is worth considering two such alternatives in these discussions of alternatives. Peper Harow, a lively community near Guildford, is one example of an open treatment environment caring for vulnerable boys. Admittedly, its clients are more able than the average offender in his mid-teens (average IQ was 125), but this school wins high commitment from its boys. The needs of 45 lads between the ages of 15 and 18 are met by a combination of close staff–pupil relationships, high academic provision and aspiration, relatively long stay (average two years eight months) and an egalitarian/therapeutic regime.

Using the criteria of probable need for security which we shall apply to the Borstal population in the next chapter, we found that about a quarter of the school's population fell into this category. A much higher proportion would have merited a place either in hospitals or the Borstal system generally had they not been admitted to Peper Harow. Much of the ability of the community in holding on to these lads came from a cohesive and highly committed boy world, and identification engendered by the therapeutic style of the institution.

The success of Peper Harow with boys after release was higher than most CHEs, but the presence of a number of middle-class boys, frequently drug offenders, may have inflated this rate. Again, success is not the issue. For some adolescents, particularly older teenagers whose disenchantment with residential life is usually deeper than for younger boys, Peper Harow illustrates that security is not necessarily the easiest way of keeping them in.

It comes equally as something of a surprise to visit the open wing of a large hospital and find that many serious and problematic offenders are under less constraint than, say, young recruits to the armed forces. These difficult men are sheltered in part of a sub-normality hospital which houses over 800 patients so this special group of patients can nestle comfortably under the blanket provided by the sub-normality of the vast majority of inmates. Sitting on the terrace on a Sunday afternoon, overlooking the sea and busy with a little occupational therapy, will be sexual offenders, the occasional arsonist, a murderer, a few violent youths who would otherwise be in Borstal, drug offenders, the high suicide risk, burglars and con-men. Indeed, it requires the pen of a Genet to describe this establishment adequately and very considerable courage to run it.

The consultant psychiatrist who initiated this unit explained:

> Naturally one had to be discreet with the local hospital board; we are, after all, a sub-normality hospital. To have sprung a forensic unit on them without preparation would have got nowhere. So we began to admit the sub-normal delinquent group. Actually, the sub-normality has been played down and we have admitted those with more serious crimes. It's beginning to remind me of Grendon Underwood.

The unit experienced some difficulty in identifying the most flexible legal category under which the offenders could be admitted to the hospital. The consultant explained,

> We began by taking them in on a Section 60 Order of the Mental Health Act. Unfortunately, the statutory after-care supervision of the patients held in

this way and then released is limited to six months. But for these sorts of lads this is clearly insufficient. Again, if they prove difficult, abscond or are violent, then it is a great problem to get them rapidly back into a secure situation. You tend to get left with the difficult young men that others, understandably, are reluctant to take on. So, in the end, we opted for a probation order.

One of the features of this experiment is the close and cordial relationships which it maintains with all the interested groups on its margins. Probation had already begun to take an active interest in the hospital's provision early on, particularly for their adolescent drug offenders or those in sexual difficulties. The police and social services were well disposed and the judiciary were open to the suggestion that this hospital could provide a viable alternative to a prison or secure Borstal. Frequently, it is assumed that magistrates and judges will be very resistant to such benign approaches as they may not see a sojourn in hospital as a sufficient deterrent for serious offenders. But the psychiatrist was less pessimistic:

Naturally, you must assure the judiciary that the patients will be under control. You must emphasise that you share their concern over public safety and point out that sometimes these young people will be with us longer than they would be serving a prison sentence. Frankly, the magistrates are not anxious to send down young people who may be suffering from some personality disorder. Sex offenders are often given to us because everyone knows that prison does them no good and other inmates give them a bad time.

The unit opened in 1966. It is one part of a large hospital and no more generously staffed than the other wards. It has nine nursing staff for 48 patients which means that there are three on duty at any one time. This staff provision is supplemented by those with duties in the wider hospital. For example, teachers skilled in remedial work visit frequently. There is also a psychologist and usually a student attached.

The ages of the offenders vary from 15 to 54, although the majority are under the age of 25. We made a study of the unit's population between July 1968 and October 1972 and found that 31 per cent of the intake was between 15 and 21. The patients were very institutionalised and many had received custodial sentences before their arrival in the hospital. Something of the hospital's sub-normality specialisation survives among the special unit population, for 30 per cent of them had IQs of less than 75. It was also found that 35 per cent of the offences committed were sexual, frequently of a serious nature, 27 per cent involving persons under the age of 13. A further 17 per cent were offences of violence and it is unlikely that the majority of these people would normally have been under open conditions.

The average length of stay in the unit was about ten months and the longest stay was 37 months. Three-quarters of the patients were discharged to the community, including 48 who were released on probation. Only 17 per cent (28 men) were transferred to other institutions because of a deterioration in behaviour. Nine of these went to prison, three to Borstal and 16 to other hospitals.

The information on reconviction for this group is, unfortunately, less reliable. It is only available for those released on probation and, unfortunately, we know very little about the 35 per cent who were released to the outside world and considered by the authorities to be capable of fending for themselves. Of those released on probation, 65 per cent were reconvicted during the period of supervision. This figure may seem high but it compares favourably with those released from open prisons and it is very likely that those who were deemed not to require supervision and discharged direct to the community of whom we have no trace will be more successful.

However, the success of the unit is not really the point at issue, for all the patients have as poor a prognosis as many of the young persons in maximum security. What is important is that despite the familiar problems of intake and management, the unit demonstrates again that many offenders whose crimes make maximum security a foregone conclusion, need not be under lock and key. As the chief male nurse commented: 'It's the word hospital that does it, we have been here for more than a hundred years. If you are mentally ill people suspend their judgement. And if you are sub-normal, then you just can't help it'.

There are, of course, many non-residential strategies for helping the adolescent offender. Two examples that should be considered are professional fostering schemes and intensive intermediate treatment. While there are no studies which demonstrate conclusively that this type of provision can replace security, the initial evidence is encouraging. Research from the Kent fostering project indicates that this form of care is more successful, even with the hardened delinquent, than might have been expected and the personal social services working party on intermediate treatment as well as the Jay committee are optimistic about the potential of community care for the persistent offender. [8]

Open alternatives to security, however, may not necessarily fulfil the wider, sometimes implicit, functions of custody and these were discussed in Chapter 9. Secure accommodation serves many different functions of which treatment is only one and non-custodial or community alternatives to long-stay units may not be practicable when other functions have priority. Let us, therefore, in closing, glance briefly at the alternative strategies available when functions other than treatment are paramount. Let us first look at the use of secure units for remand.

Remand of children while awaiting further decisions

We pointed out earlier in this book that one of the main sources of concern to magistrates and police about provision for offenders is the problem of holding young persons while further decisions are made about their future. Almost every day a magistrate criticises the lack of secure remand facilities within the child-care system and immature adolescents are placed in prison department establishments. The government has stressed repeatedly the need to remove such young people from prisons.

Our researches have confirmed the importance of some secure remand facilities for young offenders but question the need for a long spell in security. Frequently, we found that the crisis of control apparent after an adolescent's arrest waned long before his court appearance. Initial rejection from the child's family and difficult behaviour by the offender led magistrates to issue an 'unruly certificate' which enabled the young person to be admitted to custody. However, once this initial crisis had cooled and as both the offender and his family came to accept the situation, we could find little reason why the young person should remain in security. The offender could easily have been sent home or to an open hostel and could have been placed under supervision. In some other cases we studied the police had to request a secure remand for homeless young offenders, a pattern which is becoming common in cities and seaside resorts. Magistrates, therefore, are forced to recommend security simply because there is so little alternative remand accommodation such as bail hostels or foster homes.

In both these cases, the time spent in security could be reduced if there were a more flexible remand policy and if a wider range of complementary provision were available. Existing secure facilities could then be employed more to contain those offenders whose previous conduct suggests that they present a danger to the public or will fail to appear in court. The viability of such a policy is confirmed by the large number of young people who are remanded in custody but who ultimately receive non-custodial sentences in court. In 1973, for example, 3,760 boys and 202 girls were remanded in custody but 40 per cent of these boys and 75 per cent of these girls were subsequently found to be not guilty or were given non-custodial sanctions.

We also have some serious reservations about the regimes of the secure remand homes for young people. For example, the legal constraints governing remand make it difficult for staff to guide and counsel the adolescent. Indeed, this is one of the complaints of many prison officers who work in remand centres. But, while there may be valid reasons for ensuring the independence of the person charged, the implications of this for immature adolescents are particularly serious. The consequences of this form of containment are likely to be more damaging to the adolescent than the effects which we explored in the last chapter.

Assessment of a child's needs and future placement

Secure accommodation is also used to hold young people while their needs and future placements are assessed. Some observation and assessment centres have such provision. Here, security not only holds the child but, unlike remand, also attempts to plan the child's welfare.

The role of secure assessment cannot be discussed independently of assessment itself and, in recent years, the theoretical assumptions behind the whole process have come under attack. The renewal of interest among psychologists such as Mischel in the situational determinants of behaviour have cast serious doubts on the value of all assessments undertaken outside the child's normal environment. [9] An evaluation of the child's needs, it is argued, must involve more than the recording of characteristics that are assumed to be consistent across a range of settings. The value of assessment has also come under scrutiny in studies of particular centres. [10] This research has revealed that the eventual placement decision could easily have been forecast from the background of the child before admission.

The addition of a secure component to the assessment process, therefore, adds to the problems we have just discussed as children's needs are greatly influenced by the social situations in which they find themselves and the most clearly perceived need of anyone in security is not to be there. We suspect that the real functions of such provision are concerned more with control than with evaluating the child's future requirements. If this is the case, there are few alternatives that we can suggest to the secure accommodation at present employed and the control functions must be frankly recognised. Indeed, it is interesting to recall that for years the classifying schools serving the approved school system operated without security and rarely had difficulties in carrying out their task. It is perhaps ironic that many boys now in the closed units on these campuses have been assessed in the open centre a few yards along the road!

Some of the pressures for secure assessment facilities may stem from management problems faced by the smaller and less experienced local authority observation and assessment units. In some cases, though not all, it is clear that the ethos of these institutions differs little from that of the old remand homes. It is perhaps significant that the annual conference of the heads of assessment establishments yields some of the least enlightened debates heard in child care and it is equally noticeable that some of their institutions are not without difficulties. [11] While it may be necessary to have some secure assessment facilities for purposes of control, in the light of this evidence, the extent of the provision required is hard to assess.

Separation of young people from others

It is perhaps misleading to talk about provision when we are exploring the management of behaviour which arises from the daily routine of residential life. We saw earlier that violent confrontations, for example, are very much the product of a complex interaction between children and staff and that some institutions can manage these more effectively than others. The use of secure accommodation for solving such disruption has, therefore, to be seen in this context. We have found that the use of separation facilities in residential homes varies widely. We have visited many establishments containing difficult adolescents which never isolated them in security and, paradoxically, it is in the larger closed units, where interpersonal tensions are exacerbated, that separation is most frequently employed. In practice, it seems very difficult to avoid punitive implications in the use of withdrawal rooms. The manhandling of an inmate towards a cell rarely has any positive effect on the institutional climate and it is difficult to accomplish in a way that is

169

viewed as therapeutic by both the recipient and the other children, especially if the separation facilities are in another building.

We often fail to realise the different opportunities for withdrawal presented to a child in a family as opposed to a public situation. Mischel, to whom we have already referred, notes that an adolescent behaves quite differently when alone with his parents than he does when with them in the company of others. In a family, the temper tantrum has an audience but after the child has chosen to withdraw, the quietening down is private, usually in a bedroom. In a residential institution, however, not only is the disruption public but the staff reactions are closely watched. Thus, departure has to be imposed on the child and the consequences are punitive. Because of a lack of privacy in CHEs, the child cannot negotiate his exit, oasis of recovery or return. An increase in privacy for children, therefore, would do much to obviate the need for secure rooms.

It is interesting to note that during our earlier researches into ordinary, independent boarding schools, which often care for middle-class casualties, security was never considered as a solution to disruptive behaviour. The hysterical or suicidal child was usually taken in by staff in order to remove him from social and academic pressures. In child-care establishments, we are perhaps not sufficiently aware of the considerable stresses that residential life puts on children. In Chapter 7 we noted how severe these can be. When we are considering the need for and uses of this type of secure provision, therefore, much would be gained from taking a closer look at the actual dynamics of the residential environment.

Protection of the public

A final function served by security is the need to guard the public from the dangerous behaviour of particular children and here, the custodial task of security must be acknowledged. While many grave offenders settle readily in open establishments, there will clearly be a residual group whose behaviour will be so threatening that they have to be locked up. But in practice, the definition of threat is not easily established and reflects wide ambiguities in public thinking. Many of the categories that we employ symbolise our preoccupations rather than reflect the true threat posed by the offender. For example, we might demand security for young people guilty of murder, rape, arson or violence yet it is the child who takes and drives motor vehicles who probably presents the greatest danger to the greatest number. In the next chapter, we shall see that of the boys aged 15 and 16 in open Borstals, 53 per cent have taking and driving away convictions and a further 24 per cent have committed arson and damage. However, it is violence and absconding that leads to a secure placement even though we have demonstrated that these are largely products of interaction.

We need, therefore, to clarify our priorities on these cases. Although there can be no alternatives to security for a proportion of children who threaten the community and themselves, the final irony stems from our preoccupation with control.

We already have considerable secure provision for boy absconders who plunder our property but seem most reluctant to provide it for personally vulnerable adolescent girls.

Conclusion

We would be the first to accept that the alternatives just described do not make much contribution to the size of the problem presented by difficult adolescents to the social services or prison departments. The paucity of alternative approaches for problematic young offenders provides yet another memorial to the strength of the residential tradition which we described in the opening chapters. We would emphasise that, in research terms, the small numbers sheltered by the examples we have given make any accurate evaluation of their work extremely difficult. All we can suggest is that they indicate a hopeful direction which wider experiments might follow.

The schemes at Penarth, Bristol and the mental hospital, as well as the work of good residential schools such as Risley and Peper Harow, indicate that security need not be the reflex response either to children's absconding or to the violent, sexually threatening and predatory behaviour of the older adolescent.

The unit at Uppercliff suggests that paternalistic structures with generous staff provision and a child-centred regime modifies the behaviour problems of neurotic, restless little boys. The experience of Risley Hall re-emphasises this point. These, with the Bristol experiment arrest status deterioration. Open treatment alternatives to security likewise provide similar encouragement. In a modest way, Peper Harow and, more ambitiously, the mental hospital offer a coherent treatment approach to high-risk young people. By a variety of structural features, they win high commitment from their clients and hold on to those boys whom others would define as in need of secure provision.

More specifically, in the child-care area which has been the focus of this book, we would urge others to imitate the special care facilities provided at Uppercliff. It does seem that such intervention checks that inexorable drift towards crisis that characterises the careers of the secure unit boys. Similar intensive care units should be tried with a wider age range and, of course, with girls whose problems demand this sort of provision.

However, it should be noted that all these alternatives spring from within the system. They have approached, usually in a very modest way, clear and widely acknowledged deficiencies in established practice. In this respect they can hardly be called radical alternatives. Possibly their survival and success has been because they do not ostensibly threaten established practice. All the experiments we have considered use custodial and secure provision for their failures and all the units are supported by the funds and resilient structures of large, bureaucratic organisations such as the Home Office, the Health Service, local authorities and and leading charities. This re-emphasises a need identified in an earlier chapter that not only should we integrate the wide variety of secure provision that is available for problematic adolescents but also incorporate into their care programmes creative alternatives to detention.

Notes

[1] See S. Millham, R. Bullock and P. Cherrett, *After Grace – Teeth*, London, Human Context Books, Chaucer Publishing Company, 1975.
[2] Advisory Council in Child Care, *Care and Treatment in a Planned Environment*, London, HMSO, 1970.
[3] S. Millham and R. Bullock, *Research at Risley Hall, some Findings to Inform Discussion*, unpublished paper, Dartington Social Research Unit, 1974.
[4] See A. Pearl and F. Riessman, *New Careers for the Poor*, New York, Free Press, 1965.
[5] See N. Hodgkin, 'The new careers project at Vacaville: a California experiment', Howard League for Penal Reform, *New Careers for ex-offenders*, 1973.
[6] S. Millham, R. Bullock and K. Hosie, 'Another try: an account of a new careers project for Borstal trainees', in N. Tutt (ed.), *Alternative Strategies for Coping with Crime*, Oxford, Blackwell, 1978.
[7] *Report on the Work of the Prison Department*, London, HMSO, 1976.
[8] N. Hazel, R. Cox, P. Ashley-Mudie, *Second Report of the Special Family Project*, Kent Social Services, 1977; Personal Social Services Council, *A Future for Intermediate Treatment*, 1977 and NACRO *Report of Working Party on Children and Young Persons in Custody*, 1977.
[9] W. Mischel, *Personality and Assessment*, New York, Wiley, 1968.
[10] Social Services Research and Intelligence Unit, Portsmouth, *First Year at Fairfield Lodge*, 1976.
[11] See, for example, the reports in *The Times* of the Llandudno conference on and around 3 February 1977 and incidents reported in social work press during October 1977 concerning two such centres.

13 Young offenders in penal establishments

It is not possible to discuss the need for secure places within the CHE system without considering the large group of young offenders who are already the responsibility of the prison department of the Home Office. The 1969 Children and Young Persons' Act had intended that the majority of young offenders in need of residential care should be placed in establishments run by the local authorities and it was envisaged that, over time, the minimum age of entry to Borstal would rise to 17 and that the junior detention centres would be abandoned. However, the rise in juvenile crime, accompanied by the difficulties experienced by social services departments in placing the older juvenile offender have led to an increasing number of 15- and 16-year-olds finding themselves in prison department institutions. In 1975, some 6,000 boys, aged between 14 and 16, experienced a spell in a detention centre while nearly 1,200 15- and 16-year-olds were received into Borstal.[1] Of these 7,000 boys, 90 per cent go to closed institutions so, contrary to popular ideas, there has been a great increase since 1969 in the number of children and young people experiencing a period in maximum security. Clearly, this tendency has considerable relevance to any discussion on the number of secure places necessary, for any numerical estimates of need for security in the child-care system will be influenced by our attitudes to the 15- and 16-year-olds already in Borstal institutions.

Most of the boys passing through detention centres will be less experienced offenders than the Borstal trainees although it seems no longer to be the case that these lads are first-time delinquents experiencing a short, sharp shock. There is little material available about boys currently entering detention centres but a survey has recently been conducted by the Home Office of 130 boys, aged between 14 and 16, whose homes are in the South West region of the prison department administrative area and surrounding counties.[2] On reception, the ages of the boys were as shown in Table 13.1.

Table 13.1
Boys' ages on reception at detention centre

Age on reception at detention centre		Estimate in numbers for national population of 6,000
14	26%	1,650
15	39%	2,340
16	35%	2,100
N= 127		N= 6,000

The characteristics of this group reveal an unexpected pattern. Half these boys have more than three previous convictions while only 11 per cent had none. Thirty per cent have been offending for over three years, one-third have been to CHEs, 20 per cent were living in a residential institution at the time of their last arrest and half of the 43 per cent who have previously experienced some form of residential care have absconded at some point. A third of the sample had only one or no previous convictions, confirming that there is a large proportion of fairly unsophisticated offenders in this group but the remainder are not dissimilar to boys placed in open Borstals and senior CHEs.

Although the sample used in this study is small, the statistics are important for they are very likely to be within 8 per cent of the national figures. There has clearly been a shift in the type of boys admitted since the early days of the 'short, sharp shock' to deter the incipient delinquent and this may explain why only 30 per cent of the boys manage to keep clear of trouble after release.

A few boys, however, will be sentenced in this way because of a failure by the local authorities to find other places in security. This is a clear misuse of these facilities as detention centres were never intended for deeply delinquent boys. Neither were these places viewed as providing secure storage for an unruly adolescent while his social worker searched out his next placement. We saw earlier that 22 per cent of our 1975 special unit population had previously been through a detention centre.

In general, however, the detention centre boys are unlikely to be candidates for places in secure CHEs although some of them have been, and will continue to be, a demand on social work resources. Few of them have committed grave crimes and their previous residential histories, although occasionally extensive, do not match the range displayed by boys of a similar age in special units.

Young offenders in Borstal, however, are likely to be a quite different group. A Borstal sentence follows crown court proceedings. This would suggest that the charges are serious and the offender experienced. We have already commented that these boys were defined as being too difficult for the old senior approved schools which could, where necessary, contain boys up to the age of 19. But, in recent years, most CHEs have reduced the age of their client group. There are now fewer places within the CHEs for the older boy. Consequently, an increasing number of offenders over the age of 15 receive Borstal sentences. As with the detention centres it is not an effective way of dealing with offenders in their mid-teens. The failure of boys released from Borstal is high and the younger the boys, the more frequently and rapidly they get into serious trouble.

Social services departments have little expertise with older offenders in their mid-teens and few locations for them. Boys are either explicitly or implicitly written off to the prison system, a solution hardly likely to delight the Home Office who, having surrendered most of their facilities and responsibilities for sheltering younger offenders, now find the boys returning in increasing numbers. The rise in the Borstal population has meant a decline in the length of time boys serve and a consequent disruption of Borstal training programmes, all of which were based on a boy's length of stay. In addition, the demands on education facilities in Borstals have put pressure on the provision because of a rapid increase in the numbers of boys who are still of school age.

Little recent material has been published about the Borstal population.[3] In particular there is little in print on the characteristics of present Borstal boys. It is, therefore, difficult to establish whether or not the young offenders now in Borstal institutions are any more problematic than they were before. It is also difficult to establish whether they differ materially from senior boys in the old approved school system. For, in the past many present Borstal boys would have been adequately contained in open establishments. However, if these 15- and 16-year-olds at present in Borstal are all hardened criminals, presenting serious dangers to the public, clearly any attempt to take this group out of the Borstal system will necessitate the provision of more than 1,000 secure places within the CHE system. If, on the other hand, these offenders are replicas of the old senior approved school boys, the majority, it would be safe to assume, could be contained in open settings. Hence, in our estimate of the needs and numbers for secure places, we first have to analyse the characteristics of the younger group of the Borstal population and then, in the light of this, suggest what could be done with them.

To investigate this problem with greater sophistication, we were able to undertake an analysis of all 15- and 16-year-olds admitted to Borstal during 1975. The Young Offenders Psychology Unit in London made available some data on all boys aged 15 and 16 admitted during this period. After further analysis of this material, we were able to explore whether or not boys' backgrounds and histories would make security an integral part of treatment if this group were to be sheltered in the CHE system. The Home Office figures included all boys admitted during 1975 with the exception of those entering the centre in Manchester, where records were only available for 42 weeks of that year. In our final estimates of the need for security, therefore, we have to increase the Manchester figures by 20 per cent to get an overall total for the whole year. This small adjustment is essential as the proportion of 15- and 16-year-olds in the total intake is higher at Manchester than elsewhere. It is also just possible that a few receptions may have been omitted from these data and the figures we present, therefore, may be fractionally below the true national figure, but the degree of error will be very small.

What, then, are the background characteristics of these younger Borstal trainees? Do they differ from the boys once sheltered in senior approved schools and, if removed from the Borstal system, would they need to be placed in secure units? Our discussions of the Home Office material should help us to answer these questions.

During 1969 and 1970, we undertook research into six senior approved schools for boys and examined the characteristics and histories of all the 324 boys sheltered in them.[4] All these schools were open establishments and the boys were between 15½ and 17½ on reception. Some of the older boys were, therefore, over 19 at the time of their release. If we compare the characteristics displayed by these senior approved school boys six years ago with the present 15- and 16-year-olds in Borstal, we can quickly establish the similarities and differences between the groups. It is, of course, possible that during the last six years, there have been changes in the characteristics of older delinquents but there is little evidence to suggest any radical transformation. While there is a dearth of material comparing changes in the intake to CHEs since the implementation of the 1969 Act, the evidence that does exist, such as our study of boys at a senior CHE in 1975,[5] fails to confirm any radical changes, although we did note an increasing tendency to use the CHE for disruptive boys who had not been particularly delinquent.

When we examine the patterns of offending and the institutional histories of the two groups of boys, we see that the Borstal population is without doubt more criminal and institutionally experienced than the old senior approved school boys. But the differences are largely quantitative rather than qualitative and are neither radical nor contrasting. The Borstal group still displays characteristics that are typical of older delinquents. For example, when we look at the number of boys' previous convictions, we can see that the Borstal population has a higher level of criminality than the approved school boys. Twenty-seven per cent of the boys in open and 47 per cent of those in closed Borstals have over five previous convictions compared with a figure of only 15 per cent for the approved school group (see Table 13.2).

Table 13.2

Number of preconvictions of Borstal and approved school groups
(figures are percentages)

No. of convictions	Borstal boys (15–16 years)		Senior approved schools
	Open	Closed	
2 or less	29	19	48
3 or 4	42	34	37
Over 5	28	47	15
N =	203	585	324

The nature of the offences, too, seems to be more grave for the Borstal population. Table 13.3 shows that there are more convictions for offences which could present a danger to the public, crimes of violence, sexual assault, arson and taking motor vehicles. Again the difference is one of degree and such offences were not unknown among the old approved school population, where 15 per cent had convictions for taking and driving away a motor vehicle. What is perhaps most significant is that the vast majority of boys' offences in both groups are still violations of property (theft, burglary, etc.) and the differences we have presented must be seen in this context. The Borstal boys may have more convictions and their crimes may threaten public safety more but these differences must not mask the fact that the majority of offenders in both groups are remarkably similar – persistent offenders against property.

Table 13.3
Types of offences committed by boys (figures are percentages)

| | Borstal boys (15–16 years) | | Senior approved schools |
	Open	Closed	
Theft, burglary	84	85	81
Violence	16	31	4
Sexual offences	1	4	3
Damage, arson	24	27	2
TDA	53	51	15
N =	321	806	324

We also find that the Borstal boys, especially those in closed establishments, are more institutionally experienced than the senior approved school boy of former years. They are more likely to have been in children's homes, CHEs and detention centres but, again, the differences must not be exaggerated or obscure the fact that the majority of boys in both groups have avoided these placements.

The figures in Table 13.4 suggest that there are few qualitative differences between the two groups of offenders and that the overall problems and presenting symptoms are very similar. The intensity and persistence of antisocial behaviour may be greater among the Borstal group, but, even here, problems such as alcoholism, drug addiction, violent behaviour, sexual deviance, suicidal tendencies and persistent absconding are relatively uncommon and only affect a minority.

Table 13.4
Previous institutional experiences (figures are percentages)

| | Borstal boys (15–16 years) | | Senior approved schools |
	Open	Closed	
Children's home	21	35	22
Approved school/CHE	21	57	20
Detention centre	54	54	9
N =	314	771	324

We can conclude, therefore, that the 15- and 16-year-olds in Borstal present more difficulties in terms of their institutionalisation and criminality than the old senior approved school boys but that there do not seem to be any radical differences in the actual nature of the problems they offer. This additional intensity in the difficulties they present may necessitate care in secure settings for some, but clearly not for all of them. The difficulty lies in deciding how many really do require security. This would involve establishing criteria by which we can select this group from the larger population.

During 1975, we find that 1,197 boys aged 15 or 16 were sentenced to Borstal training. This figure cannot be absolutely accurate because of the small correction we have applied to compensate for the shorter period covered by the evidence for the Manchester reception centre and the absence of data on a few admissions. However, the totals we provide should be very near the national figure. Of these 1,197 boys, 462 (38 per cent) were aged 15 on sentence and 735 (62 per cent) were 16. It usually takes about two weeks for a boy to arrive at his training Borstal, so a boy sentenced when 15 years 11 months may be 16 when he begins his training.

The Borstal authorities make their own assessment of the need for placement in a secure setting and, in general, the younger the boy, the more likely he is to be placed in a secure, as opposed to an open institution. In spite of local authority rejection of these 15-year-old offenders as being too difficult for CHEs, 22·9 per cent were allocated to open establishments implying that, even by Home Office criteria, these boys can be handled in open environments. For those boys aged 16 when sentenced, the ratio is higher and 32 per cent are placed in open institutions. In all, therefore, 341 (28·5 per cent) of the 1,197 boys will go to open Borstals while the remaining 856 (71·5 per cent) spend their training period in secure settings.

Table 13.5 lays out the complete details of placements for various categories of age on sentence and it can be seen that as the boys get older, they stand a greater chance of finding their way to open environments. This table also demonstrates the rise in the number of admissions for boys over 16½ on sentence. Many of these boys will be over 17 for much of their stay and the large numbers of boys included in this group confirm the significance of cut-off age for any estimates of secure places needed to treat these offenders in the CHE system.

Table 13.5
Placements for various categories of age on sentence

Age on sentence	Total receptions	Allocated to open Borstal		Allocated to closed Borstal	
		No.	%	No.	%
15–15½	207	33	16	174	84
15½–16	255	73	29	182	71
16–16½	319	91	29	228	71
16½–17	416	144	35	272	65
	1,197	341	28·5	856	71·5
Aged 15	462	106	22·9	356	77·1
Aged 16	735	235	32·0	500	68·0

The Home Office, then, direct 71 per cent of the 15- and 16-year-olds to closed institutions but the criteria they employ for establishing a need for security are far less discriminatory than those used to admit boys to Redbank, Redhill or Kingswood special units. In the first place, most of the Borstal provision is secure. Home Office establishments tend to be more specifically custodial so that absconding and violence are tolerated far less than would be the case in a CHE. There is also a long tradition of training offenders in large, closed institutions and it would, therefore, be unwise to equate a Home Office definition of need for security with placement in a special unit of the type we have described in this report. We can clearly eliminate for the purposes of our estimates the 341 boys placed in open Borstals as they have absolutely no need for care under secure conditions. Many of the boys sheltered in secure Borstals, on the other hand, require neither the levels of custody nor the intensity of supervision provided in the special units we have studied, although other Borstal boys certainly do need both security and control. The issue is into which categories do the remaining 856 boys in secure Borstals fall? How many need maximum security and how many do not?

To make an accurate estimate of the need we have just described, we compiled a scale consisting of various behaviour and characteristics that would *probably* necessitate security when treatment programmes are arranged. The persistent absconder is usually one such case; those displaying violent behaviour in previous placements another. In the scale, we also took into account the nature of the boy's offences so that convictions for dangerous crimes of violence, arson and sexual assault are included. We also added the 10 boys who had attempted suicide on three or more occasions although, with these tragic cases, it seems to be intensive supervision rather than security that is needed.

It is important to stress that we do not necessarily believe that security is the best way to meet the behaviour categorised in this scale. For example, we have included the persistent absconder in spite of our previous argument that running away could be much modified by changes in institutional practice. Obviously, some boys run even from benign regimes. However, it should be made clear that if serious attempts are made to meet the needs of absconders under open conditions and they have some success, then these *probable* estimates are slightly inflated. In the same way we have suggested that aggressive behaviour is much influenced by institutional expectations and Derek Miller maintains that the rehabilitation of violent young offenders is hindered by maximum security.[6] But decision makers may not agree and, in any case, have to work under different constraints. The fact that items are included in the following scale does not imply that we think the behaviour is best met by a secure placement.

The scale used to measure *probable* need for care in secure settings was compiled as shown in Table 13.6 and alongside each heading we provide the proportions of 15- and 16-year-old Borstal boys displaying each characteristic.

These categories are, of course, far too vague to imply that security is essential when they are present. Such assertions would be naïve. However, they are criteria which, in our opinion, should be influential when secure placements are under consideration. It is interesting to see that only a small proportion of the Borstal population displays these features. It is also important to note that other possible items were excluded from the scale. The number of offences that a boy has committed, for example, has not been included in the scale because the frequency of boys' offences is similar amongst trainees in both open and closed Borstals. Even when we employed an item of more than seven convictions in our criteria for probable security, we found that a large number of boys from open Borstal actually qualified for security. We, therefore, decided to include in our scale the *types* rather than the number of offences.

Table 13.6

Scale of probable need for care in secure settings, Borstal boys (15-16)
(figures are percentages)

	Open	Closed
Over 11 abscondings from open institutions	2	15
Absconding from Home Office or police custody	1	7
Violent behaviour in previous institutions	2	16
Sexual deviance	0	1
Convictions for grave crimes*	2	17
Arson involved in offences	1	5
Over 3 suicide attempts	0	1
N =	321	807

*Murder, attempted murder, manslaughter, death by dangerous driving, wounding, GBH, rape, attempted rape, indecent assault, sexual assault on children, arson.

There are several other features such as drug addiction, alcoholism and TDA offences which might have been included in our scale for these do indicate a *possible* need for security. We therefore applied a second scale to the Borstal population: the measure of *possible* need for security and included these factors along with all the items used in the previous scale, at the same time reducing the qualifying levels to five abscondings from open establishments and to two suicide attempts (see Table 13.7). The scale of *possible* need for security is therefore wider than the scale of *probable* need but, clearly, all who qualify on the *probable* scale are automatically included in the possible group. The details are laid out below and the frequency of these characteristics among the Borstal population is given alongside each heading.

We applied each of the two scales to the 1,174 boys (aged 15 or 16 on sentence) for whom we had information, to see how many in each age group would qualify for security. Each individual record was examined and both scales were applied. If the boy displayed any *one* of the items included in the scales he became a *probable* or a *possible* candidate for security. Very few (6 per cent) of the boys in open establishments recorded features found in the scale of probable need for security but 24 per cent of this group found themselves included when the measure of possible need was applied, suggesting that the true need for security is far nearer the figure derived from the *probable* than the *possible* scale. The details of the application of the scales are as shown in Table 13.8.

Table 13.7

Scale of possible need for care in secure settings, Borstal boys (15-16)
(figures are percentages)

	Open	Closed
Over 5 abscondings from open institutions	3	27
Absconding from Home Office or police custody	1	7
Violent behaviour in previous institutions	2	16
Sexual deviance	0	1
Convictions for grave and serious crimes*	18	47
Arson involved in offences	1	5
Over 2 suicide attempts	0	2
Alcoholic/drink problem	2	4
N =	321	807

*Offences included in previous scale with the addition of possession of weapon with acquisitive offence, robbery with violence, over 3 offences of TDA.

Table 13.8

Numbers of boys needing security on the criteria of each scale
(figures are percentages)

	In closed Borstals				In open Borstals			
Age on sentence	Admissions	Poss. & Prob.	Prob.	Neither possible nor probable	Admissions	Poss. & Prob.	Prob.	Neither possible nor probable
15–15½	174	46	71	29	33	12	21	79
15½–16	182	45	72	28	73	5	21	79
16–16½	228	36	66	34	91	5	21	79
16½–17	272	38	64	36	144	6	28	72
	856	40·4	67·9	32·1	341	6·5	23·3	76·2

This table shows quite clearly that the proportion of boys falling into the *probable* category falls as the boys get older. Forty-six per cent of the boys sentenced before the age of 15½ qualify for security compared with only 38 per cent of the 16½–17 group. On the other hand, the actual number of 15-year-olds is small and it must be remembered that the ages given in this table are those at sentence, so that a boy admitted at 15½ will be over school leaving age on release. The increasing number of admissions among the 16-year-olds also indicates the importance of the cut-off age as a factor influencing our estimates of need. If, then, we expand Table 13.5, we now have a statistical basis with which we can estimate the number of secure places needed in the CHE system to shelter the 15- and 16-year-olds at present in Borstal (see Table 13.9).

Table 13.9
Number of secure places needed at any one time

Age on sentence	Total receptions	Placed in closed Borstals	Per cent needing security on probable scale	Number of secure places needed each year on probable scale
15–15½	207	174	46	81 (46% of 174)
15½–16	255	182	45	82 (45% of 182)
16–16½	319	228	36	82 (36% of 223)
16½–17	416	272	38	103 (38% of 272)
	1,197	856	40·4	348

Two factors will affect our numerical estimates, the cut-off age we mentioned previously and the expected length of stay in security. The length of Borstal training has now fallen to nine months but this is largely a response to the pressure of numbers. We noted in an earlier chapter that there is little consensus among the staff in special units as to an optimum length of stay. It may be that a boy of 15 needs to stay longer than a 16-year-old, but the existing special units fail to offer much guidance. Staff at Redbank believed that absconding could be counteracted within six months whereas at Kingswood and St Charles stays were longer. Suppose, therefore, that we put forward a suggestion that the youngest, 15–15½, group should remain until 16 – that is an average stay of 9 months, and the rest say only eight months, we can use the figures presented in Table 13.9 to estimate the number of secure places that need to be available at any one time. This is done as shown in Table 13.10.

The scale of *probable* need suggests a need for 239 secure places whilst the *possible* need measure puts forward a figure of 403. As we know that the real need will be nearer the first figure, it seems that just under 300 places should be available at any one time to cater for these boys for the length of time mentioned and to provide vacancies which accommodate turnover. If we want the length of stay to be longer, say 15 months for the 15–15½ group and 12 months for the rest, our calculations become as follows, and the figures obtained are 366 and 609, suggesting a realistic estimate of 400 places.

Table 13.10
Estimate of need for secure places

Age on sentence	Number needing security each year on probable scale	Intended length of stay	Places needed at any one time	Places needed based on probable and possible scale
15–15½	81	9 months	61	91
15½–16	82			
16–16½	82	8 months	178	302
16½–17	103			
		Total:	239	403

Clearly, the precise number of places will depend on the significance accorded to various factors outlined in the preceding paragraphs but, at least, we now have some basis on which to make a realistic estimate of the security required for the young Borstal population. The implication for planning is clear: before numbers can be arrived at, there has to be a clear decision on the maximum age of admission for boys and their expected length of stay. We have seen that the message from the secure units we have studied is largely that how long you stay depends on what staff see security as achieving. Generally, as we saw in Chapter 9, the more institutions believe that they are offering treatment, the longer staff expect boys to stay and the more security boys experience. Thus, the number of secure places required is inextricably linked to the approach units adopt towards the difficult child.

Conclusions

We have considered the increasing numbers of young offenders moving to Borstal simply from a needs and numbers perspective. Naturally, it is not part of our function to argue whether or not these young people should remain the responsibility of the Home Office. Any change in the minimum age at which boys can enter Borstal or detention centres would be influenced by a wide number of factors. It is unlikely that research would be among the most cogent of these. However, from our visits to Borstals and remand centres many impressions linger, although in no sense are they research findings.

It does seem that the increasing number of young boys in Borstals is causing them considerable problems. The institutions link a Spartan, regimented ethos to a demanding trade training programme. In style it is not, and never was, intended to meet the emotional and educational needs of younger boys, many of whom are physically and mentally immature. As almost all the younger boys coming to Borstal will have been in residential care previously, most are allocated to closed institutions. Indeed, we have already noted that the younger boys are the more likely to be in closed rather than open provision. A number of closed Borstals are located in old prisons, such as Rochester and Portland, and while modifications in the buildings have been made, it does mean that young boys still spend much of their time in prison surroundings.

One has every admiration for the efforts of Borstal staff who have the unenviable task of accepting all boys that the courts send, yet they still try to make the experience beneficial. Unfortunately there is little sign that the efforts achieve very much. There is no indication that in influencing long-term recidivism, the Borstal system is particularly successful and for younger boys, there is every indication that it is quite ineffective.[7] Sixty-four per cent of trainees released in 1972 were reconvicted within two years (three-quarters of them within the first year) and for boys under 17 on sentence, the figure is even higher, 79 per cent.

Several years ago we commented that the needs of offenders in their mid-teens required much more consideration than they received.[8] While the old senior approved schools did not offer boys much, their regimes contained them adequately and, at least, spared them a premature penal experience.

It is quite possible to argue that returning the persistent offender of 15 and 16 years to the child-care system will achieve no more, with regard to long-term success, than allowing boys to go on to Borstal. Our evidence from the secure units and the old senior approved schools would certainly support this view. Reconviction rates in the approved schools were not markedly better than in the Borstals and only one-third of older boys managed to remain clear of trouble on release from senior schools. This is why we have consistently urged that there should be a reappraisal of the role of residential care for boys in their mid-teens. A much more flexible approach is needed, possibly imitating the community service projects and alternatives to Borstal initiated by the Home Office. Changing administrative responsibility for these young offenders without changing the nature of boys' experience will achieve very little. Apart from the recent Jay committee report on the younger adolescent offender, there seem to be few ideas on what to do with them.[9] There is little to encourage us when the plight of these boys has rapidly deteriorated.

Notes

[1] *Report on the Work of the Prison Department*, London, HMSO, 1976, Cmnd 6542.
[2] Young Offender Psychology Unit, Home Office, *A Survey of the Characteristics of Junior Detention Centre Trainees Whose Home Areas are in the Prison Department South-West Region or Adjoining Counties*, unpublished mimeo-

graph, 1977.

[3] There are several studies of the Borstal population in the 1950s and 1960s. See, for example, T. C. N. Gibbens, *Psychiatric Studies of Borstal Lads*, Institute of Psychiatry, London, monograph no. 11, Oxford, University Press, 1963; A. G. Rose, *Five Hundred Borstal Boys*, Oxford, Blackwell, 1954 and D. Lowson, *City Lads In Borstal*, Liverpool, University Press, 1970.

[4] S. Millham, R. Bullock and P. Cherrett, *A Comparative Study of Eighteen Boys' Approved Schools which compares their Stylistic Variety and the Commitment of Boys and Staff*, unpublished report, Dartington Social Research Unit, 1972.

[5] S. Millham, R. Bullock and K. Hosie, *Research at North Downs*, unpublished report, Dartington Social Research Unit, 1975.

[6] D. Miller, 'The biology and psychology of juvenile violence: its implications for prediction and treatment', paper presented to Association for the Psychiatric Study of Adolescence, Edinburgh Conference, 1976.

[7] *Report on the Work of the Prison Department*, op. cit., p. 46.

[8] See S. Millham, R. Bullock and P. Cherrett, *After Grace – Teeth*, Human Context Books, Chaucer Publishing Company, 1975, Chap. 17.

[9] National Association for the Care and Resettlement of Offenders, *Report of the Working Party on Children and Young Persons in Custody*, 1977.

14 Summary and conclusions

This study of secure provision has attempted to view the issue in a number of ways. It has resisted the temptation to linger over the many theoretical issues raised by security because these do not immediately concern people faced with making difficult decisions on problem children. It has looked at the custodial inheritance of child care and the ways in which the discomforts of reform frequently engender reaction and demands for more coercive measures. We have suggested that criticisms of the 1969 Act spring from wider and deeper issues than any supposed ineptitude in dealing with difficult children. This may provide some belated comfort to local authorities who have had to suffer considerable ill-informed criticism.

Our examination of entry to the secure units and the wider functions that such custody has for the child-care system raises a number of disquieting conclusions which are supported by other research. It is clear that the majority of adolescents in the special units are casualties of the care system and that this damage is unevenly distributed. Admission to security depends on making a sufficiently cogent case, a brief which relies almost entirely on a candidate's inconvenient behaviour in other residential institutions. This is in marked contrast to hospital units where the criteria for admission are specific, where treatment has been validated and where both rest on a widely accepted theoretical base. We find it difficult to envisage entry procedures for secure units overcoming these problems of selection, particularly when decisions about placement are increasingly left to social services departments. At the moment, it seems that the demand for security reflects the requirements of inadequate open institutions and community services rather than the needs of difficult children.

This study has also looked at some aspects of children's presenting behaviour, particularly violence and absconding. Our evidence suggests that much of this difficult conduct is identifiable early, amenable to intervention and that its incidence in residential institutions varies widely. The perspectives of staff on this behaviour also differ and the institution plays an important role in creating much of its deviance. We have also noted that some children arrived in the secure units convicted of grave crimes. The rise in the number of such convictions, the length of time these offenders spend in detention, their arrival, departure and legal rights should be a cause of some concern.

This study has also illustrated the ways in which secure provision differs. We have noted that the units vary in size, task, style and length of stay. They all face problems in providing an adequate therapeutic environment for children; they are subject to vicissitude, isolation and external hostility. But they do confer some benefits on the children. They break the persistent absconding patterns and extreme withdrawal of some neurotic children and, contrary to popular opinion, the young people are not hostile to the caring aspects of the regime. It seems unlikely that they suffer psychological damage from a short incarceration and the experience can confer on them physical and educational advantages.

We noted that the reconviction rates for delinquent boys in secure units were high, that is, when failure is defined as further offending. Within a short time, the great majority of children released find themselves in another custodial institution. We have acknowledged that the units safeguard the child while he is enclosed, that the clients of security are unpromising material and that staff make every effort to help, but these apologia should not obscure the failure of security to modify, in the long term, boys' criminal behaviour. For the majority of boys, the secure units provide a brief sojourn in an expensive ante-room to the penal system.

We have discussed alternatives to security and noted that the earlier the intervention with high-risk children, particularly in open intensive care units, the greater are the chances of eventual success. It is also clear that some open situations can effectively shelter young people and adults who on many criteria seem to present a considerable risk to the public. Unfortunately our institutional heritage, both in thought and provision, has limited the exploration of alternatives while the ever-increasing costs of residential facilities inhibit experiment.

An analysis of the population sheltered by the units and recent applications for places would suggest that there is little need *within the child-care system* for a rapid increase in secure places. This is a view supported by senior staff in the secure units and many external professionals. However, this does not mean that the extent of secure provision is entirely adequate. There may be a need for short-term secure remand facilities and there are clearly gaps in secure treatment facilities in certain geographical areas. It is also difficult to estimate the numbers of girls in need of security but it is likely that the provision at the new Birmingham youth treatment centre will meet these demands more adequately. However, we would stress that the different functions of security should be kept separate because units find it very difficult to create a viable regime when some children are sheltered for more intensive care while others are there simply for custody.

We have suggested that much of the external pressure for an increase in secure places, from press, judiciary and police, is concerned with the persistent male offender in his mid-teens. There seems little consistency between local authority social services departments in their readiness to assume responsibility for these boys and they have gathered in increasing numbers in Borstals and detention centres. The prison system, whatever its strengths, cannot adequately meet the emotional and educational needs of younger boys, a deficiency which the authorities readily admit. The original intention of the 1969 Act was to remove all boys under 17 from Borstal, a system in which, in any case, considerable changes were envisaged. But the reluctance to implement this legislation, on both political and practical grounds, has had the unintended consequence that many more boys are thrust early into the prison system. If and when the social services are prepared to assume responsibility for these offenders, it is here that the need for considerable increase in secure accommodation exists.

Naturally, it is not our task to comment on issues of such political moment, but

187

we have at least made clear the criteria which should be used in estimating the number of secure places this young Borstal population requires. Our estimates are less than the number of secure places at present occupied by these young Borstal boys. We have suggested the number of secure places needed by social services departments, depending on these boys' probable need for security and the length of time it is intended that they stay in custody. However, we would emphasise that, without some new, radical ideas on the provision which the social services departments offer, taking back this group of young Borstal boys into child care will solve nothing. The long-term success of this group when sheltered in the child-care system was little better than in the present Borstals. We ourselves have repeatedly emphasised that much more thought should be given to the plight of the older offender and more care offered to the early identifiable, vulnerable recidivist. In an earlier study, we commented that, 'In the senior schools, any observer can see the debris of countless, ineffective, institutional placements floating out with a tide of rejected, defeated older boys towards Portland Borstal'.[1] If anything, the tide is running even more swiftly today. With the exception of one or two courageous experiments, there is no evidence that, generally, local authority social services departments are concerning themselves with the deeper issues raised by these children. It is, in fact, singularly depressing to find how much this study of secure provision has corroborated our previous research conclusions.

Superficially, estimating the need for secure accommodation might seem an easy exercise. However, this study has shown security to be a complex issue. At theoretical levels, we have glimpsed the ways in which institutions maintain, fortify and extend their position. In contrast, we have identified the host of empirical problems that security creates, but the identification of a confused situation at least indicates where action might be taken. We shall close with a few practical suggestions on the ways in which local authority social services departments should approach the development of any special facilities.

Initially, any local authority social services department, faced with demands for more secure accommodation, should seek to improve the whole range of facilities offered to high-risk children. In the case of their residential institutions, a number of models have been developed which seem to us to be effective. These CHEs can be visited and certainly are not theoretical utopias conjured by social workers. Such homes shelter a number of very difficult children and have greatly diminished their provocative behaviour.

If increased efforts are made in the community with better supervision, imaginative intermediate treatment schemes and short-term sheltering, many of the children who still find their way into residential care could be adequately helped outside. There is no evidence that more high-risk children are now in CHEs than previously and we commented in 1972 that about half the boys in CHEs need not have been there. The fewer the children admitted to CHEs, the better are the chances that intensive care will be given to the vulnerable group of children who need residential help. A reduction in the numbers taken into residential care would enable more adolescents in their mid-teens to be accepted into open child-care settings. This may check a deterioration in these children's behaviour or, at least, will render it less visible, thus reducing demands for security. Naturally, some secure accommodation will be necessary but it should be part of a programme of care, it should have a clearly defined task and it should cease to act as a crisis-postponing device.

The tasks of the secure units will vary: they may have long-term treatment aims; they may offer intensive care for a few months or they may simply act as a cooler for the explosive child. Whatever the task is, it should be limited and precise because units cannot operate well with a motley group of problem children. If the units' function is to be specific, so must their approach. They must focus on the child's anxiety, isolation and feelings of inferiority or rejection. We can see little to recommend in a 'school' regime which elbows aside psychotherapeutic approaches and diminishes the contribution of child-care staff. However fashionable the three Rs might be at the moment, lack of them does not correlate with disturbance or a need for maximum security. Hence, more trained child-care staff should be recruited, more women given key roles in the institution and consistent psychiatric help provided. Above all, lingering aspects of the prison must go. Slopping out, the repeated locking and unlocking of doors, the use of cells for isolation, frequent body and room searches, the scrutiny of literature and mail, are all degrading and largely unnecessary. If labelling experiences do exist, then surely these must be among the most cruel. We would suggest that a more benign approach to the visits of parents or friends should be adopted and more provision made for this. The social services departments should scrutinise all these issues and insist that these considerable improvements are made and maintained.

When local authorities are planning secure units, they should take note of the accumulating experience of senior staff in the existing secure units and the approach adopted at the youth treatment centres. This may help modify the difficulties that all units seem to experience during their early years. Nevertheless, local authorities must be prepared for a succession of problems and crises because small institutions, even those sheltering normal adolescents, are very unstable. Secure units need considerable external support and encouragement; otherwise they feel themselves to be isolated and unappreciated.

We have noted that it is difficult to attract staff to work in secure settings or to find senior staff with sufficient experience to set them up. This could face local authorities with considerable problems. The challenge of a job in security demands people of stability, ability and confidence. Therefore, much more thought ought to be given to training, although present training courses have little expertise to offer here. But much could be gained from interchange of staff or encouraging them to spend placements in a wide variety of institutions sheltering vulnerable children. Experience of adolescent units and secure wings in hospitals, of child guidance or youth treatment centres, even of the closed Borstals such as Feltham, would provide staff with a wider reference group and diminish the anxiety enhanced by their isolation and lack of proper training. It would prevent staff from treating a neurotic adolescent who runs away as an embryonic psychopath.

Frequently, and justly, research is reproached for its theoretical preoccupations and esoteric language. This largely reflects the interests of its most appreciative audience – other academics. While we still need to know much about children at risk, we certainly could use what is already known much more effectively. It is sad that of the scales we develop, the significant relationships that research laboriously reveals and the categories that are identified, few are employed on a day-to-day basis. For example, it should not be beyond the capabilities of local authority research departments to reapply many of these scales or explore many situations in ways clearly laid out in research methodologies.

Regional plans need to know the number of high-risk children they actually have in care. By 'high-risk' we mean those who have started to offend or to be aggressive and troublesome from an early age. How many show marked mood swings or run away during primary school years? By gathering material about the children who accumulate long periods in residential care, who are frequently transferred and who have little home contact, the authorities can identify which children are going to create problems as adolescents. It should also be the task of local authority research units to tell social services departments which institutions have high absconding rates, high transfer rates and low success. They should identify which areas of the service are making the most demands for secure accommodation or any other special facility. Without this information, decision making must reflect the passing fashions and transitory preoccupations of the social services.

Local authorities, clearly informed, must then act to remedy the situation. They should not wait for scandals to force their hand or wilt before the pressures exerted by various professional lobbies. It is a rather depressing reflection on those institutions that care for children that much more concern is expressed over falling numbers, over truancy and absconding and over aggression, than is ever voiced over poor success, even when success is defined in institutional terms. In contrast, in the much maligned independent boarding schools the law of the market place operates in a way that is very beneficial, maintaining standards and meeting parental expectations in spite of an inadequate external inspectorate. Unfortunately, parents of children in care are not well placed to exert similar pressure on the homes that shelter their children. This puts an even greater obligation on the social services department to be vigilant.

Finally, the local authority social services departments need to know how many 15- and 16-year-old boys are going to Borstal. From these figures and by making estimates of probable need for security in ways demonstrated in Chapter 13 planners can arrive at some reasonable figure for the secure places required. Naturally, this raises all sorts of wider policy issues but, at the moment, fate seems rather capricious for some 15-year-olds when a number of social services departments are eagerly shouldering this burden of responsibility, while others are passing their young offenders on to the Home Office.

Few regional planning groups seem to ask these key questions and the number of secure places planned seems to be a reflection of the number of applications made for such accommodation over the past few years; not in itself the most reliable of indices. The approach to mixing the sexes of children in the units, for example, is naïve and the site chosen for a unit largely determined by some long-standing obligation to rebuild a remote and crumbling CHE.

A forward-looking regional plan would be thinking along other lines. It would be developing small, open, intensive care units similar to those we have described and attaching them to good CHEs in the region. Here, the high-risk children identified in the ways just suggested, could be placed. The social services departments would be experimenting with hostel-like accommodation, possibly a couple of terraced houses in a reasonably diverse urban setting. Here a stable married couple could support a number of adolescents in their mid-teens who would otherwise be in Borstal. Older children in care would be encouraged to participate in community work or attached to job creation or work experience projects. Considerable encouragement is also provided by the success of professional fostering and intermediate treatment with certain vulnerable children in care. Above all, there would be alternatives available, a care programme, flexibility and imagination.

Indeed, the final message from any study of secure provision should not be one of confusion and misdirected resource. Decisions have been taken in the light of the little information available and the very pressing problems of difficult children. We do need the secure accommodation we have at the moment; we must just ensure that it is used effectively for those children who need it. These are the highly disturbed or neurotic absconders who will not settle in the best of open care situations and a number of young people who are clearly a danger to the public. There is no evidence that, in the past, the welfare of the child has been disregarded for administrative or political convenience. We may not make quite the same decisions today as were made in the early 1960s but research can always be clever when looking backwards. In fact, there is some cause for comfort. The careful scrutiny now exercised by the DHSS on applications for secure places could well be much extended. The reluctance of the central authorities to approve many ill-considered schemes for security is entirely supported by this study. What could have been an avalanche of imprisoning children has not taken place. At least, security has not become a well-established monolith with its own staffing structure, sectional interest and political stance. This, from our wider knowledge of institutions, is an enormous advantage since it still allows everyone freedom for manoeuvre. It is also clear that the hesitation to expand secure provision springs not only from desires for economy but also from the moral and spiritual disquiet we all feel at locking up children.

Note

[1] S. L. Millham, R. Bullock, P. Cherrett, *After Grace – Teeth*, London, Human Context Books, Chaucer Publishing Company, 1975, p. 279.

Index

193